Self-Crowned Laureates

Self-
Crowned
Laureates

SPENSER
JONSON
MILTON
AND THE
LITERARY
SYSTEM

Richard Helgerson

University
of California
Press
Berkeley
Los Angeles
London

University of California Press
Berkeley and Los Angeles, California

University of California Press, Ltd.
London, England

© 1983 by
The Regents of
the University of California

Library of Congress
Cataloging in Publication Data

Helgerson, Richard.
    Self-crowned laureates.

    Includes bibliographical references.
    1. English poetry—Early modern, 1500–1700—History
and criticism. 2. Poets, English—Early modern, 1500–
1700—Biography. 3. Spenser, Edmund, 1552?–1599—
Authorship. 4. Jonson, Ben, 1573?–1637—Authorship.
5. Milton, John, 1608–1674—Authorship. 6. Authorship—
History. I. Title.

PR531.H4   1983   821'.3'09   82-8496
ISBN 0-520-04808-3   AACR2

Printed in the United States of America

1 2 3 4 5 6 7 8 9

86-B75

To my mother and father

Contents

Acknowledgments This book has benefited from the generous assistance of more people—students, friends, and colleagues—than I can here thank individually. But four names do demand mention. Michael O'Connell has been involved in the project from the beginning; Mark Rose got drawn in soon after; Jackson Cope and Daniel Javitch have been active in its last stages. The advice of all four has improved the book, and their encouragement has made its writing a more pleasant experience. I am also indebted to the National Endowment for the Humanities for a fellowship that allowed me a year of uninterrupted work, to the Academic Senate at the University of California, Santa Barbara, for travel, research, and secretarial assistance, and to the editors of *PMLA* and *ELH* for permission to reprint material that first appeared in the pages of those journals.

Santa Barbara
March 1982

Introduction

—

"I take it for a rule," Thomas Mann wrote in the diary he kept while reading *Don Quixote,* "that the greatest works were those of the most modest purpose. Ambition may not stand at the beginning; it must not come before the work but must grow with the work, which will itself be greater than the blithely astonished artist dreamed; it must be bound up with the work and not with the ego of the artist. There is nothing falser than abstract and premature ambition, the self-centered pride independent of the work, the pallid ambition of ego."[1] This book is about three English Renaissance poets who broke Mann's rule, three poets whose ambition preceded and determined their work, three poets who strove to achieve a major literary career and who said so. The first is Edmund Spenser. In 1579, at the age of twenty-seven, he presented himself to the reading public as the New Poet, the English successor to Virgil. Two decades later and at the same age, Ben Jonson let it be known that he might henceforth be regarded as the English Horace. And in 1628 the nineteen-year-old John Milton broke off the Cambridge vacation exercise over which he was presiding to reveal his intention of one day singing "of kings and queens and heroes old" as "wise Demodocus" had done at the feast of Alcinous. The ambition so "prematurely" announced—the

1. Thomas Mann, "Voyage with Don Quixote," in *Essays of Three Decades,* trans. H. T. Lowe-Porter (New York: Knopf, 1947), p. 460.

ambition not only to write great poems but also to fill the role of the great poet—shaped everything these men wrote in the remainder of their active and productive literary lives. As well as presenting poems, masques, plays, and pamphlets, they were always presenting themselves.

But neither "great" nor "major" quite gets at what Spenser, Jonson, and Milton were attempting. They did seek to be better than other English poets and thus different in degree. But they also wanted to be different in kind. Theirs was to be a role apart. But apart from what? A "different" kind implies other kinds. Indeed, it implies the existence of a system whose individual elements take meaning from their relationship to the whole. The success of these poets' self-presentation thus depended on more than individual talent and an individual desire for greatness. It depended as well on a system of authorial roles in which that ambition might make sense.

This book is also about that system, a system which stands in particular need of description. For where others that intersected it—the system of genres, modes, and styles in poetics or the system of ranks, offices, and guilds in society—possessed well-established and widely accepted sets of names and definitions, it had none.[2] Neither Plato nor Aristotle had talked of authorial roles and their relation to one another, nor had Horace, Quintilian, or the medieval encyclopedists, though they had talked of other things—most significantly the differences between nature and convention, between logic and rhetoric, between the philosopher and the sophist—that would contribute greatly to its articulation. Rather than being a settled and stable structure, perpetuated by education and the rules of society, the system of authorial roles was only emerging in late sixteenth-century England. Though literary and cultural

2. For a brilliantly suggestive discussion of some of these other systems, see Claudio Guillén, *Literature as System: Essays Toward the Theory of Literary History* (Princeton: Princeton Univ. Press, 1971), pp. 375–419.

theory were committed to imitation and revival, a sudden increase in the production of poetry was bringing into existence
an essentially new configuration of what Michel Foucault has
called "author-functions."[3] Identifying themselves with Virgil,
Horace, and Demodocus, the poets themselves labored to deny
the newness. But Virgil had known nothing of Renaissance
courtiership or of courtly love; Horace had never written for
the public theaters; Demodocus was no literary latecomer in a
generation of cavalier poets. Thus even as the new writers
proclaimed their ancient lineage, they were contributing to the
manifestation of a system that had no precise counterpart in
antiquity.

Among the problems that faced them was the lack of a
word that could be relied on to designate the role they wished
to play. It was easy enough to name a pastoral or a duke, but
what was one to call a writer of this particularly ambitious
sort? "Poet" had, they felt, been taken over by lesser men
performing a lesser function, and there seemed no way of getting it back. The repeated efforts of Spenser, Jonson, and
Milton themselves and of such other English defenders of poetry as Sidney, Puttenham, or Webbe either to find some name
that would suit the dignity to which the poet was ideally entitled or to clear away the muck that made the usual name
unsuitable do, however, speak eloquently of their concern.
They dismissed the usurpers as poetasters, versifiers, or riming
parasites and elevated the great writers as *vates*; they translated
"poet" into "maker," equated it with "priest," "prophet,"
"lawmaker," "historiographer," "astronomer," "philoso-
phist," and "musician," and adorned it with adjectives like
"good," "right," and "true." But all their efforts to establish a
single term that would unequivocally denote the function they

3. Michel Foucault, "What Is an Author?" in *Textual Strategies: Perspec-
tives in Post-Structural Criticism,* ed. Josué V. Harari (Ithaca: Cornell Univ.
Press, 1979), pp. 141–160.

strove to exercise ended in failure. The necessary distinction could thus be made only with the circumlocution of self-presentational gesture.

It is perhaps worth noting, as an index of our difficulty with these poets, that we still have no satisfactory way of designating them. Hence the "laureate" coinage that gives my book its title. The other most obvious possibilities seem to me either too narrow, too loaded, or too broad. *Vates,* the term Virgil revived to distinguish himself from the mere *poetae* of his age, works no better now than it did in the sixteenth century. Though it clearly affected Spenser's and Milton's conception of their role, it excludes Jonson, who had no prophetic ambition. Jonson would again be excluded were we to borrow from the system of genres and use "epic" or "heroic." In the Renaissance, role and genre were closely associated. But even for Spenser and Milton, genre was secondary—a sign of the role rather than the role itself. The term *public poet* that occasionally appears in modern criticism has at least the virtue of excluding no one, but it leads too readily to an opposition with *private man,* an opposition the poets would have been the first to deny.[4] There may, in fact, have been such an opposition, though I suspect that the conflicts we attribute to it originate more often within the role itself or within the man who chose it than between the two, but, wherever we finally agree to locate the conflicts, we should not adopt a term that answers the question before we ask it. As for the still more common *professional,* it is still more objectionable. Sometimes, as in John Buxton's *Elizabethan Taste,* it assumes its etymological sense and refers to "professed" poets, to the exclusion of publicly less ambitious writers like Dekker, Heywood, and Shakespeare—writers who, in Buxton's words, were "hors concours" to the world of courtly patronage. But just as often, as in G.E.

4. See, for example, George Parfitt, *Ben Jonson: Public Poet and Private Man* (London: Dent, 1976).

Bentley's *Profession of Dramatist in Shakespeare's Time* (and in the remainder of this book), "professional" specifically excludes the "professed" poets and is reserved instead for the Dekkers, Heywoods, and Shakespeares, the writers who made their living from the public theater. And sometimes, as in J. W. Saunders' *Profession of English Letters,* it means either or both indiscriminately.[5] Yet the differences between Buxton's professionals and Bentley's are significant enough to require the introduction of a second term like *laureate.*

Second terms spring from difference, opposition, antithesis. As I have been suggesting, opposition is essential both to the construction of a system, like the system of authorial roles, and to the meaning of any particular utterance, including the utterances of authorial self-presentation, that derives from it. Mann's dislike of "premature ambition" is a function of one such system, the system of Romanticism and its Modernist descendant. The adjectives I have been reviewing, however inadequate they may be, map one corner of another. To list the second terms they imply is to locate more precisely the point toward which our poets were tending. *Great* opposes itself to *small, mediocre,* or *poor; vatic* to *poetic* (obviously a problem, especially for Spenser and Milton); *epic* to *lyric* or *dramatic* (a problem for Jonson); *public* to *private* (private poet as well as private man); *professional* to *amateur.* From this play of opposing terms, the shadowy image of the Elizabethan literary landscape begins to emerge even before we consider the historical individuals who peopled it. Nor would it be difficult for anyone familiar with the period to name actual small poets, lyric and dramatic poets, private poets, and amateurs. Were any of these functions left unfilled, we would notice the gap.

5. John Buxton, *Elizabethan Taste* (London: Macmillan, 1963), pp. 317 and 335; G. E. Bentley, *The Profession of Dramatist in Shakespeare's Time, 1590–1642* (Princeton: Princeton Univ. Press, 1971), pp. 11–37; and J. W. Saunders, *The Profession of English Letters* (London: Routledge, 1964), pp. 31–67.

The Elizabethans would also have noticed it. They did, in fact, see many such gaps in the 1570s and 1580s and hurried to fill them. Before Spenser occupied it, the role of great English poet was repeatedly said to be vacant. The system thus recruited the man, but it remained for the man to show that he met the requirements of the system. Could he pull this particular sword from its stone?

Not only *vatic* and *epic,* but each term, taken in the net of its differences, points to an area of difficulty, to a question the poet had to answer in the course of his self-presentation. What relation has his greatness to that of other significant cultural protagonists, literary and nonliterary? What is the nature of his inspiration and thus of his authority, and is that authority compatible with poetry? What are the literary genres appropriate to his role? What contribution does he make to the collective interests of the nation and the state? What is his source of income and what does he owe those who supply it? Left by his scrivener father with a small but adequate fortune, Milton was able to ignore the last of these questions, but he had to deal with the others. Spenser and Jonson had to face them all.

Born of its opposition to *professional, laureate* too suggests questions: What recognition could such a poet hope for? And what position might he expect to fill? For clearly the poets themselves thought of both recognition and position in the quasi-official terms implied by the word *laureate.* "Thou shalt ycrouned be" is the promise held out in *The Shepheardes Calender* and the image of crowning echoes not only through Spenser's work but through that of his successors as well. Jonson spent half his nights and all his days, or so he said, "To come forth worth the ivy or the bays," and Milton imagined himself sitting "with the ivy and laurel of a victor." In the reigns of Elizabeth, James, and Charles, the laureateship had, however, no settled institutional basis. Academic crownings of the sort that made Skelton "poet laureate" of Oxford and Cambridge had fallen out of use (though Jonson did get an honorary M.A. from Oxford), and the office of Poet Laureate had not yet been officially established. By the time it was, with the appointment of Dryden in 1668, a split had opened between the idea of a laureate poet and the possibility of any office that could be granted by a mortal king. The publication of *Paradise Lost* in 1667 announced the split, and it widened with each new royal nomination, until in 1757 Thomas Gray could refuse the succession, remarking that "the office itself has always humbled the professor."[6] Little more than a decade earlier, Pope had elevated the then current incumbent, Colly Cibber, to the bad eminence of chief dunce of *The Dunciad*. By the mid-eighteenth century, to be Poet Laureate had come to mean that one was quite decidedly *not* a laureate poet. Thus a man who aspired, as Pope did, to stand in the line of true greatness might in this new age make opposition to the official Laureate a powerful sign of his own authorial integrity.

But neither Spenser nor Jonson could have foreseen the full measure of that future separation and decline. Not even Milton could foresee it, though the example of his career helped bring it about. For all three the laureate crown figured not the *translatio stultitiae* of Pope's *Dunciad*, but rather the *translatio studii* of the *Aeneid* and of the Renaissance itself. Instead of the ignominy of Shadwell, Tate, Eusden, and Cibber, they would have remembered the Renaissance fervor of Petrarch's Capitoline coronation. Spenser and Jonson both advertised the near relation of poet to monarch and both accepted royal pensions. As a defender of regicide, Milton could hardly have done as much (Davenant was the poetic pensioner of Milton's generation), but, until the writing of *Paradise Lost,* he too conceived of the great poet as the anointed spokesman of the nation. It

6. Thomas Gray quoted by Kenneth Hopkins in *The Poets Laureate* (Carbondale: Southern Illinois Univ. Press, 1954), p. 79.

was in his official capacity as Latin Secretary to the Council of State that he wrote his *Defense of the English People,* a work he compared to an epic poem and thought would secure his literary fame. In this expectation he was wrong, but his mistake grew naturally from an idea of the great writer that he shared with Spenser and Jonson, an idea implied by the word *laureate.*

These writers lived, as Laurence Manley has demonstrated, in a time of unusually acute "normative crisis."[7] Humanist and Protestant reform had broken the continuity of European history, calling into question the bases on which art, society, and the self reposed. Was their ultimate sanction nature—absolute, immutable, and universal—or merely transitory custom? In their laureate self-presentation, Spenser, Jonson, and Milton all found themselves pulled toward the absolutist side. A laureate could not be a timeserver. Rather he was the servant of eternity. In his work and in his life, he felt constrained to express the orthodox ethical norm not only of his time but of all time. The suspicion that there might be no such entity rendered his undertaking particularly doubtful, even Quixotic. Dryden, the first official Poet Laureate, was already much closer to the opposite pole.[8] The opening of his most famous poem suggests the difference:

> In pious times, ere priestcraft did begin,
> Before polygamy was made a sin . . .

The exquisitely complex irony of these lines derives in part from the fact that they are not altogether ironic. There *was* a time when polygamy was not a sin. Values *do* change. Right and wrong vary from age to age, from place to place, from party to party. "Wit and fool," it can now be admitted, "are

7. Laurence Manley, *Convention, 1500–1750* (Cambridge: Harvard Univ. Press, 1980), p. 137.
8. See Manley's interesting discussion of Dryden's criticism, pp. 290–321.

consequents of Whig and Tory."[9] Dryden is the first English poet of laureate ambition to strike so casual a pose. By his own admission, he wrote *Absalom and Achitophel* to serve a political faction, and, though he thought it, "in its own nature, inferior to all sorts of dramatic writing," he wrote comedy to satisfy popular taste. "I confess my chief endeavors are to delight the age in which I live. If the humor of this be for low comedy, small accidents, and raillery, I will force my genius to obey it, though with more reputation I could write in verse."[10] No previous laureate would have allowed himself such a confession. Nor would any have modeled his self-presentation, as Dryden did, on Montaigne's. A self *ondoyant et divers,* a shifting, unstable self whose adherence to the governing political and religious norms of the age was only a matter of convenience required by a generally corrosive scepticism, would have been regarded as incompatible with a laureate's profession.

From their attempt to maintain an ethically normative and unchanging self arise the deepest tensions in the work of Spenser, Jonson, and Milton—tensions that reveal themselves in such persistently problematical episodes as the destruction of the Bower of Bliss, the punishment of Mosca and Volpone, and the deflation of Satan. In each, readers have long felt that the poet was of the antagonist's party without knowing it. The seductive, exuberant, self-regarding energy the laureates condemn bears a troubling likeness to the energy of their own art. Surely Spenser owes as much to the sensual delight of Acrasia, Jonson to the Protean role playing of Volpone, Milton to the rhetorical brilliance and heroic rebelliousness of Satan as any of them does to the counterforces of morally righteous judg-

9. *The Poems of John Dryden,* ed. James Kinsley, 3 vols. (Oxford: Clarendon Press, 1958), I, 215.

10. John Dryden, *Of Dramatic Poesy and Other Critical Essays,* ed. George Watson, 2 vols. (London: Dent, 1962), I, 145 and 116.

ment. It is precisely here, in this involvement of the poet as conscious prosecutor and unconscious defendant that such passages differ from an otherwise similar episode in Shakespeare, the rejection of Falstaff. Shakespeare does not get rid of Falstaff; Hal does. Judgment comes from within the play as a function of Hal's kingly office, not from without as a function of Shakespeare's poetic one. Shakespeare is simply not there. The laureates are. Like Hal, they have an office to fill and an identity to establish. Spenser along with Guyon destroys the Bower of Bliss; Jonson puts "the snaffle in their mouths that cry out, we never punish vice in our interludes"; and Milton pronounces judgment on Satan. Their laureate self-fashioning demanded rigorous exorcism and denial of them, for the threat was always the same: metamorphic loss of identity.

To define himself and to fend off change, the laureate isolated one part of himself, which was also a part of the collective cultural structure by which he was constituted, and treated it as "the other"—that against which his particular rectitude might best be known. "Self-fashioning," as Stephen Greenblatt has written, "is achieved in relation to something perceived as alien, strange, or hostile. This threating Other ... must be discovered or invented in order to be attacked and destroyed."[11] Greenblatt presents this as a general phenomenon in the Renaissance, and to the extent that Renaissance men and women felt it necessary to construct an identity (rather than, for example, merely inheriting one) that is so. But that necessity lay with particular weight on poets of laureate ambition. An official self of the sort they aspired to embody required more decisive excision of the other than did less seriously manifested selves. In the late sixteenth century, differences between the serious and the ludic self were a principal feature of the system

11. Stephen Greenblatt, *Renaissance Self-Fashioning From More to Shakespeare* (Chicago: Univ. of Chicago Press, 1980), p. 9.

of authorial roles, and they will consequently be a principal subject of my first chapter. But here we can more easily define the particular quality of the Renaissance poets by another glance into the Laureate future. Dryden, too, identified various reprehensible others—royalists when he was a Cromwellian, Catholics and Puritans when he was an Anglican, Anglicans when he was a Catholic. But then, as often as not, he openly went over to the other's side—particularly when the other attained power. This accommodating pliancy, associated from Dryden's time on with the official Laureateship, opened him and his eighteenth-century successors to repeated attacks on their integrity, and it still makes them seem at best marginal members of the true laureate company.

In one respect, however, both Dryden, the first official Laureate, and Pope, the first anti-Laureate laureate, bear a striking resemblance to the Renaissance forebears from whom their separate lines diverge. Both invested much effort in their self-presentation. Pope's is conspicuous enough to have prompted several recent studies devoted to it alone, and Dryden's provoked Swift (in the person of his Grub Street hack) maliciously to remark: "Our great Dryden . . . has often said to me in confidence that the world would have never suspected him to be so great a poet if he had not assured them so frequently in his prefaces that it was impossible they could either doubt or forget it."[12] Like Pope and Dryden, Spenser, Jonson, and Milton felt it necessary to keep reminding the world of their greatness. But even as we recall the sometimes annoying obtrusiveness of these assurances, we should remember too that they are often an integral part of the laureate's finest poetry. Self-presentation has its supreme triumphs as well as its costs. Without it we would have no Colin Clout. Nor would we have the invoca-

12. Jonathan Swift, *A Tale of a Tub*, ed. A. C. Guthkelch and D. Nichol Smith (1920; 2d ed. Oxford: Clarendon Press, 1958), p. 131.

tions to Books 1, 3, 7, and 9 of *Paradise Lost* or the great moment in the Cary-Morison ode when the poet's own name bridges the stanzas like a mythical giant joining heaven and earth.

> Call, noble Lucius, then for wine,
> And let thy looks with gladness shine.
> Accept this garland, plant it on thy head,
> And think, nay know, thy Morison's not dead.
> He leaped the present age,
> Possessed with holy rage,
> To see that bright eternal day,
> Of which we priests and poets say
> Such truths as we expect for happy men.
> And there he lives with memory and *Ben.*
>
> ### The Stand
> *Jonson,* who sung this of him, ere he went
> Himself to rest,
> Or taste a part of that full joy he meant
> To have expressed.

"Ben" is with memory and Morison, "Jonson" here below with Cary.[13] The laureate mediates between the eternal realm of perfect form and the temporal realm of death and birth. Whether it is Jonson bestriding the stanzas or Colin piping to the Graces on Mt. Acidale or Milton receiving the "nightly visitation unimplored" of his Celestial Patroness, such a poet presents a self whose authority derives from inner and outer alignment with the unmoving axis of normative value. His laureate function requires that he speak from the center.

He does not, however, get to that still point easily. For a poem like the Cary-Morison ode to work, the poet's name must already mean something. "Who knowes not Colin

13. See Richard S. Peterson's discussion of this point in *Imitation and Praise in the Poems of Ben Jonson* (New Haven: Yale Univ. Press, 1981), p. 221. I follow Peterson in printing the full stop after *"Ben."*

Clout?" Spenser asked in reintroducing his pastoral persona in the new context of *The Faerie Queene*. Such gestures suppose the prior achievement of an acknowledged position, as Milton's allusions in *Paradise Lost* to his blindness and political isolation suppose our recognition of him as the man who spent his sight "In liberty's defense, [his] noble task, / Of which all Europe talks from side to side." Only a poet whose career had become a public fact could successfully imitate, as both Spenser and Milton did, the Virgilian (or pseudo-Virgilian) *Ille ego,* "I am the poet who in times past . . . ," or refer, as Jonson did, to the "shutting up of his circle." At such moments, the poet draws on an account to which he has been making deposits for many years.

But how did he establish the credit to open the account in the first place? And how does he maintain that credit in periods of crisis? These are questions that particularly preoccupy me in this book. I give more attention to how the poet gets to his laureate destination than to what he does when he gets there, more attention to such liminal works as *The Shepheardes Calender,* the three Comical Satires, and the *Poems* of 1645 than to *The Faerie Queene, Volpone,* or *Paradise Lost.* For in those crossings of the threshold, when the author first appears before his audience, the pressure on self-presentation is greatest. To some extent, each beginning—beginnings of individual works as well as beginnings of careers—brings a renewal of self-presentational pressure. I thus talk often of proems, prefaces, and prologues. Pressure falls too on endings and on intermediate passages of transition or challenge, when the role seems no longer to fit the world, and these will also demand attention. Whenever the voice of the poem becomes in some fairly explicit way the voice of the poet, whenever the speaking becomes a justification of the speaker and his authority, then we will want to pay special heed. That such occasions do arise so much more often in the work of poets like Spenser, Jonson, and Milton than in that of their amateur and professional contemporaries is one of the best signs of their relation to one another and of the distinctness of the role they sought to play.

As laureate poets, Spenser, Jonson, and Milton closely resemble one another. As members of distinct literary generations, they are, however, quite unlike. Though each presented himself as a poet of the laureate sort, each had also to relate his self-presentation to the demands of a particular moment, a moment shared with other writers (whether aspiring laureates or not) born in the same span of years. Each had to speak to his own time in a language it might be expected to understand, even if only to say that he was of all time. Without making some such accommodation, he could hardly hope to perform the mediating function that was ideally his. Instead he would appear merely absurd, like Thomas More's philosopher, reciting Seneca's speech to Nero from the *Octavia* in the midst of a comedy by Plautus. But if, realizing this absurdity, he took his cue, adapted himself to the drama in hand, and acted his part neatly and well, could he retain his identity as philosopher?[14] More struggled with this dilemma, and so did the Renaissance laureates. Truth is one, but times change. The poet who hopes to present a normative self is caught between the two.

In the course of my work on this book, precise temporal location has come to seem more and more important, and so has the shared quality of that temporal location. Some of the resulting interest in generations has spilled over into a separate paper on generational theory and the generational structure of English Renaissance literature.[15] But much of it remains in this book where its products include most of those arguments in the

14. I here paraphrase Robert M. Adams' translation of *Utopia* (New York: Norton, 1975), p. 28.
15. "The Generations of English Renaissance Literature," presented at the Modern Language Association Convention in Houston (December, 1980).

chapters on Spenser, Jonson, and Milton that depart furthest from our usual understanding of these writers. It seems to me that very little in their self-presentation is gratuitous and far less is the product of individual temperamental vagary than is commonly thought. I do not, for all that, pretend to reduce each to a point at the intersection of two lines, one labeled "laureate" and the other "generation." Only a part of their meaning can be read from so restricted a perspective. But it is a part we often miss. Limited as it is, this bilinear charting does serve to locate social and cultural constraints that do not appear on other maps and to discover significance in gestures that before seemed empty or odd. A generation is the temporal location in which a certain language is spoken. "I am a laureate" is the statement each of our poets wanted to make. The problem that faced them was whether that statement could be convincingly made in the language of their own particular generation. An appreciation of that problem can only make their accomplishment more humanly important, more relevant to the struggle of men and women in any age to achieve a position of individual authority and preeminence. These poets sought to play an exemplary role. In studying that effort and the difficulties it encountered, we make them exemplary in a way they could not have fully intended. We make them examples of the very human placement in time and in culture that they strove to transcend.

In the late sixteenth and early seventeenth centuries, a large number of the brightest and most energetic young Englishmen were drawn to the collective project of creating a national literature. Following the lead of the Greeks and Romans, the Italians had developed a significant vernacular literature in the fourteenth century and massively renewed it in the early sixteenth. In the 1540s the French and the Spanish undertook similar projects. Now it was the turn of the English. Sidney was only one of many to ask "why England (the mother of excellent minds) should be grown so hard a stepmother to poets"[16] and only one of many to help, by the strength of his own poetic contribution, remove that unflattering title from England's name. And if England needed a literature, it also needed a laureate poet—a Homer, a Virgil, an Ariosto, or a Ronsard. With the position so obviously open, many men showed they had considered applying, and several, besides Spenser, Jonson, and Milton, entered a serious claim: Chapman, Daniel, Drayton, Wither, Davenant, and Cowley. Of these, Wither, who probably expended more energy on self-presentation than any English poet before Wordsworth, falls between the generations that most concern me and thus receives only cursory notice. The others get more. Chapman, Daniel, and Drayton figure along with Spenser and Jonson in the first chapter, which deals with the initial articulation in two dynamic lead generations of the system of authorial roles, and Cowley and Davenant share a section in the chapter on Milton, where I talk about the erosion of that system in a belated generation.

But to confine attention to the laureates, even to this expanded group of laureates, would be to miss the larger matrix of authorial roles within which theirs was distinguished. I have thus examined the self-presentation of some ninety-five English writers born between the late 1530s and the early 1620s. Not all of them are quoted or discussed individually in the following pages. For reasons of expository economy, one has often to stand for many. But all participated in the systems of role type and generation that I describe. And the thousands of individual gestures they made in presenting themselves provide the only access to those systems. Our task will be to avail ourselves of that access, to move from gesture to system and back again, hoping that in the circling (not to say "circularity") of argu-

16. Sir Philip Sidney, *An Apology for Poetry*, ed. Geoffrey Shepherd (1965; rpt. Manchester: Manchester Univ. Press, 1973), p. 131.

ment that is an inevitable part of most humanistic research we will come better to understand what greatness of the sort the laureates sought means—*what* it means and *how* it means.

As many readers will by now have remarked, this book is itself a part of a collective project—a project that is engaging the energies of my generation of American literary scholars in something of the way that poetry engaged the generation of Elizabethan courtiers to which Spenser and Sidney belonged. I speak, of course, of semiotics and its application to the study of literary discourse. In company with a growing number of students, I find myself borrowing heavily from the insights of structural linguistics in an effort to uncover the symbolic codes on which the institution of literature has been based. This was not my intention when I began work on this book. I started rather with an historical question. In an earlier study of the writers who dominated English literature in the 1580s—the decade that first thrust England toward the mainstream of European Renaissance literature—I found the marks of an extraordinary and quite surprising uncertainty about the whole literary enterprise. These men had been taught by their fathers and schoolmasters that poetry was wasteful folly and that folly led inevitably to repentance. At first they rebelled against this iron law, but in the end they submitted and gave up writing, condemning all they had done as the outbreak of licentious youth. In doing so they were fitting their own literary activity to the commonplace definition of a poet as a young man culpably distracted from the real business of life. Obviously this self-image left no place for a fully developed poetic career. How then, I wondered, did Spenser, the immediate contemporary of these men, achieve such a career? My first inclination was to look for antecedents, to study the tradition of the great poetic career diachronically, tracing this element of Spenser's self-presentation to Virgil, that to Chaucer, and still another to Ariosto. But gradually the axis of my interest rotated from the diachronic to the synchronic. Spenser did not ignore the other writers of his generation to make himself over in the image of some illustrious predecessor. Rather he was constituted by the same set of relations as were his coevals, different though their careers might be. His self-presentation was a function of theirs. From here it was a short and perhaps inevitable step to full engagement in the project of semiotic analysis.

That engagement does not, however, mean that I have left behind either my interest in history and historical change or my sense that men like Spenser, Jonson, and Milton possess an irreducible and active individuality—though both inclinations go against the grain of much current semiotic theory and practice. To some, a semiotic history seems a contradiction in terms. As critics have repeatedly remarked, the fundamental semiotic notion of system is ahistorical, perhaps even antihistorical. Semiotics provides tools for analyzing synchronic relations, but not change. Yet change is an undeniable part of our historical experience. My emphasis on generations is meant to address this problem. Though change is constant in literature, as in society and culture generally, its rate is not. There are moments when, for men of a similar age, a configuration of relations holds still, allowing them to make it the enabling basis of their collective self-presentation. As Emile Benveniste has said (with no reference to generations), "The legitimacy of diachrony, considered as a succession of synchronies, is thus reestablished."[17] In defining a generation as the temporal location in which a certain language is spoken, I had this succession of synchronies in mind. Each generational synchrony lends itself to semiotic analysis. Nor do we necessarily leave the realm of semiotics in asking how one is transformed into an-

17. Emile Benveniste, *Problems in General Linguistics*, trans. Mary Elizabeth Meek (Coral Gables, Florida: Univ. of Miami Press, 1971), p. 5.

other, for often such transformations are themselves the intended source of meaning. A new generation defines itself with reference to the old. The legitimacy of synchrony, considered as a system of diachronic differences, is thus in turn reestablished.

As for the irreducible and active self, it impresses itself on the consciousness of anyone who spends much time in the presence (I use the word advisedly) of my three poets. Clearly, they each speak as well as being spoken through. If one swing in our interpretive circling from gesture to system tends to dissolve the single intending self, the swing back reconstitutes it. Meaning is in difference, the possibility of meaning in a system of differences. But someone must be there to make and to mark the difference. Some one particular person says what has not been said before, what would not be said in the same way, if at all, were he not there—and someone else understands. Without those two agents (who may on occasion be one), there can be no communication. This is not to posit a transcendental self, a self of whom it could be sensibly asked, "What would he do were he living now?" Move the birth of a Spenser, Jonson, or Milton by a few years, or a few miles, or a few notches on the social scale and he would cease to be. Of the codes that constituted him only the genetic would survive. The literary works of these men were made possible by the situations in which they occurred. Their meanings could not have been imposed unless they were understood, unless the conventions that made understanding possible were already in place.

I have paraphrased these last two sentences from Jonathan Culler, who, though he accepts as an accomplished fact "the death of the author," has recently noticed "a paradox inherent in the semiotic project and in the philosophical orientation of which it is the culmination"—a paradox that readmits the prematurely deceased author to life. For, as Culler writes, "our whole notion of literature makes it not a transcription of preexisting thoughts but a series of radical and inaugural acts: acts of imposition which create meaning."[18] Such acts, I think we may safely assume, have authors, though authors who are themselves authorized by the systems that make those acts possible. Neither the author nor the system can be discarded. Each deconstructs the other, but each also constructs the other. If we are to understand literary utterances, including the utterances of authorial self-presentation, we must know, whether implicitly or explicitly, the literary system. But we must also know Spenser, Jonson, and Milton. They, after all, make our knowledge of the system worth having.

18. Jonathan Culler, *The Pursuit of Signs: Semiotics, Literature, Deconstruction* (Ithaca: Cornell Univ. Press, 1981), p. 39.

The
Laureate
and the
Literary
System

In dedicating the *Seven Books of the Iliads of Homer* to Essex, George Chapman spoke of poetry as "this poor scribbling, this toy . . . being accounted in our most gentle and complimental use of it only the droppings of an idle humor; far unworthy the serious expense of an exact gentleman's time." Yet of this "fruitless, dead, and despised receptacle," the human soul has, Chapman declared, made "her earthly residence . . . to reverse [poetry's] appearance with unspeakable profit, comfort, and life to all posterities." Chapman nicely defines the laureate's task: to make of a gentleman's toy something of unspeakable profit. His laureate contemporaries may not all have shared his Neoplatonic belief that the soul would, in some miraculous way, do the transforming, but they did agree that, if it were to serve their ambition, poetry required transformation. Though the Renaissance had given new life to the idea of the poet's high calling, the practice of poetry, particularly in England, had, it seemed to the aspiring laureates, fallen into the hands of dilettantes and hacks. Spenser complained that in his unheroic age even a poet "of the old stocke" must "rolle with rest in rymes of rybaudrye"; Drayton despaired of being read "at this time, when verses are wholly deduced to chambers"; Daniel disputed "the received opinion" of poetry which

> Hath so unseasoned now the ears of men,
> That who doth touch the tenor of that vein,
> Is held but vain;

and Jonson, after defining "the offices and function of a poet," lamented "that the writers of these days are other things, that, not only their manners, but their natures are inverted, and nothing remaining with them of the dignity of poet, but an abused name, which every scribe usurps."[1]

We have learned to disregard such statements. "Conventional" or "formulaic" we call them. And so they are. They are the formulae of literary self-presentation. Chapman, Spenser, and the rest use them in imitation of other poets, ancient and modern, whom they hope to resemble. But they also use them to distinguish themselves from their amateur and professional contemporaries—contemporaries they would perhaps have had to invent had they not existed, but who, in fact, existed in such numbers that they dominated the literary scene. In the 1570s, when Spenser began to write, his fellow English poets were all amateurs. By the 1590s, when Jonson got started, the situation had changed. The expansion of the literary market, particularly the market for plays, had brought into existence a small but active group of true professionals, men who depended on writing for a livelihood, and Spenser's own, still uncompleted career was providing an English example of that

---

1. *The Works of George Chapman*, ed. R. H. Shepherd, 3 vols. (London: Chatto and Windus, 1892), II, 8; *The Works of Edmund Spenser: A Variorum Edition*, ed. Edwin Greenlaw, C. G. Osgood, et al., 11 vols. (Baltimore: Johns Hopkins Univ. Press, 1932–1957), VII, 98; *The Works of Michael Drayton*, ed. J. William Hebel, 5 vols. (Oxford: Shakespeare Head Press, 1933), IV, v *; *The Complete Works in Verse and Prose of Samuel Daniel*, ed. A. B. Grosart, 5 vols.

quintessentially humanist construct, the laureate poet. But still the amateurs remained ascendant. There was thus some plausibility to the laureates' charge.

The name of poet had been usurped, and poetry had been made a toy, a vanity, a thing of ribaldry fit only for private chambers. And if we do not see things quite this way now, it is nevertheless a fair representation of the received opinion in at least some influential circles—circles whose approbation the laureate required. The very context of these quotations should be enough to tell us that they were meant seriously, for each is part of a much larger exercise in public self-definition and each has many echoes elsewhere in its author's work. These men recognized that a laureate career would be intelligible only if presented in relation to other literary and nonliterary careers. It necessarily defined itself by means of a series of similarities to and differences from other ways of writing and other modes of being. But was the field of poetry large enough to hold differences of such magnitude? If Elizabethans understood poetry to be merely a fugitive and licentious toy—and, however loudly poetry was sometimes praised, such a view was widespread—then the laureate might have no way both to distinguish himself and to retain his title to poetry. Bend too close to contemporary practice and he would topple from his laureate eminence to "rolle with [the] rest"; but hold to that eminence with too little concession and he would, as Drayton discovered, lose his readers, and perhaps even the name of poet. "A good honest man," Jonson said of Daniel, "but no poet." The readiness with which such anathemas come to Jonson's lips testifies to his sense of the perilous exclusivity of the term, as does his half-

---

(London, 1885), I, 227; and *Ben Jonson*, ed. C. H. Herford, Percy Simpson, and Evelyn Simpson, 11 vols. (Oxford: Clarendon Press, 1925–1952), V, 17–18. I have modernized spelling and, to a lesser extent, punctuation in all quotations except those from Spenser. Subsequent references to these editions will be noted in the text.

ironic insistence on its application to himself. "In his merry humor he was wont to name himself the poet" (I, 132 and 150).

Self-definition and *self-presentation* are the prime operative terms here. For the laureate, writing was a way of saying something about himself. He wanted not only to be a laureate, but also to be known to be one. Like any other meaningful communication, this required a system of conventional signs— a system that stands to the particular self-defining gestures accomplished by the various writers as, to use terms made familiar by Saussurean linguistics, *langue* stands to *parole*. An individual utterance *(la parole)* can have meaning only because certain possibilities exist within the competence *(la langue)* of the speaker and his listeners. In like manner, a set of poems and the various verbal and nonverbal gestures surrounding it could be the manifestation of a laureate career only if certain possibilities existed within the literary system that the writer shared with his audience. But Spenser and Jonson had reason to doubt that in their case the requisite possibilities did exist.

The laureates were, in effect, reviving a dead language. And though there might be a general inclination to regard that language as more noble than any then spoken, it remained nevertheless largely unintelligible. On occasion the poets were themselves uncertain whether they had gotten it quite right, uncertain whether the career on which they had embarked could be accomplished by the actions they were performing. Concern of this kind marks *The Shepheardes Calender* and occurs again in Daniel's *Musophilus*. But more often they felt that they were misunderstood, that the fit audience was few indeed. "In these jig-given times," Jonson wondered, who will countenance either a legitimate poem or a legitimate poet? "Thou pourest them wheat," he told himself on another occasion, "And they will acorns eat" (V, 431, and VI, 492). His image recalls Ascham's comparison of modern rime to ancient quantitative meter. "Surely to follow rather the Goths in riming than the Greeks in true versifying were even to eat acorns with swine when we may freely eat wheat bread amongst men."[2] Both Ascham and Jonson relate their claims to the Renaissance program of classical rebirth. But what if the old language, the old roles, and the old gestures were Greek to the dark, ignorant, and swinish present? The wheat bread of quantitative meter found little favor. Who could say that readers would not reject the laureate with similar disdain, leaving him to sing angry odes to himself? However exalted their notion of their role, however thorough their imitation of the great poets of antiquity, Spenser, Jonson, and the other English Renaissance laureates had finally to conform to the actual body of current literary practice. And that meant linking their self-presentation to the self-presentation of their amateur and professional contemporaries.

Laureates and Amateurs

We can, however, leave the theatrical professionals temporarily aside. In its Spenserian phase, laureate self-fashioning was related only to the amateur, and even later amateur patterns continue to dominate. Furthermore, throughout these years, public self-presentation through poetry was largely confined to the amateurs and laureates. Both used their literary work to say something about its author, and in doing so they necessarily conformed to principles familiar in semiotics—principles that would not much help us in discussing the career patterns of the professionals.

Meaning in the Elizabethan system of literary careers, as in any sign system, derives from relations and oppositions between the elements of that system. To write in a certain genre or

2. Roger Ascham, *The Schoolmaster,* ed. Lawrence V. Ryan (Ithaca: Cornell Univ. Press, 1967), p. 145.

to speak of one's work in a certain way or to establish a certain relationship with booksellers, stage managers, or patrons was to associate oneself with one group of poets and to dissociate oneself from another. But the analogy between the system by which a sixteenth-century English poet declared his literary identity and the most common semiotic model, the linguistic, breaks down at one crucial point, for the meanings generated by the literary system depend to a far greater degree on history. The literary past was present to Renaissance readers and writers as ancient sound shifts and semantic displacements never are to the users of a language. The synchronic thus included an awareness of the diachronic. A sense of the literary past was part of their structure of apprehension. Without some recollection of Virgil or Horace the laureates would have been nearly unintelligible, as would the amateurs without Petrarch (the Petrarch of the *Canzoniere*) or Ovid. It is, however, easy to exaggerate the importance of this diachronic dimension, to mistake the identification of sources for an analysis of the literary system. Allusions to earlier writers are significant gestures, but no more significant than many others—than, for example, attitudes toward print, a matter on which the ancients were of necessity silent. Though Spenser was called "our Virgil" and Sidney "the English Petrarch," neither much resembles his presumed model. Each presents himself in opposition to a set of contemporary expectations—expectations similar enough to those against which Virgil and Petrarch presented themselves to make those earlier poets usable, but different enough to alter significantly the resulting pattern.

The expectations against which the English amateurs defined themselves were, for the most part, not literary at all. They were rather those associated with gentle birth and a humanist education—in particular the expectation that the end to which a man so born and so educated should direct himself was service to the commonwealth. Now, of course, the humanists themselves admired poets and poetry and gave literary studies a central place in their curricula. Castiglione's courtier, Elyot's governor, and the pupils of Ascham's schoolmaster were all expected to turn out verse. But as the century progressed and as humanism moved northward, the active life of civic service and the contemplative (or concupiscent) life of literary withdrawal came more and more into conflict. The place of poetry in Elyot is already narrower than in Castiglione, and it narrows still further in Ascham, who classes poets as "quick wits," those hasty, rash, heady, brainsick, riotous, and unthrifty young men who, in Ascham's opinion, rarely "come to show any great countenance or bear any great authority abroad in the world." Against these Ascham sets the dutiful "hard wits," the men best suited for public service: "grave, steadfast, silent of tongue, secret of heart; not hasty in making, but constant in keeping, any promise; not rash in uttering, but ware in considering, every matter, and thereby not quick in speaking, but deep of judgment, whether they write or give counsel, in all weighty affairs." These, he concludes, "be the men that become in the end both most happy for themselves and always best esteemed abroad in the world."[3] Nor is Ascham's ideal idiosyncratic. It echoes the prescriptions of the chief ancient sources of ethical precept, Isocrates' *Ad Demonicum*, Cato's *Distichs,* and Cicero's *De Officiis,* and is in turn echoed in the advice of such Elizabethan figures of paternal and governmental authority as Sir Henry Sidney and Lord Burghley.[4] Ascham's grave and hard-witted counselor is the man Sidney, Spenser, and their contemporaries were taught to be.

The Elizabethan amateurs presented themselves as poets in

---

3. Ascham, pp. 22–24.

4. Sidney's advice to his son Philip has been reprinted in James M. Osborne, *Young Philip Sidney, 1572–1577* (New Haven: Yale Univ. Press, 1972), pp. 11–13. Letters of advice from Burghley to his sons Thomas and Robert can be found in *Advice to a Son,* ed. Louis B. Wright (Ithaca: Cornell Univ. Press, 1962), pp. 1–13.

opposition to such teaching. They made a place for poetry and created an identity for the poet by systematically inverting the values of midcentury humanism. In their literary self-presentation, gravity gave way to levity, work to play, reason to passion, public accomplishment to private delight, misogyny and antiromantic prejudice to love. The very generic forms they most favored—the love sonnet, the pastoral, the prodigal-son fiction—express the opposition between poetry and duty. But, curiously, even in their self-defining rebellion, the amateurs confirmed the values of midcentury humanism. They rarely began without an apology or ended without a palinode. They thus enclosed and rejected the self-as-poet in order to reveal the dutiful and employable self-as-civil-servant. They publicly anatomized their own wit to show themselves in a glass of government. Their ultimate recognition of the claims that they made poetry deny declared them to be members of the class of the humanistically trained, prodigal sons who were ready to return. For them, poetry came to be a way of indicating their fitness for precisely the sort of service against which they were rebelling, a way of proclaiming a serious self by shamefully displaying its opposite. "If any ask thee what I do profess," one of the least of the amateurs told his verse, "Say that of which thou art the idleness."[5]

The laureates began in close association with the amateurs. They attended the same schools, visited the same great houses, wrote poems to the same noble patrons, and sought preferment in the same royal court.[6] They shared, moreover, the same idea of the end to which their lives should be directed. Educated, like the amateurs, in the tradition of civic humanism, the laureates agreed that they could properly fulfill themselves and dis-

5. Thomas Bastard, *Chrestoleros, Seven Bookes of Epigrames*, Spenser Society (1888; rpt. New York: Burt Franklin, 1967), p. 83.
6. See John Buxton, *Elizabethan Taste* (London: Macmillan, 1963), pp. 317–338.

play their gentility only in the active service of the common-wealth.[7] The two groups differed, however, in how they hoped to accomplish that service—the amateurs as churchmen and statesmen, the laureates as poets. For the amateur, poetry was, as we have seen, a way of displaying abilities that could, once they had come to the attention of a powerful patron, be better employed in some other manner. For the laureate, poetry was itself a means of making a contribution to the order and im-provement of the state. This difference resulted naturally in differing attitudes toward the circulation of their work and in literary careers of markedly different shape. The amateurs avoided print; the laureates sought it out. The amateurs wrote only in youth or, more rarely, in the interstices between busi-ness; the laureates wrote all their lives.

In their self-presentation the laureates made much of these differences. But they first emphasized their similarity to the amateurs. So firm was the amateurs' hold on the name of poet that the laureates could not wholly reject amateur attitudes. Nor could they wholly accept them. Thus, as a role-preserving compromise, they selected certain works, usually those written in the minor genres most practiced by the amateurs, and pre-sented them with the familiar amateur self-disparagement. Daniel, in characterizing *Delia* as "the private passions of my youth . . . things uttered to myself and consecrated to silence" (I, 33), sounds as reticent and shamefaced as any amateur. Likewise, Chapman, who elsewhere calls himself the "grave and blameless Prophet of Phoebus," can, in introducing his Ovidian *Banquet of Sense,* claim not to "profess . . . sacred poesy in any degree" (III, 9, and II, 21), as can Drayton in the comic *Owle:* "We . . . leave the laurel unto them that may" (II,

7. For a particularly relevant illustration of the humanist insistence on the active life, see Lodowick Bryskett, *A Discourse of Civil Life,* ed. Thomas E. Wright (Northridge, Calif.: San Fernando Valley State College, 1970), pp. 4–25. Spenser is one of the speakers in Bryskett's dialogue.

478). Even Spenser doubted whether he should publish his *Shepheardes Calender* and spoke of his love poetry as "lewd layes . . . [made] in th' heat of youth" (IX, 5, and VII, 213). If the amateur—a Gascoigne, Sidney, Lodge, Hall, or Donne—advertised a tension between the poetry of youth and the business of age, a tension that often led to literary repentance, the laureate displayed a similar conflict between his work in the "amateur" genres and his work in those larger, more public forms on which his laureate claim depended. In *The Faerie Queene,* Spenser transformed but retained the conventions of amateur love poetry; in *The Civil Wars* and *Poly-Olbion,* Daniel and Drayton abandon them altogether. On one side of the great divide were sonnets of youth and love; on the other, serious public poems of history and topography—poems that corresponded in the career of a laureate to the active public service of the amateur.

In Daniel's motto, *Aetas prima canat veneres postrema tumultus,* the laureate finds his answer to the amateur's abandonment of singing for fighting. Like the amateur, the laureate presents himself as having been betrayed into verse by youthful passion and exposed in print by a piratical publisher. But, like the amateur's, his private and licentious poems plead indulgence, for they too give promise of more respectable future accomplishment. "Favored by the worthies of our land," he will "grow / In time to take a greater task in hand" (Daniel, III, 27). This movement from one kind of poetry to another could easily be given an appearance of Virgilian continuity ("Lo I the man . . ."), but I suspect that imitation of the amateurs was no less decisive than imitation of the ancients. In combination, the two provided a gesture of extraordinary subtlety and power, for by its means a writer like Spenser or Daniel or Drayton could at once satisfy expectation and redirect it. He could show himself to be a poet in the Elizabethan sense, while he simultaneously assimilated that modern role to the ancient one of

Roman laureate. He thus made the familiar amateur formula say something new. But without that formula, he would surely have found less use for Virgil.

Jonson marks his originality, an originality that distinguishes him even from the other laureate poets of his age, by rejecting any compromise, however limited, with amateur self-disparagement. For the first twenty years of his career, he wrote in no genre that he considered unworthy, or at least in none that he could not elevate, and, though he silently suppressed some of his juvenilia, he apologized for nothing he wrote. His epigrams (not songs and sonnets, to be sure) he presented defiantly as "the ripest of my studies" (VIII, 25). No English poet, whatever his pretension, had made such a claim for such poems. Bastard had called his epigrams "the accounts of my idleness," and Weever his "a twice seven hours . . . study."[8] Davies and Guilpin adopted similar attitudes toward theirs, and Donne did not allow his to be printed. Even Martial, Jonson's Roman model, had denied entry into the "theater" of his verse to any stern Cato; he feared the moralist's disapproval— a sentiment echoed, according to Thomas Moffet, in Sidney's literary repentance: "Having come to fear . . . that his *Stella* and *Arcadia* might render the souls of readers more yielding instead of better," Sidney, that most nearly laureate of amateur poets, "very much wished to sing something that would abide the censure of the most austere Cato."[9] So, continues Moffet, he translated "the *Week* of the great Bartas" and "the psalms of the Hebrew poet." For Jonson, there could be no such amateur self-depreciation, no shame, no repentance, and no reparation. "In my theater," he proclaimed, "Cato, if he lived, might enter

8. Bastard, p. 4; John Weever, *Epigrammes in the Oldest Cut and Newest Fashion*, ed. R. B. McKerrow (London: Sidgwick and Jackson, 1911), p. 1.
9. Thomas Moffet, *Nobilis, or a View of the Life and Death of a Sidney*, trans. and ed. Virgil B. Heltzel and Hoyt H. Hudson (San Marino, Calif.: Huntington Library, 1940), p. 74.

without scandal" (VIII, 26). A true poet, in Jonson's view, must be a poet without a palinode.

In opposing his work so uncompromisingly to the amateurs', Jonson only made more apparent the fundamental laureate strategy. If the Elizabethan amateur molded himself like a negative image on the template of midcentury English humanism, the laureate reversed the process, taking his form from opposition to the amateur. He thus restored to poetry a face resembling that of the humanist progenitor. When Jonson complains that the manners and nature of the writers of his time are "inverted," he points to this negative likeness between what he would call "poet" and "poetaster." Such likenesses are of course, never exact. Indeed, they may, to an eye not trained to see them, be scarcely perceptible. Poems and plays are crossed by so many systems with which we are more familiar—social, economic, psychological, philosophical, and literary—that quite fundamental relations in career type are easily obscured. But more often the differences on which authorial self-definition was based are readily apparent. What is less apparent is that the differences are functional, that they are the intended source of meaning. As critics, we use such differences to help us define by contrast the particular quality of each poet, but we do not often recognize that they are signs as well as symptoms, that they came to be there because they helped the poet define himself to his audience. In the production of meaning, as Saussure insisted, "il n'y a que des différences."[10] The differences are the poet's meaning.

Consider, for example, Joseph Summers' characterization of Donne and Jonson in terms of "opposed ideals and practices."

Besides the private and the public, the amateur and the professional, the individual and the general, one thinks of extravagance and sobri-

10. Ferdinand de Saussure, *Cours de Linguistique Générale* (1915; rpt. Paris: Payot, 1976), p. 166.

ety, excess and measure, spontaneity and deliberation, immediacy and distance, daring and propriety, roughness and elegance, tension and balance, agility and weight. And one can go on to expression and function, ecstasy and ethics, experience and thought, energy and order, the genius and the craftsman—ending with those inevitable seventeenth-century pairs, passion and reason, wit and judgment, nature and art.[11]

These differences are not, I would suggest, merely the fortuitous product of dissimilar temperaments, though temperament surely had something to do with them. If Donne appears extravagant, excessive, and spontaneous, it is in part at least because he wished to define himself as poet in opposition to humanist ideals of sobriety, measure, and deliberation. And if Jonson seems more sober (in verse, if not at the Mermaid), measured, and deliberate, it is because he presented himself in accord with those humanist ideals and in opposition to amateur extravagance, excess, and spontaneity—qualities that characterize the objects of his satire in both the epigrams and the plays.

The differences between Donne and Jonson are thus not primarily individual. Taken together, the terms on Donne's side could as easily serve as a description of Ascham's "quick wits," while those on Jonson's perfectly fit the "hard wits." They constitute opposed paradigms of rebellion and duty, of amateur and laureate. Sidney, Harington, Marston, or Nashe, different as they are from one another, could each be substituted for Donne with no change at all. And if changes would be needed to replace Jonson with Spenser, Daniel, Drayton, or Chapman, most of the terms would nevertheless fit, particularly if one thought only of those larger works on which they based their laureate claim. "Wild, madding, jocund, and irregular," the "wanton verse" of Drayton's *Idea* belongs, with the

11. Joseph H. Summers, *The Heirs of Donne and Jonson* (New York: Oxford Univ. Press, 1970), p. 39.

amateur juvenilia of other laureates, in the Donne column. But for the dutifully laureate *Barons' Wars,* Drayton sought rather Jonsonian "majesty, perfection, and solidity" (I, 485, and II, 4). To be sure, style follows genre, but both follow career type. Only a poet of a certain kind writes a poem like the *Barons' Wars.* Less adequately described by the Jonson terms is Spenser, whose attempt to reconcile amateur and laureate values goes much further than Drayton's movement from one mode to the other. But even applied to Spenser, the terms are not so much wrong as incomplete. In his self-presentation, Spenser did not perhaps oppose reason to passion, but he did try to reconcile the two in a way that would still distinguish him from the amateurs—not reason versus passion, but reasonable passion versus unreasonable passion. Though the distinction is less absolute than Jonson's, Spenser's laureate identity depended on it.

"But such a marshalling of abstractions can," Summers points out, "be misleading." It makes us forget how much Donne and Jonson had in common. To jog our memories, Summers borrows a sentence from Douglas Bush: "Both poets rebelled, in their generally different ways, against pictorial fluidity, decorative rhetorical patterns, and half-medieval idealism, and both, by their individual and selective exploitation of established doctrines and practices, created new techniques, a new realism of style (or new rhetoric), sharp, condensed, and muscular, fitted for the intellectual and critical realism of their thought."[12] In sum, Donne and Jonson are alike in that both are members of a single literary generation, a generation that defined itself in opposition to the generation of Sidney and Spenser. Taking both career identification and generation into account, we can express the relation of these poets to one another as a four-part equivalence.

12. Summers, p. 40.

Spenser : Sidney :: Jonson : Donne

But perhaps Jonson's position would be better appreciated were Donne replaced by Marston. Donne is in some ways more conservative than his generation and thus more resembles Sidney. With Marston as representative amateur, we see more fully the shift that separates Jonson from Spenser, the shift in literary form from poetry to drama, in mode from romance to satire, in fictional scene from pastoral to urban, in center of fashion from court to the inns of court, and in *magister amoris* (when love is not simply rejected) from Petrarch to Ovid.

On each side of this generational divide, the amateurs dominate, establishing a literary system particularly designed to express their own rebellious poetic identity. The task of the laureates was to take this system and make of it a vehicle for a very different sort of identity. If Chapman, Daniel, and Drayton seem not quite to have addressed themselves to this problem, it may be because of their intermediary position. Born midway between Sidney and Donne, they no longer saw the former as problematical and were too set in their Elizabethan manner to meet the challenge of the latter. They took, with varying degrees of dependence, Spenser's accomplishment as a model, a model imperfect only in its admixture of amateur attitudes, without realizing that the strength of Spenser's work as living poetry derived from that admixture. Instead of transforming the amateur themes and genres, as Spenser had done and as Jonson was to do, they sought in topography, history, and translation a laureate purity that left them alienated from the dominant literary fashion of their age—"the remnant of another time," as Daniel was already saying of himself in 1605.

An Official Self

So far I have said little of the professionals, and with good reason, for they said little of themselves. In the theater the professional dramatist was visible, if at all, only as an actor. And when, on rare occasions, his work got into print, it was likely to be anonymous. In neither their acted nor their printed form were his plays exercises in self-presentation. But despite the professional's reticence, his activities were made a signifying part of the Elizabethan system of literary careers. The responsibility for this assimilation belongs largely to the amateurs.

At first glance, the union of amateur and professional may appear highly improbable. In terms of education and social standing, they were at opposite ends of the scale—the amateur at the top, the professional at the bottom. Yet that very contrast served the amateur assimilation, for how could a gentleman better declare his truancy than by writing for the public theaters? If poetry represented a dereliction of duty, drama was worse. Thus where the quick wits in Gascoigne's *Glass of Government* speed their way to destruction with poems, the prodigal in Greene's *Never Too Late* does it still more spectacularly with plays. And what happened in fiction could, the authors intimate, happen in life. Both Gascoigne's book and Greene's are transparently autobiographical. Moreover, Greene was not alone in his public-theater prodigality. Like him, Marlowe, Peele, Lodge, Nashe, Marston, and Beaumont all made play writing a part of an amateur career—a career that in each case served to define the writer to his audience. It was against this amateur assimilation and against the preexisting attitudes which made it possible that Jonson had to struggle in using drama as a main vehicle for his laureate career. And, as always, the struggle was to make meaning by significant opposition. Thus, if we examine the common attitudes of amateurs and professionals, we should see the laureate more clearly.

If play writing could so easily be made to occupy the place more commonly taken in an amateur career by verse making, it was because both were supposed to be equally frivolous. Neither private verse nor public drama made the claim to literary greatness that distinguishes the laureate and his work. The courtly amateur claimed to write only for his own amusement and that of his friends; the professional, for money and the entertainment of the paying audience. The similarity between them is reflected in a trait we have already noticed, their common reluctance, whether feigned or true, to have their work printed. Though the "kind" would not have been the same, most amateurs and professionals could have echoed Heywood's protest: "It never was any great ambition in me to be in this kind voluminously read."[13] Their reasons no doubt differed—the amateur feared loss of face, the professional loss of income—but they resembled one another in lacking a desire to give permanent form and wide, printed circulation to the products of their wit. In this both differed from the laureates, who not only allowed their writings to be printed, but took great care that they be printed as handsomely as possible.

When they called their poems and plays "works," Daniel and Jonson defined the fundamental pretension of the laureate. (Suckling read this signal aright and in his "Sessions of the Poets" had Jonson tell "them plainly he deserved the bays, / For his were called *Works,* where others' were but plays.") Amateurs and professionals spoke rather of literature—or at least of the literature they wrote—as play. It occupied either the idleness of the writer or the idleness of the spectators, "that they may return to their trades and faculties with more zeal and earnestness, after some small, soft, and pleasant retirement."[14]

13. *The Dramatic Works of Thomas Heywood,* 6 vols. (1874; rpt. New York: Russell and Russell, 1964), VI, 5. In this address to the reader, prefaced to his *English Traveler* (1633), Heywood distinguishes himself particularly from Jonson: "True it is that my plays are not exposed unto the world in volumes to bear the title of *Works* (as others)."

14. Thomas Heywood, *An Apology for Actors,* ed. Arthur Freeman (New York: Garland, 1973), sig. F4. Heywood does of course argue that this retirement is in various ways morally improving.

A professional, like Heywood in his *Apology for Actors,* or an amateur, like Sidney in the *Defense of Poesy,* could, in good humanist fashion, make a far higher claim for drama or poetry, but he rarely presented himself or his own work—as the laureates habitually did—in such lofty terms. Few of Heywood's many plays were printed and, of those that were, very few include any prefatory self-presentation. Typical of these last is the dedication of *The Fair Maid of the West* to John Othow of Grey's Inn: "I must ingenuously acknowledge a weightier argument would have better suited with your grave employment, but there are retirements necessarily belonging to all the labors of the body and brain." As for Sidney, he allowed none of his literary productions to be printed and referred to the *Arcadia,* the most ambitious of his undertakings, as his "toyful book" to be read by his sister and her friends "at your idle times."[15] Even in their defensive treatises, Heywood and Sidney maintain their characteristic attitudes, the self-effacement of the professional and the humorous *sprezzatura* of the gentleman amateur. "I have been ever too jealous of mine own weakness willingly to thrust into the press," writes Heywood, "nor had I at this time, but that a kind of necessity enjoined me to so sudden a business"; while Sidney says of himself, "I know not by what mischance in these my not old years and idlest times having slipped into the title of a poet, [I] am provoked to say something unto you in defense of that my unelected vocation."[16] Needless to say, no such necessity or provocation was called on to explain the existence and publication of *The Faerie Queen, The Civil Wars, The Poly-Olbion, The Whole Works of Homer,* or *The*

15. Heywood, *The Fair Maid of the West,* ed. Robert K. Turner, Jr. (Lincoln: Univ. of Nebraska Press, 1967), p. 3; Sidney, *The Countess of Pembroke's Arcadia (The Old Arcadia),* ed. Jean Robertson (Oxford: Clarendon Press, 1973), p. 3.

16. Heywood, *Apology,* sig. A4; Sidney, *An Apology for Poetry,* ed. Geoffrey Shepherd (1965; rpt. Manchester: Manchester Univ. Press, 1973), p. 95.

Works of Ben Jonson. Their authors professed an elected vocation.

Toy, pastime, play, retirement—these terms were applied to their writings by amateur and professional alike, "for," as Dekker said of his *Shoemaker's Holiday,* "nothing is purposed but mirth."[17] Such mirth might be reprehended by the Catos of Court and City, by the Burghleian humanists and the burgher Puritans, but society generally was more lenient. The amateur was excused because he would ultimately renounce poetry for more serious pursuits, and the professional because, having little claim to gentility and its duties, he made it his humble occupation to provide for the recreation of others. Both thus enjoyed a freedom denied the laureate, a freedom from seriousness.

It may, however, seem absurd to talk of the freedom from seriousness of groups that in Jonson's time included Donne on the one side and Shakespeare on the other. The seriousness of either would, in the opinion of most modern readers, outweigh that of a whole theater of Daniels, Draytons, or even Jonsons. But Donne's and Shakespeare's is a seriousness of a very different sort from the laureates'—not the seriousness of a man writing in conformity to the dictates of truth and duty, but rather a seriousness discovered in play. We see this most readily in Donne, in the histrionic excess of his wit, searching out through image and attitude roles for the performing self, but it is perhaps still more fundamental to Shakespeare. For two decades in comedy, history, tragedy, and romance, Shakespeare explored the indirect ways by which his playful mimetic art touched on a grace beyond the reach of the professors of seriousness. His stolid Romans may speak of poets as "jigging fools," unfit for the serious business of war, but Shakespeare

17. *The Dramatic Works of Thomas Dekker,* ed. Fredson Bowers, 4 vols. (Cambridge: Cambridge Univ. Press, 1953–1961), I, 19.

ironically undercuts those same Romans in every serious pose they strike. Not they, but rather the Hals, the Rosalinds, the Hamlets—the characters who give themselves up, if only for a holiday, to the games of disguise—achieve full seriousness. Though bracketed with the imaginings of lunatics and lovers, the poet's story of festivity and dream "grows to something of great constancy." Critics have been no more successful than Hippolyta in defining that "something." At the serious center of the professional's work, as of the amateur's, lies an enigma that neither feels obliged to resolve. It possesses greatness and constancy, but, like Bottom's dream, it has no definable bottom, no external referant, no unambiguously ascertainable meaning. It has rather the elusive autonomy of game.

By contrast, the something of great constancy at the center of the laureate's work is easily defined. It is the poet himself. His deliberately serious poetic is grounded on a serious, centered self. As Daniel suggests in *Musophilus,* his poem of renewed self-consecration, the laureate's self, muse, and art are so intimately dependent on one another as to be virtually indistinguishable. They are separate facets—the doer, the doing, and that which is done—of a single being. "I . . . here present," he writes,

> the form of mine own heart:
> Where, to revive myself, my Muse is led
> With motions of her own, t'act her own part,
>   Striving to make her now contemned art,
> As fair t'herself as possibly she can;
> Lest, seeming of no force, of no desert,
> She might repent the course that she began.
>   (I, 223)

To avoid the repentance that was the mark of an amateur's career, the laureate returns to his heart to find there the beauty, force, and desert that justify his elsewhere "transformed verse, apparelled / With others passions or with others rage." Spenser makes a similar return in response to a similar provocation in Book VI of *The Faerie Queene,* as Jonson does in the two odes to himself.

> Let this thought quicken thee,
> Minds that are great and free,
>   Should not on fortune pause,
> 'Tis crown enough to virtue still,
>   her own applause.   (VIII, 174)

For the laureate, the something of great constancy is the poet's mind, "great" and "free." Jonson embraced with a fervency only to be equalled by Milton the ancient notion that the poem referred to the poet and that both referred to an abstract, atemporal concept of virtue. "For," as Jonson wrote in the preface to *Volpone,* "if men will impartially, and not asquint, look toward the offices and functions of a poet, they will easily conclude to themselves the impossibility of any man's being the good poet without first being a good man" (V, 17).

The derivation of Jonson's sentence from classical rhetoric tells us something more of the peculiarly uncomfortable position of the laureate, trying at once to be a poet and to distinguish himself from the poets of his age. For the amateur and the professional, rhetoric was primarily a source of pleasure; for the laureate, it was rather (and of necessity) an instrument of persuasion. "In moving the minds of men and stirring affections," the poet, and particularly the comic poet, most clearly resembled, in Jonson's view, the orator (VIII, 640). For both, persuasion depended on self-presentation. "Persuasion," Aristotle explained in his *Rhetoric,* "is achieved by the speaker's personal character when the speech is so spoken as to make us think him credible. We believe good men more fully and more readily than others."[18] There was, however, a danger in Jon-

---

18. Quoted by Robert M. Durling in *The Figure of the Poet in Renaissance Epic* (Cambridge: Harvard Univ. Press, 1965), p. 13. Durling goes on (pp. 13–43) to distinguish between Horace and Ovid in terms of their relation to the

son's identification of poet and orator, the danger that the former might be lost in the latter. Sidney, who, like Jonson, based his serious defense of poetry on its moving force, caught himself in time. "Methinks I deserve to be pounded for straying from poetry to oratory."[19] For the laureate it was much harder not to stray. Without the persuasiveness of the orator, he could scarcely hope to accomplish his didactic undertaking—the undertaking that justified his claim to be fulfilling his humanist obligation toward the active life through poetry. Only by rhetorical persuasion could he "effect the business of mankind" (Jonson, V, 17). The amateur or professional, who accepted no such serious obligation, had likewise no need either to present himself as a good man or to risk his identity as poet.

The goodness of the laureate was not to him merely another pose. It was rather the truth that underlay all the poses of his fictive art, the immovable center of his work as of his being. When Jonson resolves to "Live to that point . . . for which I am man, / And dwell in my center, as I can" (VIII, 219), he makes a particularly laureate affirmation of serious selfhood.[20] Depart from that centered self and the laureate would, as Daniel remarked,

> with these times of dissolution, fall
> From Goodness, Virtue, Glory, Fame and all.   (I, 223)

Detached role playing unites amateur and professional. The professional's negative capability, which allows autonomy to a realm of created selves, corresponds to the amateur's first-person assumption of a variety of often rebellious parts. For both,

rhetoric of persuasion. The differences between them are remarkably similar to those between the Elizabethan laureates and amateurs—a fact that Jonson had already noticed and used in *Poetaster,* where he presents himself as Horace and the amateurs as Ovid.

19. Sidney, *Apology,* p. 139.

20. See Thomas M. Greene, "Ben Jonson and the Centered Self," *SEL,* 10 (1970), 325–348.

the world is a stage on which they too are merely players. The laureate defines himself differently. "I have considered," Jonson wrote in *Discoveries,*

Our whole life is like a play wherein every man, forgetful of himself, is in travail with expression of another. Nay, we so insist in imitating others, as we cannot (when it is necessary) return to ourselves: like children, that imitate the vices of stammerers so long, till at last they become such and make the habit to another nature, as it is never forgotten.

But then he goes on to excuse one class, the one to which he, as good man and good poet, belonged, from this otherwise universal "we":

Good men are the stars, the planets of the ages wherein they live and illustrate the times. God did never let them be wanting to the world, as Abel . . . Enoch . . . Noah . . . Abraham . . . and so of the rest. These, sensual men thought mad, because they would not be partakers or practicers of their madness. But they, placed high on the top of all virtue, looked down on the stage of the world and contemned the play of fortune. For though the most be players, some must be spectators.   (VIII, 597)[21]

Characterized by a superlunary constancy, the laureate is removed from and opposed to the mad mimicry of the world, a mimicry that embraces amateur and professional alike.[22]

21. Jackson I. Cope refers to these passages in the course of an interesting discussion of the way in which Jonson presented himself in *Every Man Out of His Humor. The Theatre and the Dream: From Metaphor to Form in Renaissance Drama* (Baltimore: Johns Hopkins Univ. Press, 1973), pp. 226–236. On the antitheatricalism suggested by the passages, see Jonas A. Barish, "Jonson and the Loathèd Stage," in *A Celebration of Ben Jonson,* ed. William Blissett et al. (Toronto: Univ. of Toronto Press, 1973), pp. 27–53. I take this antitheatricalism to be a function of Jonson's laureate self-presentation.
22. Compare Patrick Cruttwell's characterization of "metaphysical or Shakespearean" self-consciousness as "dramatic, that of the actor, who can let himself go—to all appearances—completely, because he knows that in reality the part he is playing need not be identified with his self: and because of that, his parts can always be changed, his range is infinite." Opposed to this, Crutt-

Jonson's list of good men again recalls Milton, who in *Paradise Lost* compiles a very similar list. The strongest link between these two seventeenth-century laureates is to be found here, in a shared sense of the good man's historic function of illuminating the age in which he lives. They agreed that virtue expresses itself most directly through the lives of these good men and that poems can be vehicles of that expression only because their authors are such men. But if the good man illuminates the world, he is also necessarily at odds with it. His separate identity depends on such opposition. Hence the intensely antagonistic bitterness of both Jonson and Milton. That this bitterness is a function of the laureate's role, of the process of self-definition, and not merely of the waspish characters of these two writers is suggested by its recurrence in Spenser and Daniel, both men of relatively gentle temper. If Richard Lanham is right, self-righteous antagonism to the world has been an integral part of the serious, centered self since its literary emergence in Plato's depiction of Socrates.

Questioning with a peculiarly modern preference for game over seriousness, Lanham asks whether Socrates' self "was especially worth knowing." "Isn't it really the testy, impatient, intolerant self of the religious zealot? . . . So full of self-importance and self-satisfaction . . . so willing to preach to others the error of their ways, is this man, whose whole life plays variations on 'Why the world should be more like me,' the perfect teacher? Is he indeed the model for Western man?" Though Lanham would say "no," Plato said "yes." Plato makes, as Lanham says, "the possibility of human seriousness depend on

---

well places Jonsonian self-consciousness, "that of someone obliged to behave according to a certain code, who would feel himself disgraced or humiliated if he went outside it." In calling the former "living and fruitful" and the latter "sterile and static," Cruttwell expresses the usual nineteenth- and twentieth-century view. *The Shakespearean Moment and its Place in the Poetry of the 17th Century* (1954; rpt. New York: Columbia Univ. Press, 1970), pp. 48–49 and 220.

Socrates, on accepting him as a referential type of self, as divinely inspired."[23] In like manner, the Renaissance laureates made the seriousness of their works depend on the seriousness of their own centered and self-knowing selves. "First give me faith," wrote Jonson to one that asked to be sealed of the Tribe of Ben, "who know / Myself a little" (VIII, 220). To join the laureate's fit audience, to be sealed of his tribe, requires a constantly renewed act of faith in the inspiration, goodness, and self-knowledge of the laureate himself—an act of faith that neither amateur nor professional demands.

Lanham refuses this faith. In the serious Socratic self, he finds not self-knowledge, but rather willful self-deception.

From the rhetorical point of view, Socrates shows signs of not really knowing himself. . . . One sees running all through the *Apology* the dramatic sanction of identity. But this rhetorical sanction at the center of his Athenian life Socrates could never see. Neither could Plato. Had he seen it, he could not have contended with the Sophists as he did. He would have realized he was partly, as we are all partly, one of them. Socrates would have recognized, had he truly known himself, the rhetorical ingredient in all human behavior, would have seen his truth as only half the human truth, half the human self.[24]

Many readers have detected just such self-deception in Jonson. It is, I would suggest, an inevitable result of the laureate enterprise. A man who plays a role that pretends to be no role at all is caught in self-contradiction of a sort that he can admit only at the price of abandoning his original pretension. Nor can he avoid the problem by giving up his dramatic self-presentation. No man can do that, the laureate still less than most. Since his self is the guarantor of his work, it requires a presentation that is of necessity dramatic. Thus the more the laureate labors to assert his ideal stasis and self-sufficiency, his godlike superior-

23. Richard A. Lanham, *The Motives of Eloquence: Literary Rhetoric in the Renaissance* (New Haven: Yale Univ. Press, 1976), pp. 45–46 and 43.
24. Lanham, pp. 45–46.

ity to all role playing, the less static and self-sufficient he appears. "An innocent man needs no eloquence," Jonson sententiously wrote, yet, like so many of his moral sentences, this condemns him, for he could never resist using all the eloquence at his command in defense of his innocence. "I might have passed by," he continues a few lines later, "yet I durst not leave myself undefended" (VIII, 604–605). Throughout his career, he, like Milton or Chapman or Drayton, felt compelled to rebuke every slight and answer every criticism, even as he pretended indifference to both. Such compulsion could scarcely be resisted by men who were fashioning not only poems, but also a poet.

To us, the amateur and the professional seem closer to truth, and to a true poetics, because they make no direct claim on truth. W. B. Yeats put the modern view nicely in his un-Jonsonian essay of Jonsonian title, "Discoveries." "If it be true that God is a circle whose centre is everywhere, the saint goes to the centre, the poet and artist to the ring. . . . The poet must not seek for what is still and fixed, for that has no life for him; and if he did, his style would become cold and monotonous, and his sense of beauty faint and sickly . . . , but be content to find his pleasure in . . . whatever is most fleeting, most impassioned."[25] Like the saint, the Renaissance laureate went to the center, the "still and fixed" center of himself, which ideally was also the center of his culture—the juncture of religious, moral, political, and artistic authority. It was a self that could best be found, not

25. W. B. Yeats, *Essays* (New York: Macmillan, 1924), p. 356. The persistence of such views is illustrated not only by Cruttwell's remarks quoted in note 22, but also, in a very different critical idiom, by Roland Barthes's distinction between "readable" and "writeable" texts, between *le lisible* and *le scriptible*. *S/Z* (Paris: Seuil, 1970), p. 10. Like Yeats, Cruttwell, and (for that matter) Lanham, Barthes rejects the fixed, static, and serious "classic" text in favor of a more open and less referential text whose reading is characterized by "désire," "volupté," and "enchantment." These values obviously suit Shakespeare better than Jonson.

by introspection, but by the careful study of Scripture and those various Greek and Roman mirrors of duty that we have noticed influencing Ascham: Isocrates' *Ad Demonicum,* Cato's *Distichs,* and Cicero's *De Officiis.* In a letter to a friend, Sidney cited the Bible and Cicero as the keys to self-knowledge and Polonius borrowed from Isocrates and Cato in composing the most famous Renaissance list of precepts, a list that ends, "This above all, to thine own self be true." In their poetry, however, Sidney and Shakespeare, the amateur and the professional, could suspend and even mock this serious, centered, referential self. As poets, they belonged rather with Yeats, masquerading on the ring of being. To distinguish himself from them, the laureate had to attach himself to duty.

Officium was for the laureate, if not for the amateur or the professional, related to poetry in its full double meaning, both dutiful action and office. As well as seeking to accomplish his duty, the laureate sought a public office, an office symbolized by the laurel crown, an office comparable to those for which the amateurs abandoned poetry. The idea of goodness on which the laureate modeled himself was riven by a paradox that required such public officiousness of him. According to a tradition that goes back at least to Plato and that was made central to the Christian idea of God, the Good is characterized equally by self-sufficient stasis and by altruistic expansion. Closed in the circle of its own perfection, goodness needs nothing outside itself; "'Tis a crown enough to virtue her own applause," as Jonson said of and to himself. Yet the Good ceases, by definition, to be good if it withhold its good; to be good, the Good must do good.[26]

In the Renaissance these contradictory principles found

26. For a discussion of this paradoxical idea of the good, see Arthur O. Lovejoy, *The Great Chain of Being* (1936; rpt. Cambridge: Harvard Univ. Press, 1942), pp. 24–66.

their fullest embodiment in Stoicism and in civic humanism, and the characteristic postures of each deeply mark every laureate career. To the poet as Stoic, his mind was kingdom enough. But to the poet as humanist, an office in the king's court was a necessity. The laureate poet thus both fulfilled and abandoned himself by becoming Poet Laureate. His civic obligation made the monarch the center of his circle, and to that center Spenser, Daniel, Drayton, Chapman, and Jonson all gravitated. Yet what they discovered there bore a troubling resemblance to the games of vanity and mimicry they had left behind. Nor could they help playing such games themselves, though they often played them with an awkwardness that betrayed their discomfort. In this respect, both the amateur, who shared the laureate's humanist ambition, and the professional, who didn't, had the advantage—the amateur because his poetry was neither a serious presentation of himself nor a serious application of that self to the business of government, and the professional because, as entertainer, he hardly had to present himself at all.

But modern readers have not until recently been much inclined to sympathize with the laureate's predicament. An official self is, almost by definition, an insincere self; an official poet, a bad poet. How can official poetry, cut off from that "rage for chaos," which the romantic temper sees as the essential basis of all art, be anything but cold and monotonous?[27] Yeats himself raised the central objection in his introduction to Spenser. "One is persuaded that his morality is official and impersonal—a system of life which it was his duty to support—and it is perhaps a half understanding of this that has made so many generations believe that he was the first poet laureate, the first salaried moralist among the poets. . . . He should have been content to be, as Emerson thought Shake-

27. Morse Peckham, *Man's Rage for Chaos* (Philadelphia: Chilton, 1965).

speare was, a Master of the Revels to mankind."[28] Like Spenser, the other sixteenth- and seventeenth-century poets of laureate pretension have all, at one time or another, been blamed for not having been content to be Shakespeare. Put this way, the reproach is unanswerable. Foolish indeed the ambition to be more! Shakespeare's accomplishment is proof enough that his was the more profitable course—as in its smaller way Donne's accomplishment seemed, a few years ago, proof of the greater profit of his.

But, as critics and scholars in the last quarter-century have been at pains to demonstrate, neither our prejudices nor our preferences were the Elizabethans'.[29] In their self-fashioning, the laureates necessarily opposed the usual sixteenth-century literary practice, but at least they were supported, indeed projected into the postures they assumed, by the governing ideals of their society. Not sharing those ideals, we read them awry. To us the association of poet and monarch means selling out to the Establishment. To them it meant fulfillment of duty. We have no trouble understanding the little flute player in Georges Brassens' song who refuses the king's offer of a title of nobility because, as he says, "On dirait par tout le pays, le joueur de flute a trahi." But we do have difficulty in understanding the very different gestures of Spenser or Jonson. Yet the laureate's search for royal favor had in its system precisely the meaning that the flute player's rejection of it has in ours. Both mean: "This artist is true to himself."

In poetry, as in all other domains, Renaissance theorists

28. Yeats, pp. 458–459.
29. Two recent studies that deal directly with the problem of the relation between poet and monarch are Michael O'Connell, *Mirror and Veil: The Historical Dimension of Spenser's "Faerie Queene"* (Chapel Hill: Univ. of North Carolina Press, 1977) and Stephen Orgel, *The Illusion of Power: Political Theater in the English Renaissance* (Berkeley: Univ. of California Press, 1975). See also Thomas R. Edwards, *Imagination and Power: A Study of Poetry on Public Themes* (New York: Oxford Univ. Press, 1971).

conceived of a hierarchy of value, and at the top of the literary hierarchy they placed the great public poet, the true poet, the laureate. Such a poet, they often argued, was as rare and as precious as a monarch. *Solus Rex aut poeta non quotannis nascitur,* runs one of Jonson's favorite Latin tags. Both king and poet, the one as governor, the other as maker, were thought to reflect on earth, in a way that distinguished them from other men, the image of God. When the civil and literary hierarchies met in one person, as Puttenham claimed they did in Elizabeth, or Jonson in James, the Renaissance man felt a particular *o altitudo*. But even when separate, their functions ideally brought them together. "Learning"—and to Jonson, who translated this passage out of Vives, learning was a prime distinguishing characteristic of the laureate poet—"learning needs rest; sovereignty gives it. Sovereignty needs counsel; learning affords it. There is such a consociation of offices between the prince and whom his favor breeds that they may help sustain his power, as he their knowledge" (VIII, 565). How could one feel disgraced in being a "salaried moralist" when the paymaster and pupil was a king? The laureates asked not whether the goal was worthy, but rather whether, given the state of poetry and of the polity in their time, it could be achieved.

"I Play the Man I Am"

In their literary self-fashioning, Spenser, Jonson, and the other laureates tested, however inadvertently, some of the deepest values of their culture—values that had given rise to the idea of the laureate poet. The idea of the laureate was, in large measure, the idea of the Renaissance. Each envisioned a rebirth of classical antiquity and, more particularly, a rebirth of the kind of man prescribed by ancient moral philosophy. By their undertaking, the laureates implicitly asked whether such a man could exist and succeed. Could an Elizabethan poet "know and be one complete man"? (Chapman, II, 434). Could he be both Stoic and humanist, true both to himself and to his civic duty? Could he create an "art of presence" (to use the term Arnold Stein has recently applied to Milton),[30] which would also be an art of moral persuasion, without losing his claim to the art of poetry as his contemporaries understood it? In seeking to give an affirmative answer to these questions, the laureates offered themselves as cultural protagonists—aspirants to glory, but unwitting preys to defeat. In a different way, the amateurs were already playing the role of cultural protagonist. "Make me your mirror," Gascoigne told the young gentlemen of England. "If you see me sink in distress, notwithstanding that you judge me quick of capacity, then learn you to maintain yourselves swimming in propriety and eschew betimes the whirlpool of misgovernment."[31] By their rebellion, the amateurs tested the narrow limits of midcentury humanism, and by their repentance, they confirmed those limits. But for most of them, both the rebellion and the repentance were too conventional to include much risk.

The amateur's testing of his culture is comedic in its outline, a conflict between youth and age that ends in reconciliation and in the reaffirmation of the basic order of society. The pattern of laureate testing is more nearly tragic, for it ends not in a predictably repentant return (the laureates had nothing to repent and had never left home), but rather in lonely disillusionment with a hypocritical society that rejects those who act out its official ideals. Taking a hint from the writers themselves, who modeled many of their fictions and self-portraits on the

---

30. Arnold Stein, *The Art of Presence: The Poet in "Paradise Lost"* (Berkeley: Univ. of California Press, 1977).

31. *The Complete Works of George Gascoigne,* ed. J. W. Cunliffe, 2 vols. (Cambridge: Cambridge Univ. Press, 1907), I, 14.

parable of the prodigal son, I have elsewhere referred to the Elizabethan amateurs as "a generation of prodigals."[32] The laureates resemble rather the prodigal's elder brother, dutiful but ignored. Jonson's complaint of ill-use after much faithful service is much like the elder brother's. "Poetry, in this latter age, hath proved but a mean mistress to such as have wholly addicted themselves to her or given their names up to her family. They who have saluted her on the by and now and then tendered their visits, she hath done much for and advanced in the way of their own professions (both the law and the gospel) beyond all they could have hoped or done for themselves without her favor" (VIII, 583). Having given their names up to poetry, the laureates understandably felt that poetry should have made some suitable return. But they saw the fatted calf of worldly consideration going instead to the amateurs.

Advancement and patronage, "a kid that I might make merry with my friends," were not all these elder brothers lacked. Mere recognition of identity, the bare admission that a valid distinction had been made, seemed often denied them. For, as Jonson continued, not only did poetry, in her neglect of the laureates, "emulate the judicious but preposterous bounty of the time's grands, who accumulate all they can upon the parasite or freshmen in their friendship but think an old client or honest servant bound by his place to write and starve." She also imitated the less grand.

Indeed, the multitude commend writers as they do fencers or wrestlers, who, if they come in robustiously and put for it with a deal of violence, are received for the braver fellows, when many times their own rudeness is a cause of their disgrace. . . . But in these things the unskillful are naturally deceived and . . . : think rude things greater than polished and

32. Richard Helgerson, *The Elizabethan Prodigals* (Berkeley: Univ. of California Press, 1976), p. 155. André Gide's adoption of the parable in his self-defining "Retour de l'Enfant Prodigue" (1907) provides additional evidence of the persistence of the attitudes toward the writer expressed by the sixteenth-century amateurs. Gide differs from them—and thus marks the difference

scattered more numerous than composed. Nor think this only to be true in the sordid multitude, but the neater sort of our gallants, for all are the multitude. Only they differ in clothes, not in judgment or understanding.   (VIII, 583)

Commons, gallants, and grands alike—*all* are the multitude. Unrewarded and misapprehended, the laureate thus stood alone at the moral center of an otherwise erring society.

Though tragedy is no doubt too strong a word for careers as outwardly successful as those of Spenser and Jonson, the laureates' sense of alienation, particularly when the fullest incorporation was what they had sought, does come near the heart of tragic experience. Despite their careful effort to achieve an identity congruent with all that seemed most worthy in their culture, these men came to feel that their serious self-presentation was not taken quite seriously—that their work was regarded as play. They were being cast in the very role from which they had dutifully sought to differentiate themselves. Champions and victims of an exalted and unworkable ethos, they, like Coriolanus, whose career theirs resemble, might have asked the society that had made them,

> Would you have me
> False to my nature? Rather say, I play
> The man I am.

Playing the men they were (or were supposed to be), Daniel drifted into prose, Chapman into querulousness, and Drayton into isolation from his audience. Even Spenser and Jonson, who had so much better understood the problem of laureate self-definition, knew disillusionment and defeat—Spenser, threatened by the Blatant Beast of envy and detraction, bitterly telling

---

between the modern and the Renaissance sensibility—by having his prodigal return not to repent and, by his repentance, confirm the established values of society, but rather to subvert them still further by enticing his younger brother into rebellion.

his verse to "keep better measure, / And seeke to please, that now is counted wisemans threasure" (VI, 149), and Jonson, neglected alike in court and theater, contenting himself with his own applause. It would take Milton and a political revolution to make the laureate's fall seem fortunate. Though Spenser, like Milton, could celebrate the paradise within, he and his laureate contemporaries were too much shaped by the values of civic humanism to find in private rectitude a satisfactory consolation for the defeat of their public ambition.

The
New Poet
Presents
Himself

—

A Ribbon in the Cap of Youth

Among his immediate contemporaries, Spenser was doubly
unique. Not only was he the best poet (*Anglicorum Poetarum
nostri seculi facile princeps,* as Camden called him), he was the
only poet of distinctly laureate ambition. Other men did, of
course, write verse. But he alone presented himself as a poet, as
a man who considered writing a duty rather than a distraction.
With the exception of a few rare and little-respected hirelings,
Spenser's literary contemporaries were gentlemen for whom
poetry was, as I began to suggest in the last chapter, a mere
ribbon in the cap of youth, a ribbon which, if paraded too
ostentatiously, threatened to expose its wearer to ridicule and
shame. Their poetic self-indulgence (for self-indulgence it was
generally admitted to be) was, in consequence, usually of short
duration and was marked, whatever its duration, by much
self-conscious defensiveness, leading quite often to repentance.
A Sidney, a Lodge, or a Harington might defend poetry in the
highest terms, proclaiming its divine origin and advertising its
civilizing effect, but when these men spoke of their own work it

was either with humorous and graceful disdain or with some more serious uncertainty. At such moments, the various elevated notions of the poet as counselor of kings and monarch of all sciences, as first bringer-in of civility, best teacher of virtue, and most potent inspirer of courage—notions that had filled their defenses of poesy, their apologies, and their honest excuses—failed them, leaving no refuge but self-depreciation or recantation. Sidney referred to the *Arcadia* as "a trifle, and that triflingly handled," and he ended his life requesting that both the *Arcadia* and his lyric works be consigned to the flames. Lodge too characterized his literary efforts as the off-hand products of a man whose true vocation lay elsewhere, and he too repented. Even Harington, for all his reputation as a wag, feared that in becoming "a translator of Italian toys" he was wasting his education. And on the accession of James, he bid his "sweet wanton Muse" farewell, recognizing that poetry, especially for a man no longer young, stood in the way of political advancement.[1] If one or the other must be sacrificed, Sidney, Lodge, and Harington would have agreed that it should surely be poetry. Of all the earlier Elizabethan writers, only Spenser might have hesitated in making the same choice.[2]

It was a choice to which they had been directed from earliest youth. Not only was service to Queen and country the path of wealth, power, and prestige, it was also the path of duty, that

1. For Sir Philip Sidney see *The Countess of Pembroke's Arcadia (The Old Arcadia)*, ed. Jean Robertson (Oxford: Clarendon Press, 1973), p. 3, and note 16 below; for Thomas Lodge see *The Complete Works*, ed. E. W. Gosse, 4 vols. (1883; rpt. New York: Russell & Russell, 1963), I, 7 *(Rosalynde)*, and III, 13 *(Prosopopeia)*; for Sir John Harington see *Orlando Furioso*, ed. Robert McNulty (Oxford: Clarendon Press, 1972), pp. 14–15, and *Nugae Antiquae*, ed. Henry Harington, 2 vols. (London, 1804), I, 333.

2. I disagree here with Muriel Bradbrook's assumption that Spenser's initial aim was a political rather than a literary career. Unlike Gascoigne or Harvey, the other figures she discusses, Spenser does not suggest that poetry is a way of displaying talents that would be used to better advantage in some other activity if the poet could only secure suitable employment. See "No Room at

"for which you were born, and to which, next God, you are most bound," as Lord Burghley put it in a letter to young Harington.[3] In the Renaissance debate between the active and the contemplative lives, the active had won. A gentleman thus had a primary obligation to express his virtue in public service. But that ideal left little place for poetry. Humanist educators might recognize that poetry brought glory to a nation, yet they remained suspicious of poets. Ascham, as we have seen, placed them in the category of "quick wits"—ebullient young men who, he argued, rarely prove "either very fortunate themselves or very profitable to serve the commonwealth."[4] And Ascham's view of the poet was taken up, repeated, and, more important, made, as his more abstract praise of poetry never was, into a role by the young men themselves—by Gascoigne in his *Glass of Government* and by Lyly in *The Anatomy of Wit.* Each of these is a prodigal-son story, a story of a witty young man or of several witty young men who disregard the prudent advice of their Ascham-like elders and come to grief. In addition to telling this story many times in a wide variety of literary forms, the writers of Spenser's generation regularly identified themselves with their prodigal protagonists—Pettie with Alexius in the *Petite Pallace,* Lyly with Euphues, Greene with Roberto in his *Groatsworth of Wit,* Lodge with the usurer's victim in the *Alarm against Usurers,* Austen Saker with his

the Top: Spenser's Pursuit of Fame," in *Elizabethan Poetry,* Stratford-upon-Avon Studies, 2 (New York: St. Martin's Press, 1960), pp. 91–109.

3. *Nugae Antiquae,* I, 134.

4. Roger Ascham, *The Schoolmaster,* ed. Lawrence V. Ryan (Ithaca: Cornell Univ. Press, 1967), p. 22. Ascham's later exhortation to "the goodly wits of England" to "give themselves to poetry" is found in the very limited and limiting, but extraordinarily influential, context of his attack on rime and plea for quantitative meter "to make perfect . . . this point of learning in our English tongue" (p. 151). As I suggest below, to Spenser and to many of his contemporaries, this narrow door seemed for a time the only one that led to anything like a fuller poetic career. Needless to say, it opened instead on quarters more cramped than those they already occupied.

Narbonus, Harington with Rogero in the Alcyna episode of
Orlando Furioso, and Whetstone with the biblical prodigal
("the lusty younker," as Whetstone calls him) in his *Rock of
Regard.*[5] And often the repentant admission of self-destructive
prodigality was coupled with a condemnation of poetry, or of
the wit that made it possible, or of the love that inspired it. Of
course not every writer presented himself as a prodigal, but
other masks—Sidney's Philisides, a lovelorn gentleman dis-
guised as an Arcadian shepherd, or Barnaby Rich's Andruchio,
an unemployed soldier parading in fantastical finery—reveal a
similar discomfort with literature.[6] Whether their excuse was
"the unnoble constitution of the age that denies us fit employ-
ments" or the overmastering sway of some amorous passion,
they did agree that poetry required an excuse, and most felt
that the best proof of contrition was a promise not to offend in
like sort again—a promise that they usually kept.

But so long as Englishmen offered their poems as mere "idle
toys proceeding from a youngling frenzy," England could
hardly hope to have a poet of the laureate sort.[7] The Elizabethan mask of the poet as a youth improperly distracted from
the serious concerns of life has, of course, not gone unnoticed.
But so intent have critics been on explaining and defending
Spenser and his greater contemporaries in terms of their high-

5. For a fuller discussion of this pattern and its place in the lives and works
of Spenser's contemporaries, see my *Elizabethan Prodigals* (Berkeley: Univ. of
California Press, 1976). Other of my *obiter dicta* in the discussion of Spenser's
English backgrounds, including my reading of Sidney, my characterization of
the nature and influence of a humanistic education, and my understanding of
the attitudes of such figures as Burghley, Ascham, Gascoigne, Lyly, Lodge,
Greene, and Harington, are also worked out in greater detail in *The Elizabethan Prodigals.*

6. Philisides is most fully presented in Sidney's Old *Arcadia,* though he
appears in the New *Arcadia* as well; Andruchio is a character in *The Straunge
and Wonderfull Adventures of Don Simonides* (1584).

7. Thomas Watson, *Hekatompathia or Passionate Centurie of Love,* ed.
S. K. Heninger, Jr. (Gainesville, Florida: Scholars' Facsimiles, 1964), p. 5.

est and most theoretical claims for poetry and so convinced
have the critics been of the independence of the created persona
from the creating artist that they have largely ignored the effect
of this role definition on the shape of Elizabethan literature, on
the choice of subjects and their treatment, and on the
configuration of the typical literary career.[8] Yet far the greater
part of the imaginative literature of the first three and a half
decades of Elizabeth's long reign respects the boundaries
erected by that definition. Only within those boundaries could
the poetic game be played freely, and even there the player
generally took care to express his self-depreciating awareness
that poetry was merely a game. In this playful and restricted
way, much poetry was written. And in the same way, poetry
and the love so closely related to it were defended—that is,
with an ironic jocularity or exaggeration that proved the author no dupe of his own sophistry. Sidney's *Defense of Poesy* is
a perfect example of this. Outside the confines of the literary
game, Sidney never repeated such arguments. The effect of the
limits can be observed as well in the actions and remarks of
writers who strayed beyond them, in Lyly's regret that he had
"played the fool so long," in Harington's aspiration "to more
serious thoughts," in Giles Fletcher's claim to the right to pub-

8. The modern attitude toward Sidney was largely established by Kenneth
Myrick, *Sir Philip Sidney as a Literary Craftsman* (1935; 2d ed. Lincoln: Univ.
of Nebraska Press, 1965). The comparable view of Spenser has been the work
of many scholars and critics—first among them, C. S. Lewis, whose *Allegory of
Love* (Oxford: Clarendon Press, 1936) is a spirited application of medieval and
Renaissance ideas to a genuine critical appreciation of Spenser's poem. A typical, and in many ways admirable, product of this tradition is Mark Rose's
Heroic Love: Studies in Sidney and Spenser (Cambridge: Harvard Univ. Press,
1968), which, as its title suggests, finds love and heroic action triumphantly
reconciled in both Sidney and Spenser. An appreciation of the more problematic relation of action to contemplation in Elizabethan literature was initiated
by G. K. Hunter in *John Lyly: The Humanist as Courtier* (London: Routledge,
1962). My thinking about these matters is indebted both to Hunter's book and
to Richard Neuse's article, "Book VI as Conclusion to *The Faerie Queene*,"
ELH, 35 (1968), 329–353, where Hunter's views were first applied to Spenser.

lish a volume of love poems even in his forties, in Barnaby Rich's mendacious predating of his *Brusanus* to put it with the romantic works of his misspent youth, and in the protracted repentance of Robert Greene, who had written far too much for a gentlemanly amateur.[9] For the poet who remained comfortably within the boundaries, self-depreciation was a conventional gesture that made poetry possible. For one who crossed them, it could become a more serious recognition of fault. But a laureate poet, a poet of the sort that Spenser hoped to be, must of necessity ignore such boundaries. To write only in youth and only of love and neglect, to accept a definition that denied poetry any hope of affecting the world in a significant way, a definition that allowed poetry only by trivializing it, this a laureate poet could not do. The New Poet thus had his task clearly laid out for him. He had to redefine the limits of poetry, making it once again (if in England it ever had been) a profession that might justifiably claim a man's life and not merely the idleness or excess of his youth.

The metaphor of boundary may, however, evoke images and ideas far less inimical to poetry than those I have been suggesting—images of gardens, and temples, and Arcadian retreats, ideas of visionary tranquillity, of "a place where the mind may project its revised and corrected images of experience and where the soul may test and enlarge itself."[10] This last quotation suggests the usual modern critical understanding of

9. For John Lyly see *The Complete Works,* ed. R. Warwick Bond, 3 vols. (Oxford: Clarendon Press, 1902), I, 65; for Harington see *Nugae Antiquae,* I, 333; for Fletcher see *The English Works of Giles Fletcher, the Elder,* ed. Lloyd E. Berry (Madison: Univ. of Wisconsin Press, 1964), pp. 74–77; for Barnaby Rich see my "Lyly, Greene, Sidney, and Barnaby Rich's *Brusanus,*" *HLQ,* 36 (1972/73), 105–118. Greene's repentance began in 1590 with his *Vision,* his *Never Too Late,* and his *Mourning Garment* and ended only with his death and the posthumous *Repentance* of 1592.

10. Harry Berger, quoted by Angus Fletcher, *The Prophetic Moment: An Essay on Spenser* (Chicago: Univ. of Chicago Press, 1971), p. 23, n. 14. See also Fletcher's discussion, pp. 14–23.

the enclosed spaces of Renaissance literature. Such spaces are at once the necessary condition and the justification of poetry. As an art of imitation and second creation (to use terms favored by sixteenth-century theorists), poetry requires a sense of demarcation, a guarantee of its own, perhaps sacred, identity. Whether it seeks to offer an ideal of life or a perspective on it or merely an escape from it, poetry can do so only by being other than life. The justification of poetry resides in the character of its enclosed space: Nature's "world is brazen; the poets only deliver a golden." Or so argued Sidney.[11] But Sidney and his generation were, at the same time, bothered by a suspicion that the golden world might be no more than the deluding product of illicit desire. The second world of poetry was allowed for its beauty, with the Neoplatonic hope that such beauty might lead to virtuous action. But the allowance was grudging and the hope slim—sufficient perhaps to justify a courtier on holiday, though even he could not visit the golden world without shame or leave without repentance. But so long as that world had no prospect larger than the one afforded by youthful fancy, neither the allowance nor the hope could justify a man who wished to declare himself a native resident rather than a mere interloper. And that, of course, is precisely what Spenser had to do if he was to be a poet in the laureate sense. He insists on this primary allegiance in the first words of his first published work: "A shepheards boye (no better doe him call)." Colin Clout could not be blamed, as Philisides could, for abandoning a higher calling to become a shepherd. But Spenser could. He, like Sidney, had been given an education that destined him for public service, an education that defined poetry not only as different from action but as opposed to it.[12]

11. Sidney, *An Apology for Poetry,* ed. Geoffrey Shepherd (1965; rpt. Manchester: Manchester Univ. Press, 1973), p. 100.
12. See Russell Fraser, *The War Against Poetry* (Princeton: Princeton Univ. Press, 1970).

The problem was thus not merely what to write but what to be. Given his wish to realize in himself as well as in his work the grand claims for poetry that various theorists had outlined, how was he to present himself? Part of the answer, particularly in an age as given to imitation as the Renaissance, was to be found in the careers of other poets. The role of lover-poet was itself the product of one such career model, the Petrarchan. Petrarch's description of himself in his *Epistle to Posterity* as led astray by youth, corrupted by young manhood, but corrected by maturer age established a paradigm that would be repeated again and again, for it continued to serve the purpose for which it was designed. It marked out a space within which the poet and his poetry might enjoy a certain autonomy— though an autonomy based on rebellion and even, for Petrarch himself and for followers like Maurice Scève or Sidney, idolatry.[13] But if the Petrarchan role permitted one kind of poet and one kind of poetry, it made other kinds inaccessible. Now there were, of course, other models, and on these Spenser drew heavily in creating his poetic self, as he drew on them in creating the poems that were the expression of that self. Spenser's poetic self-image could in fact be described with some accuracy as a compound of Petrarch, Mantuan, Ariosto, Tasso, and Virgil. But such a description moves too easily from the English to the European context. The various models of a poetic persona and of a poetic career were not merely so many costumes hanging in the New Poet's wardrobe, ready to be put on and then taken off as he liked. Or if they were costumes, they were costumes that did not quite fit either his temperament and talent or the prevailing fashion of his time and place. And for him to have pinned a Virgilian ruff or an Ariostian sleeve on the by now quite anglicized Petrarchan suit would have been to appear as a

13. See John Freccero, "The Fig Tree and the Laurel: Petrarch's Poetics," *Diacritics*, 5 (1976), 34–40.

clown in motley. Nor could Spenser do as Jonson was later to recommend, "to make choice of one excellent man above the rest, and so to follow him, till he grow very he."[14] Even Jonson could not so abstract himself from the constraints of English literary fashion, though in *Poetaster* he tried. As for Spenser, however closely he followed Ariosto's poem, he always differed from Ariosto in his presentation of himself as poet.[15] Without Ariosto and other vernacular writers and without the great example of Virgil, Spenser's laureate self-creation is unthinkable. But those inspiring precedents could not solve for him the problems he faced as an Elizabethan who aspired to a major poetic career.

How then did he manage to distinguish himself as laureate from his amateur coevals? At first glance, particularly when the glance is taken in retrospect, the formula for his success seems absurdly simple. It consisted of two steps. The first was publicly to abandon all social identity except that conferred by his elected vocation. He ceased to be Master Edmund Spenser of Merchant Taylors' School and Pembroke College, Cambridge, and became Immerito, Colin Clout, the New Poet. No other writer of his generation was willing to take such a step. His contemporaries all hung on to some higher hope or expectation. But where they were lowered by poetry, Spenser, who never tired of insisting on his personal humility, was raised by it. This strategy had, of course, a certain autobiographical plausibility. Unlike Sidney, heir apparent to the earldoms of Leicester and Warwick, or Harington, the Queen's godson, or even Lodge, son of a knighted Lord Mayor of London, Spenser was, whatever his connection with the Spencers of Althorp, a

14. *Ben Jonson*, ed. C. H. Herford, Percy Simpson, and Evelyn Simpson, 11 vols. (Oxford: Clarendon Press, 1925–1952), VIII, 638.

15. See Robert Durling, *The Figure of the Poet in Renaissance Epic* (Cambridge: Harvard Univ. Press, 1965).

gentleman only by education. He had attended Merchant Taylors' School as a "poor scholar," and Cambridge as a sizar. In presenting himself as a shepherd-poet, he suffered no major *déclassement*.

The second step was the accomplishment of virtuous action through poetry. Though the poet may not himself be an actor in the world, his poetry does make others act. Having abandoned his own public pretension to gentility and its obligations, he proposes nevertheless that "the general end" of his major work is "to fashion a gentleman or noble person in virtuous and gentle discipline." Now other writers, of course, also argued for the didactic value of their work, but rarely did they go beyond expressing the self-defeating hope that other young gentlemen might learn from the poet's experience to avoid the like excess. The lesson of poetry was thus to stay away from poetry and from everything associated with it. Even Sidney, whose claims most nearly resemble Spenser's, ends by revealing both in the *Arcadia* and in *Astrophel and Stella* that "beauty... [is] more apt to allure men to evil than to frame any goodness in them."[16] And it is in these terms, according to both his Elizabethan biographers, that Sidney abandoned his work and willed its destruction. But not only did Spenser maintain his view with a resolutely sage seriousness, as Sidney never did, he also illustrated it triumphantly in the first three books of *The Faerie Queene*.

A confidence of purpose and a sureness of moral design, not to be found in the work of his contemporaries, mark these books. And the effect is achieved without sacrificing any of the beauty, love, or romance that were to Spenser's age the essen-

16. Fulke Greville, *Life of Sir Philip Sidney,* ed. Nowell Smith (Oxford: Clarendon Press, 1907), pp. 16–17. See also Thomas Moffet, *Nobilis, or a View of the Life and Death of a Sidney,* trans. and ed. Virgil B. Heltzel and Hoyt H. Hudson (San Marino, Calif.: Huntington Library, 1940), p. 74.

tial characteristics of poetry. If Cupid had, as Sidney said, ambitiously climbed even to the heroic, making even that noblest genre as indefensible as the rest,[17] Spenser would leave Cupid there yet would still uphold the virtuous effect of poetry. He did this by making distinctions and identifications of a sort that other writers of his generation could not maintain—distinctions between Una and Duessa, Medina and Acrasia, the true and the false Florimell and identifications between love and virtuous action, both in the particular instances of Redcross, Arthur, and Britomart and in the overall concept of the poem, its devotion to a Faerie Queen who is both Gloriana and Belphoebe, sovereign over the twin realms of politics and love. Only Spenser could, with no ironic qualification and no repentance, hail the

> Most sacred fire, that burnest mightily
>   In living brests, ykindled first above,
>   Emongst th'eternall spheres and lamping sky,
>   And thence pourd into men, which men call Love;
>   Not that same, which doth base affections move
>   In brutish minds, and filthy lust inflame,
>   But that sweet fit, that doth true beautie love,
>   And choseth vertue for his dearest Dame,
> Whence spring all noble deeds and never dying fame.
>
> (III.iii.1)[18]

17. Sidney, *Apology*, p. 125. The contradiction between this statement, which I take more seriously than do most other critics, and Sidney's praise of Heliodorus' "sugared invention of that picture of love in Theagenes and Chariclea" as "an absolute historical poem" (p. 103) provides one more example of the difficulty English poets experienced in placing foreign-inspired poetic monuments in an English moral landscape. What Heliodorus had done Sidney could do only at the risk of moral rebuke.

18. Quotations are from *The Works of Edmund Spenser: A Variorum Edition*, ed. Edwin Greenlaw, C.G. Osgood, et al., 11 vols. (Baltimore: Johns Hopkins Univ. Press, 1932–1957). I have regularized the letters *u, v, i,* and *j* and printed proper names in roman type. Otherwise spelling follows that of the *Variorum*.

And only Spenser could construct a fiction that set forth this exalted vision of love and beauty without losing hold of the world of Elizabethan political reality—a matter of both imagination and "just memory."

So confident is the assertion of beauty's claims in these first three books of The Faerie Queene, and perhaps in the fourth book as well, that Spenser had no need to feel self-consciousness about his role as poet. The poem imposes itself and supplies its own justification. There is thus no suggestion that writing it may have been an unworthy activity. On the contrary, the poem lifts its maker above his usual state, raising his "thoughts too humble and too vile" (I.proem.4). As Robert Durling has remarked, the unity and the justification of Spenser's poem and of his speaker derive from "the transcendency which spoke through him."[19]

Yet skirting about the periphery of even the triumphant first installment of The Faerie Queene is a slight, but ominous, reminder of the more usual Elizabethan estimate of poetry and its relation to the active life of public service. It emerges most clearly in the dedicatory sonnet to Lord Burghley, the leader of the Queen's government and a man notoriously unsympathetic to poets and to poetry.

> To you right noble Lord, whose carefull brest
>   To menage of most grave affaires is bent,
>   And on whose mightie shoulders most doth rest
>   The burdein of this kingdomes governement,
> As the wide compasse of the firmament,
>   On Atlas mighty shoulders is upstayd;
>   Unfitly I these ydle rimes present,
>   The labor of lost time, and wit unstayd.

Confronted with the statesmanlike gravity of Lord Burghley, Spenser forces himself back into the mold of the prodigal poet,

19. Durling, p. 234.

the unstaid wit whose work is the product of idleness and lost time. The pressure on Spenser to define himself and his work in these conventional terms was considerable, for they provided, as I have been arguing, the clearest and most widely understood notion of what a poet was and did. The triumphant realization of another idea of the poet in the first three books of *The Faerie Queene* can hardly be appreciated without some sense of those pressures—a sense that is, I think, best achieved by looking to either side of the assured work of the 1580s, to those passages in *The Shepheardes Calender,* the minor poems, and the last books of *The Faerie Queene* in which Spenser presents himself as a poet. What I hope to show by this examination is that Spenser was indeed aware of the situation that I have been describing and that he formulated his poetic identity in response to the challenge it posed.[20]

In the Labyrinth of Love

As everyone knows, the publication of *The Shepheardes Calender* was a carefully planned literary event. Not merely another collection of poems, the *Calender* marked the debut of the New Poet. The argument supposed by the poems and by E. K.'s introduction to them was already familiar in 1579 and was to become still more familiar in the decade between this

20. Since the original publication of this essay, several articles have appeared that in various ways confirm, modify, and/or extend its central argument. See Louis Adrian Montrose, "'The perfecte paterne of a Poete': The Poetics of Courtship in *The Shepheardes Calender,*" *TSLL,* 21 (1979), 34–67; Richard Mallette, "Spenser's Portrait of the Artist in *The Shepheardes Calender* and *Colin Clouts Come Home Againe,*" *SEL,* 19 (1979), 19–41; and, especially, three articles by David L. Miller: "Authorship, Anonymity, and *The Shepheardes Calender,*" *MLQ,* 40 (1979), 219–236; "Abandoning the Quest," *ELH,* 46 (1979), 173–192; and "Spenser's Vocation, Spenser's Career," *ELH* (forthcoming).

promise and its realization in the first books of *The Faerie Queene*. England lacked a poet. "There are many versifiers," as one contemporary remarked, "but no poet."[21] Italy and France had theirs, as did Greece and Rome before them. Why not England? The English language was as fit for poetry, the glory of the English nation as worthy of celebration. Yet there was no English Homer or Virgil, no English Ariosto or Ronsard. Englishmen could, of course, look back to Chaucer, but Chaucer had lived in a time and written in a language too remote from their own to be more than a distant inspiration. But now, at last, the English Poet had appeared. His fledgling work could not yet fully validate his claim to laureate greatness, and so his identity, like that of a still unproven knight of chivalric romance, was for a time to remain hidden. But he was, E. K. assured his audience, clearly beginning in the right way, with the pastoral,

following the example of the best and most ancient poets, which devised this kind of writing . . . at first to try their abilities: and, as young birds that be newly crept out of the nest, by little first to prove their tender wings, before they make a greater flight. So flew Theocritus, . . . Virgil, . . . Mantuan, . . . Petrarch . . . Boccace . . . Marot, Sanazarus, and also diverse other excellent both Italian and French poets. . . . So finally flyeth this our new poet, as a bird, whose principals be scarce grown out, but yet as that in time shall be able to keep wing with the best.

An extraordinary claim, but there was much in the volume to support it. Not only do the poems contain, as Sidney was to say, "much poetry, . . . indeed worthy the reading," they constitute a deliberate *défense et illustration* of the English language—a restoration of true English diction and a display of the range of poetic forms that English could handle.

Yet for all its pretension and real accomplishment, the book

21. *Sola quia interea nullum paris Anglia vatem?* / *Versifices multi, nemo poeta tibi est.* C. Downhale in Watson's *Hekatompathia*, p. 12.

is rife with intimations of failure, breakdown, and renunciation—intimations that arise most often in conjunction with the
commonplace Elizabethan notion of the poet as a youth be-
guiled by love. Even E. K., in defining "the general drift and
purpose of [these] eclogues," falls back on the usual etiology
and the usual defense: "Only this appeareth," he tells us, "that
his unstaid youth had long wandered in the common Labyrinth
of Love, in which time to mitigate and allay the heat of his
passion, or else to warn (as he saith) the young shepherds . . .
his equals and companions of his unfortunate folly, he compiled these xii eclogues." Here too poetry derives from the
youthful folly of love and serves either to relieve its author of
the effects of that folly or to warn others against it. But if this
cure prove successful, why should he ever write again? What is
to be his new source of inspiration and what is to be his purpose? These are not questions that occur to E. K. He is content
to repeat the commonplace without considering its implications. But clearly they do occur to Spenser. He knows his power
and has no hesitation in declaring it. He does not, however,
know quite how else to use it, or whether indeed it can be put to
any further use. Though *The Shepheardes Calender* is meant to
distinguish the New Poet from all other writers of English
verse, it finds no role for him to play other than the familiar
self-defeating one that limited the poetic careers of all his contemporaries.

The series opens with Colin Clout, "under whose person,"
as we are repeatedly told, "the author self is shadowed," breaking his pipe and abandoning his muse, and it ends twelve eclogues later with a near echo of this gesture of renunciation, as
Colin declares his muse hoarse and weary and hangs his pipe
upon a tree.[22] Whatever may be true of Spenser, Colin seems

22. John W. Moore, Jr., "Colin Breaks His Pipe: A Reading of the 'January'
Eclogue," *ELR*, 5 (1975), 3–24, reviews previous criticism of this aspect of
The Shepheardes Calender and suggests that the January eclogue and, more

destined for no further accomplishment. There is no prospect here of a tomorrow promising "fresh woods, and pastures new," as there will be in Milton's pastoral of poetic self-consecration. On the contrary, having wasted his year on the love that began in January, Colin will have no second chance. Winter has come again, "And after Winter commeth timely death." His experience thus confirms that common moral admonition so fundamental to the Elizabethan pattern of a poetic career: "All the delights of love, wherein wanton youth walloweth," as E. K. puts it in glossing the March eclogue, "be but folly mixed with bitterness, and sorrow sauced with repentance." The pattern finds perhaps its most explicit application to poetry midway through the *Calender* in the June eclogue, where Colin talks of how he sang of love until

> yeeres more rype,
> And losse of her, whose love as lyfe I wayd,
> Those weary wanton toyes away did wype.
> (11. 46–48)

But it recurs elsewhere, attached now to Colin, now to some other of the shepherds. One finds it in old Thenot's comments on youth and love in "February" (11. 69–70 and 87–90), "April" (1. 155), and "November" (11. 3–4), in Willye and Thomalin's emblems in "March," and in the characterization of Perigot and his love in "August" (11. 1–22). The pattern of youthful folly touches even the more topical satiric eclogues, shaping the debate between Palinode and Piers in "May" (11. 17–18) and the allusion to Paris in "July" (11. 145–151). So pervasive is the notion that a poet must fit this pattern that even Chaucer, rather incongruously, succumbs to it.

---

particularly, Colin's breaking of his pipe with which it ends "introduces us to the issue which gives unity to the *Calender*"—the nature of Colin's poetic vocation and the question of his fitness for it. I agree and would further suggest that the series as a whole fails either to resolve the issue or to answer the question.

He, whilst he lived, was the soveraigne head
Of shepheards all, that bene with love ytake.
("June," 11.82–83)

Given the ubiquity of these references linking poetry, love,
youth, and folly, it is difficult to imagine how the promised
emergence of the New Poet was to be accomplished.

Yet played against this conventional image of wanton
youth is a suggestion of responsibility neglected—responsibility that in Colin's case is specifically poetic. *The Shepheardes
Calender* centers on the same conflict between duty and desire
that informed all Sidney's works and that shaped as well the
poetic careers of most of Sidney and Spenser's contemporaries.
But in *The Shepheardes Calender* poetry figures on both sides
of the conflict. Colin's duty is literary. Love may inspire lyric
poetry, but it keeps the poet from other, more worthy, kinds—
didactic, panegyric, historical, and divine. Hobbinoll and
Thenot, both wise and virtuous shepherds, complain of this in
the April, June, and November eclogues, as does Cuddie,
Colin's poetic alter ego, in "October."

He, were he not with love so ill bedight,
Would mount as high, and sing as soote as Swanne.

Only in this last instance does love find a defender, and he is
swiftly put down. To Piers's suggestion that "love does teach
him to climbe so hie, / And lyftes him up out of the loathsome
myre," Cuddie replies,

All otherwise the state of Poet stands,
For lordly love is such a Tyranne fell:
That where he rules, all power he doth expell.
(11. 89–99)

And the evidence of the *Calender* supports him. Before he
loved, Colin had sung the praises of the shepherd's god, Pan,
and of the queen, Eliza. With love's fading, his verse once again

71

achieves something like disinterested exaltation in the visionary elegy for Dido. But under love's influence, he can manage only melodious self-pity.

The Shepheardes Calender thus contains a forceful critique of the conventional poet-as-lover, revealing that poetry written under such a guise is solipsistic, self-indulgent, and fruitless—that it leads inevitably to its own renunciation. Though the point is hardly less familiar than the role itself, we may be surprised to find it here in the book that launched the New Poet. We may be still more surprised to find it associated particularly with the New Poet's pastoral persona, Colin Clout. A great many other works of Spenser's generation teach the same lesson, but they usually announce, not the author's consecration of himself to poetry, but rather his renunciation of poetry in favor of some more serious pursuit. Spenser also talks of more serious pursuits, but these too, as I have said, are literary. Are we then to conclude, as A. C. Hamilton and Robert Allen Durr did some twenty-five years ago, that in the end Spenser separates himself from Colin, "cast[ing] off his shepherd's weeds," to "emerge as England's heroic poet"?[23] E. K. does deliver a clarion blast worthy of such an epiphany, but the poems fail to echo it. On the contrary, they express, along with a towering ambition and a sense of unique poetic power, much uncertainty about both the practical and the moral implications of a poetic vocation.

Particularly in the October eclogue, the one that deals most directly with these matters, we find a formidable array of barriers in the way of a modern poet. In the first place, poetry does

23. A. C. Hamilton, "The Argument of Spenser's *Shepheardes Calender*," *ELH*, 23 (1956), 175. See also Robert Allen Durr, "Spenser's Calendar of Christian Time," *ELH*, 24 (1957), 294–295: *"The Shepheardes Calender* is the young Spenser's declaration to the world that he knows to what heights he is called, to what purpose he has been graced, and that he is ready to undertake the task ... Colin is not Spenser; at most he is what Spenser or any other gifted poet, or pastor, might become. Colin is ruined, but Spenser is not."

not pay. Unlike a pastime, a vocation requires financial support. "But ah Mecoenas is yclad in claye" (1. 61). And were money forthcoming, support of another, still more vital, sort would nevertheless be lacking. As an art of imitation, heroic poetry requires heroic models. But "great Augustus long ygoe is dead: / And all the worthies liggen wrapt in leade" (11. 62–63). In a stooped and fallen age, poetry must either follow fashion and "rolle with rest in rymes of rybaudrye" or "it wither must agayn" (11. 73–78). In the Renaissance, such complaints are legion. E. K. tells us that Spenser borrowed his from Mantuan and Theocritus. But they are no less relevant for that. If Spenser was to "emerge as England's heroic poet," he did need money and he did need to believe that his age was capable of something approaching heroic accomplishment. Not that the age had to furnish all his material. The true poet makes his time as well as mirrors it, for he is the repository of "a certain . . . celestial inspiration." Such, E. K. tells us, was the argument of Spenser's own "book called the *English Poet.*" But in the October eclogue, inspiration is a matter more of uncertainty than of confident assertion. We have already noticed what short work Cuddie makes of Piers's argument that love and the "immortall mirrhor" of beauty should raise the poet's mind "above the starry skie." Cuddie's own claim for Bacchic inspiration fares no better; his comically bombastic, mock-heroic flight ends, rather, with an inglorious fall: "But ah my corage cooles ere it be warme" (1. 115).

To reverse history and reincarnate in his time the idea of the laureate poet, Spenser needed particularly the life-giving breath of inspiration, for it was in losing his divine inspiration that the ancient laureate had degenerated into the modern amorous maker. According to E. K.,

The first invention of poetry was of very virtuous intent. For at what time an infinite number of youth usually came to their great solemn feasts . . . some learned man . . . would take upon him to sing fine verses to the people, in praise either of virtue or of victory or of immortality or such like. At whose wonderful gift all men being astonished and as it were ravished, with delight, thinking (as it was indeed) that he was inspired from above, called him *vatem*: which kind of men afterward framing their verses to lighter music . . . found out lighter matter of poesy also, some playing with love, some scorning at men's fashions, some poured out in pleasures, and so were called poets or makers."[24]

Other English critics agreed that divine inspiration characterized the *vates,* but their writings suggest still greater uncertainty about the precise relation of the two poetic roles. Sidney, for example, could in one place defend poetry by identifying it with its vatic function, instancing "David's Psalms" as "a divine poem"; yet in another context, more nearly touching current poetic practice, he could as readily reverse himself and set vatic and what he now calls "right" poetry in quite different classes, specifically denying the latter an "inspiring of a divine force, far above man's wit."[25] And William Webbe, who was as eager as Sidney to defend poetry by recalling its ancient dignity and who also spoke of the *vates* as "inspired with some divine instinct from heaven," saw an equally sharp distinction in the original use of the two terms. In antiquity, Webbe remarked, "they which handled in the audience grave and necessary matters were called wise men or eloquent men, which they meant by *Vates*; and the rest which sang of love matters, or other lighter devices alluring unto pleasure and delight, were called *Poetae* or makers."[26] In a passing comment an Elizabethan might use the terms synonymously. Downhale does just that in the lines quoted in note 21 above, but when he has done so he feels that he must introduce still a third term, the unflattering *versifices,* for the English poets of his own time. A poet should

24. *Variorum,* VII, 100.   25. Sidney, *Apology,* pp 98–99 and 130.
26. William Webbe, *A Discourse of English Poesie* (1586), rpt. in *Elizabethan Critical Essays,* ed. G. Gregory Smith, 2 vols. (Oxford: Clarendon Press, 1904), I, 231.

be a *vates,* and his work should be marked by vatic inspiration. But, that being so, England has no poet. The flounderings of Piers and Cuddie over the question of poetic inspiration suggest that they experience (as perhaps their inventor experienced) a similar difficulty in effectively reasserting poetry's vatic claim now and in England. Yet such a claim was an essential element of the Virgilian model on which Spenser particularly relied, the model that offered him his best hope of an escape from the constricting Elizabethan pattern of a poetic career.

Lacking financial support, at odds with his age, unsure of his inspiration, the New Poet seems less securely set on his way than E. K. would have us think. And underlying his particular uncertainties, is a more general and more serious doubt, that poetry of the sort that he was prepared to write could, whatever his inspiration, ever be lifted to the vatic heights of religious, political, and moral perfection. *Perfection* is not, I think, too strong a word. E. K., Sidney, and Webbe differ in the precise role they assign the *vates,* but they agree that his inspired utterances must remain uncontaminated by all "lighter devices" of love and pleasure. On occasion these writers— Sidney most fully and most effectively—do argue for something like a Neoplatonic reconciliation of beauty and virtue, or, at the very least, for an Horatian mingling of pleasure and profit. But, as we have noticed in the October eclogue, such arguments quickly break down, the "both/and" resolving itself into an "either/or"—Mars *or* Venus, "Princes pallaces" *or* "baser birth," heavenly inspiration *or* amorous distraction. In part this is a matter of literary decorum, each genre having its accepted function. But the effect is to make the higher genres, those which must be mastered by a laureate poet, inaccessible to one whose inspiration belongs primarily to the lower.

Hobbinoll tries to overcome such objections in the June eclogue, as Piers does in "October," but to no avail. He suggests, for example, that even Calliope, the muse of heroic poetry, found herself "outgone" by Colin's art, but Colin himself will have none of it.

> I never lyst presume to Parnasse hyll,
> But pyping lowe in shade of lowly grove,
> I play to please my selfe, all be it ill.
> (11. 70–72)[27]

His verse is essentially private, and thus can aspire neither to a public function nor to public fame. And when, in a passage as suggestive of *The Faerie Queene* as anything in the October eclogue, Hobbinoll urges Colin to seek inspiration away from the site of his amorous bewitchment and near the centers of economic and, presumably, political power, Colin refuses to see any significant difference. Both are equally contaminated by pleasure. The exchange is worth quoting at some length. Hobbinoll directs Colin to a land where

> . . . frendly Faeries, met with many Graces,
> And lightfote Nymphes can chace the lingering night,
> With Heydeguyes, and trimly trodden traces,
> Whilst systers nyne, which dwell on Parnasse hight,
> Doe make them musick, for their more delight:
> And Pan himselfe to kisse their christall faces,
> Will pype and daunce, when Phoebe shineth bright:
> Such pierlesse pleasures have we in these places.

But Colin answers,

27. I agree with Paul Alpers that "it is simply absurd to say, as recent critics do, that the poet who speaks [these] lines has abandoned his calling." But I think that Alpers goes too far in writing them off as "the traditional diffidence of the literary shepherd." There is too much genuine uncertainty, particularly when these lines are read in the context of the June eclogue and of *The Shepheardes Calender* as a whole, to dismiss as a merely conventional stance the problematic aspect of Spenser's presentation of himself as poet. See "The Eclogue Tradition and the Nature of Pastoral," *College English,* 34 (1972/73), 365.

And I, whylst youth, and course of carelesse yeeres
Did let me walke withouten lincks of love,
In such delights did joy amongst my peeres:
But ryper age such pleasures doth reprove,
My fancye eke from former follies move
To stayed steps.   (11. 25–38)

Here it is Hobbinoll who reminds us of Spenser, while Colin strikes rather the pose of the repentant prodigal. Not only does Hobbinoll's speech look forward to the visionary land of nymphs and faeries that for so many readers is the most attractive feature of *The Faerie Queene,* but it also looks back to the April eclogue in praise of Eliza, the poem that, in Hobbinoll's then unchallenged opinion, represented the proper and dutiful use of Colin's gift. If "ryper age" deny the New Poet even this, he can hardly go on. Yet the specific placement of the exchange within *The Shepheardes Calender* does seem to support Colin's renunciation. For Hobbinoll's description of the world of poetic accomplishment recalls both Palinode's praise of May games in the preceding eclogue and Morrell's praise of the heights in the succeeding one, yet both Palinode and Morrell are sharply reproved for their views and in terms that leave no doubt that they are meant to get the worst of the argument. Now, both the May and July eclogues consider the shepherd as pastor rather than as poet. Perhaps what is wrong for one is right for the other, perhaps the poet enjoys a license denied the pastor? If so, Hobbinoll neither makes the argument nor could Colin accept it. In a mood of righteous reaction against youthful folly, Colin will entertain no such fine distinctions. All poetry touched by delight seems suspect. And no other poetry is conceivable.

Distracted by Spenser's later success and by the later success of English poetry, we are not likely to appreciate the seriousness of the concerns expressed in *The Shepheardes Calender.* But to ignore them is to suffer a failure of historical imagination. Though Spenser was already at work on *The Faerie Queene* in 1579, it was only one of several projects he had under way. And it was the one that Harvey, who shared many of Spenser's values, thought least promising. Moreover, the early version was undoubtedly a very different poem from *The Faerie Queene* that emerged a decade later—a poem, if the speculations of J.W. Bennett and W.J.B. Owen are to be trusted, far less well suited to answer the doubts raised by *The Shepheardes Calender*.[28] It seems likely, in fact, that the *Faerie Queene* we know was stamped in the mold of those concerns. Though this likelihood is posited on the critically heterodox assumption that concerns expressed in a pastoral fiction can be attributed directly and personally to the author, the assumption does not seem particularly hazardous here. We have, after all, the testimony of E.K., who simply tells us that Colin represents Spenser and Hobbinoll represents Harvey, that the advice Hobbinoll gives Colin in the June eclogue "is no poetical fiction, but feignedly spoken of the poet self," and that even Cuddie in "October" may be "the author self." And, more important, we have the evident probability that doubts like those in *The Shepheardes Calender* would naturally preoccupy an aspirant to the laurel in a land where for many years that plant had obstinately refused to grow. Spenser had good reason to worry about the contrast between what English poets in his generation in fact were—the role they played and the kind of poems they wrote—and what a laureate poet ideally could and should be.

His published correspondence with Harvey, written at precisely the same time as *The Shepheardes Calender*, is full of similar concerns. The young Spenser wonders whether he should publish at all, fears that his work may bring contempt

28. Josephine Waters Bennett, *The Evolution of "The Faerie Queene"* (Chicago: Univ. of Chicago Press, 1942) and W.J.B. Owen, "The Structure of the *Faerie Queene*," *PMLA*, 68 (1953), 1079–1100.

on himself, and worries that it may be "too base for his excellent Lordship, being made in honor of a private personage unknown." Here is precisely that conflict between private inspiration and public function which divided the two notions of the poet. Still more to the point is the Latin verse epistle in which Spenser swings back and forth, now regretting his attachment to love and begging Harvey to lead him away from it, now denying Harvey "the sacred name of a time-honored poet" for his too great seriousness.[29] "Whoever wishes," he says, "to ennoble his forehead with bands of laurel and, by pleasing the people, to win their applause, learns to play mad and reaps the base praise which rewards ignominious nonsense." But, as in "October," this is only to condemn the age and suggest the impossibility of true poetry. From here he seeks a middle way, a "both/and" to reconcile the "either/or," and ends by repeating Horace's *Omne tulit punctum, qui miscuit utile dulce.* But then he quickly admits that for him the formula does not work: "Long ago the gods made me the gift of delight, but not of the useful. O would they had given me the useful, even now, along with delight." And so he ends, burdened with his poetic gift, unwilling to waste it, not knowing how to use it.

Harvey too, in his lumbering and pedantic way, testifies to the reality of such concerns. He takes Spenser at his word, plays Cato, and reproves love. "Credit me," he says, "I will never linne baiting at you, till I have rid you quite of this yonkerly and womanly humor."[30] "Yonkerly" is among Harvey's favorite words. He uses it again for Spenser's Latin poem. "A goodly brave yonkerly piece of work," he calls it. For Harvey, as for his contemporaries generally, love and the poetry of love were toys of youth, no more. Nor, for all his interest in prosody, does he attribute to poetry any use more suitable for riper years. In his

29. Spenser's Latin epistle is translated in the *Variorum*, X, 256–258.
30. *Variorum*, X, 444.

own life, he follows rather the accepted pattern, promising to abandon poetry for the more serious business of law. And when he does lapse into verse, it is with an uneasy, if ponderously jocular, self-consciousness. "God help us, you and I are wisely employed, (are we not?) when our pen and ink, and time, and wit, and all runneth away in this goodly yonkerly vein, as if the world had nothing else for us to do, or we were born to be the only *nonproficients* and *nihilagents* of the world." Let's give it up, he goes on to say. *Cuiusmodi tu nugis, atque naeniis nisi una mecum . . . iam tandem aliquando valedicas.*[31] No one believed more firmly in Spenser's talent than Harvey (though he believed still more firmly in his own), but not even Harvey could think of poetry as the central business of any man's life, whatever his gift.

Harvey's and Spenser's fascination with classical prosody, a fascination inherited from Ascham and shared with Sidney, Dyer, Drant, and a good many others, is, I think, best understood in terms of this persistent uncertainty about poetry. The decline of learning and the depreciation of the poet were associated in their minds with the barbarous habit of rime. If the poet was to be restored to his vatic eminence, his poems must rid themselves of that Gothic tinsel and wear instead the ennobling garb of ancient meter.[32] The feeling originated perhaps in Petrarch, though for him the contrast was between Italian and Latin, between the amorous *Rime (In sul mio primo giovenile*

31. *Variorum,* X, 473. The passage as a whole shows not only Harvey's feeling that poetry should be abandoned for more serious pursuits but also his sense that Spenser might not agree. It is translated in F. I. Carpenter, *A Reference Guide to Edmund Spenser* (Chicago: Univ. of Chicago Press, 1923), p. 58, as follows: "Do, I beg you, except with me (and I am bound by a solemn oath and vow to give up the cup of love and at the very first opportunity to drain the cup of law)—do, I repeat, bid farewell to nonsense and trifling songs of this kind (which, nevertheless, I believe, will seem to you one of the things that cannot be done)."

32. See Ascham, p. 145.

errore) and the heroic *Africa.*[33] And it still recurs in Milton, in his defense of blank verse as a liberation from "the troublesome and modern bondage of riming." So Spenser, at the turning point of his career, having made his pastoral debut and having hung up his oaten pipe, wonders "why a God's name may not we, as else the Greeks, have the kingdom of our own language" and speaks disdainfully of his "old use of toying in rimes."[34] Milton's experiment worked; those of Petrarch and Spenser didn't. But each was a step into the unknown, an attempt to revive in a new world a moribund power. The risk of failure was naturally great. And the same risk belonged to their attempted reinvention of the role of laureate poet. Both the revival of the laureate and the revival of quantitative meters did find sanction in the general Renaissance desire to restore the classical past, but there was no assurance that every attempt would succeed. In some instances the world had simply changed too much.[35] Perhaps the role of youthful lover-poet had become as inescapable a part of English poetry as accentual meter and rime. And so when men like Spenser, who felt themselves drawn to the ancient vocation, measured English syllables, they were at the same time measuring the chances of a poetic career.

In 1580 for Spenser to have simply declared himself a poet,

33. In discussing Petrarch's own title for the *Rime, Rerum vulgarium fragmenta,* Nicola Zingarelli remarks, "Le cose volgari o in volgare sono poesie in lingua italiana; ma volgare implica anche un senso inerente alla passione giovanile ed erronea, come dicesse 'poesie amorose.' . . . In volgare si fanno soltanto poesie di amore." *Le Rime de Francesco Petrarca* (Bologna: Zanichelli, 1964), p. 27.

34. *Variorum,* X, 16.

35. Compare the political dreams of revived *imperium,* frustrated for Petrarch in the misadventure of Cola di Rienzo and hardly more successful in the later pretensions of Charles V, Henri III, Henri IV, or Elizabeth. See Frances A. Yates, *Astrea: The Imperial Theme in the Sixteenth Century* (London: Routledge, 1975).

making no other provision for his maintenance, would have been both morally and practically unthinkable. Only one educated as a gentleman would be sufficiently imbued with the values of classical civilization to aspire to the laureate role. But for the gentleman, the profession of letters, as a *gagne-pain,* did not yet exist. Neither the theater nor the court afforded the means of support that they would supply, however sparingly, in the next generation to Ben Jonson. Thus, unable to live by his pen alone, Spenser undertook a succession of positions of the more usual sort, as secretary to Young, Leicester, and Grey, and as Clerk of the Council of Munster. Yet, though he did not earn his living by writing, he, rather than Jonson, deserves to be called England's first professed, if not fully professional, poet. Through all the years of minor civic occupation, and well past the age when most men of his generation stopped writing, he pursued his poetic ambition. So that in 1590 he could complete his imitation of Virgil and emerge indeed as his nation's heroic poet, as the first English laureate.

> Lo I the man, whose Muse whilome did maske,
>> As time her taught in lowly Shepheards weeds,
> Am now enforst a far unfitter taske,
>> For trumpets sterne to chaunge mine Oaten reeds.

Looser Rimes and Lewd Lays

To leap, as I must now do, from the beginning of Spenser's poetic career to its end is to leave out much of the most important part. I count on the reader's acquaintance with the great accomplishment of the 1580s, the first books of *The Faerie Queene,* to keep the picture I am drawing from distortion. In these books there is little of the struggle between the love poet and the vatic poet that we have observed in *The Shepheardes Calender* and in the Harvey correspondence. Both dissolve into the poem, which contains the passion of the one and the vision of the other in a romance that is also a prophecy. Of the poet's self we hear only the humble fear that he may prove unworthy of his great argument or that his audience may mistake his work for mere "painted forgery, . . . th' aboundance of an idle brain." But these are minor doubts. Properly understood, the poem justifies both itself and its maker. This self-justifying union does not, however, hold together. Although the last books show no radical change in character and certainly no lessening of poetic power, the two poets, or the two ideas of poetry, no longer cohere. The private poet rebels against his public duty; the public poet can find no use for his private inspiration. But before looking at the indications of this split in *The Faerie Queene* itself, I would like to glance at some of the smaller poems that Spenser wrote in the 1590s, where, freed from the pressures of his epic task, he gives fuller expression to his more intimate concerns.

The minor poems show first that the material fears expressed in the October eclogue were, despite Spenser's poetic accomplishment, amply realized. Again and again, he complains that his work has gone unrewarded, that his expectation has been vain, that his "idle hopes . . . still doe fly away/Like empty shaddowes."[36] And if, in 1579, it had seemed that there might be no heroic virtue worth celebrating, that feeling too had gained substance in the intervening decade. When we think of the Armada, Drake's circumnavigation of the globe, or the Cadiz expedition (the last of which came, of course, too late to have much effect on Spenser), his attitude may seem odd, but his attention was focused rather on Ireland and England's relation to Protestant Europe, and in those areas his party made little headway. Moreover, the men who had led that party, men with whom Spenser had been long associated and who had

36. *Prothalamion*, 11. 8–9. Cf. *The Ruines of Time*, 11. 435–448; *The Teares of the Muses*, 11. 79–90; and *Mother Hubberds Tale*, 11. 892–918.

patronized his work—Raleigh, Grey of Wilton, Leicester, Warwick, Walsingham, Sir Henry and Sir Philip Sidney—were, by the 1590s, either in disfavor or dead. The episodes of Timias and Belphoebe in Book IV of *The Faerie Queene* and of Arte-gall and the Blatant Beast in Book V join certain of the minor poems, *The Ruines of Time, Virgils Gnat, Mother Hubberds Tale, Astrophel, Colin Clouts Come Home Againe, Prothala-mion,* and perhaps *The Teares of the Muses,* in testifying to Spenser's involvement with these men and their policies and to his feeling of loss at their passing. Even in *The Shepheardes Calender,* despite uncertainties about his role as public poet, Spenser had addressed ecclesiastical and political issues with a confidence bred of his identification with an active and aggressive party. But by the 1590s he had lost most of what had sustained that confidence. And to make the loss still greater, Lord Burghley, who opposed militant action on behalf of continental Protestants and who disdained both poetry and Spenser, remained vigorously in power, supported now by his son Sir Robert Cecil. If the dedicatory sonnet to Burghley in the 1590 *Faerie Queene* was meant to placate him, it failed, as the opening stanza of the second installment reports:

> The rugged forhead that with grave foresight
> Welds kingdomes causes, and affaires of state,
> My looser rimes (I wote) doth sharply wite,
> For praising love, as I have done of late,
> And magnifying lovers deare debate;
> By which fraile youth is oft to follie led,
> Through false allurement of that pleasing baite,
> That better were in virtues discipled,
> Then with vaine poemes weeds to have their fancies fed.

Here is the very conflict between affairs of state and looser rimes that Spenser had been so intent on avoiding. In Burghley's opinion, which the poet rejects but cannot ignore, Spenser's work was more likely to lead youth to folly than to virtuous and gentle discipline.[37] Spenser was thus thrown back on the defensive.

But opposition did not come only from Burghley. Even friends and patrons, like the Countesses of Cumberland and Warwick, reproved the licentiousness of his earlier work, causing him to "retract" (even as he published) his hymns of Love and Beauty. Critics have disagreed whether the second pair of hymns, those addressed to Heavenly Love and Heavenly Beauty, complement or contradict the first pair, but there is no question that Spenser pushes them, as he was perhaps pushed himself, into the familiar mold of repentance.

> Many lewd layes (as woe is me the more)
> In praise of that mad fit, which fooles call love,
> I have in th' heat of youth made heretofore,
> That in light wits did loose affection move.
> But all those follies now I do reprove.[38]

Nowhere else does Spenser sound quite so much like a repentant prodigal. And even here he rejects Love and Beauty only to reestablish them on a firmer ground, though a ground that excludes even the idealized and chaste love that is celebrated in the first two hymns and that formed the basis of the reconciliation of love and heroic endeavor, and thus of the two models of

37. Spenser had, of course, given Burghley more direct cause for offense in *Mother Hubberds Tale.* But for the poet to have alluded to that political source of disfavor would have been to cast himself in the role of satirist—a role that he studiously avoided except in a few passages of *Colin Clouts Come Home Againe,* and even there, as Thomas R. Edwards has remarked, "satire is an inadequate vehicle for the whole of Colin's experience" (*Imagination and Power: A Study of Poetry on Public Themes* [New York: Oxford Univ. Press, 1971], p. 58). Spenser keeps Colin out of the satiric eclogues of *The Shepheardes Calender* and goes to quite elaborate lengths to dissociate himself as poet from *Mother Hubberds Tale.* In this he differs markedly from poets of the next generation—Hall, Marston, and Jonson—who seize on satire as the best way of escaping the Elizabethan role of lover-poet.

38. *Hymne of Heavenly Love,* ll. 8–12. Cf. *Hymne of Heavenly Beautie,* ll. 288–294.

the poet, in the first books of *The Faerie Queene*. No wonder if Spenser saw himself less as a new Virgil and more as the Ovid of the *Tristia*, abandoned by his friends for his *carmen et error*.[39]

Nor is it surprising, given what may well have been a double sense of failure—the practical failure of the policies he favored and the moral failure of the beauty he celebrated—that Spenser should have wearied of his epic task. Through the first books of *The Faerie Queene* fatigue had been the greatest burden, ease after toil the greatest temptation. Redcross was overcome when, like Diana's nymph, he "sat downe to rest in middest of the race" (I.vii.5); Guyon weakened when he heard fair ladies singing of "the Port of rest from troublous toil" (II.xii.32); and even Britomart could be surprised, though not tempted, when "through . . . weary toil she soundly slept" (III.i.58). And most often, as in each of these instances, sensual pleasure combines with rest to oppose heroic activity. So in the Bower of Bliss, Verdant, the green youth (think of Spenser talking of "the greener times of [his] youth" when he wrote his hymns of Love and Beauty), sleeping in the arms of Acrasia, emblematically represents the courtly lovers, and by extension the courtly makers, the prodigal love poets, of Spenser's generation.[40]

39. The following inscription, based on Ovid's *Tristia* (I.ix.5), occurs in a manuscript of Gower owned in the sixteenth century by the Countess of Warwick.

> Tempore foelici
> multi numerantur amici } Spenserus
> Cum fortuna perit
> nullus amicus erit

Rosemond Tuve has argued for Spenser's authorship of the inscription and has related it to the retraction of his hymns of Love and Beauty. See "'Spenserus,'" in *Essays in English Literature . . . Presented to A. S. P. Woodhouse,* ed. Millar MacLure and F. W. Watt (Toronto: Univ. of Toronto Press, 1964), pp. 3–25, rpt. in *Essays by Rosemond Tuve,* ed. Thomas P. Roche, Jr. (Princeton: Princeton Univ. Press, 1970), pp. 139–163.

40. Though Spenser does not identify himself with Verdant or with any other victim of Acrasia's sensuality, there is, as I suggest in the Introduction, an

His warlike armes, the idle instruments
  Of sleeping praise, were hong upon a tree,
  And his brave shield, full of old moniments,
  Was fowly ra'st, that none the signes might see;
  Ne for them, ne for honour cared hee,
  Ne ought, that did to his advancement tend,
  But in lewd loves, and wastfull luxuree,
  His dayes, his goods, his bodie he did spend:
O horrible enchantment, that him so did blend.   (II.xii.80)

Of course not all the love portrayed in the first three books is of this lazy sort. The love of Redcross for Una, of Arthur for Gloriana, of Britomart for Artegall, leads rather to heroic accomplishment. And Spenser does continue to distinguish between concupiscent and heroic love in the minor poems. But in his own case, weariness, love, and sensual delight combine to draw him from his heroic duty, the completion of *The Faerie Queene.*

In two of the *Amoretti* he refers to his unfinished poem, and each time it is with a sense of weariness. "Taedious toyle," he calls it. The two sonnets do, however, divide on the question of what relation his private love has to his public poetic duty, one taking the position that Cuddie had argued in the October eclogue, the other agreeing with Piers. In *Amoretti* 33 love cancels duty while in *Amoretti* 80 it raises the poet's "spirit to an higher pitch," thus preparing him to return to *The Faerie Queene* with renewed inspiration. But even here, the amorous resting place is sharply cut off from the world of "strong endevour"; it is a "pleasant mew" where he can "sport [his] muse

---

echo of the conflict central to Spenser's laureate self-presentation in the violence of Guyon's destruction of the Bower of Bliss. Here the poet apparently felt compelled to overreact. His integrity and perhaps the integrity of the very culture that he, as laureate, sought to embody depended on it. For a discussion of the threat posed by Acrasia and the Bower of Bliss, see Stephen Greenblatt, *Renaissance Self-Fashioning from More to Shakespeare* (Chicago: Univ. of Chicago Press, 1980), pp. 157–192.

and sing [his] loves sweet praise," a "prison" from which he "will break anew."[41] The "anew" refers, I would suspect, to his first escape from the prison of private poetry in the early 1580s. But this second time he seems not to have made good his promised escape, at least not as a poet. In *Amoretti* 80 he says that his work on *The Faerie Queene* is "halfe fordonne," six books having been completed. Though he had still some five years to live, he seems never to have finished another. His last "useful" work was not a poem but, rather, a treatise on the *Present State of Ireland.* Thus the end of his literary career does have the bifurcated look that we observe in the careers of his contemporaries. Once again poetry serves the truant passion of love, while expository and argumentative prose does the work of the active world.

The split was never, of course, absolute or irrevocable. In *Prothalamion,* the last of Spenser's minor poems and perhaps, depending on the date one assigns to the Mutability Cantos, the last poem he wrote, he casts a valedictory glance back over his career—his birth in London, his service to Leicester, his "long fruitless stay" at court—with the regretful air of a man who would still join in the affairs of the great world if the great world would have him. When he says that "some brave muse may sing" the glories of the new champion, Essex, it is hard to tell whether he is putting himself definitively out of contention or bidding for the job. But in the refrain, with its insistence that the day is short and that his song will continue only while the Thames runs softly, we hear the sound of an ending, an impending withdrawal from the public world that this poem still celebrates. Spenser's magnificently unique "both/and," which

41. It is curious that, though love does oppose public duty in the *Amoretti,* it does not oppose religion. See *Amoretti,* 9, 22, 53, 55, 58, and 61. Only in *Amoretti* 72 is there anything approaching a conflict between the two, and even here it is extraordinarily muted. In this too, Spenser is very unlike his contemporaries.

had made it possible for him to be England's New Poet, had not wholly given way to the familiar "either/or," but disappointment was clearly pushing in that direction.

Encounter on Mt. Acidale

Something of that "either/or" can already be found in the last two books of *The Faerie Queene*. Book V is the most uncompromisingly public book, the one that seizes most directly on current or near-current affairs, and Book VI is the most private.[42] Yet this fundamental and quite obvious difference depends on a still more fundamental, though somewhat less obvious, similarity. In neither book does Spenser relate love and heroic action in a positive way, as he had done earlier. To accomplish their quests, Artegall and Calidore must leave their loves, Britomart and Pastorella. For them, love is a distraction rather than an inspiration. Having ambitiously climbed even to the heroic, Cupid must now climb back down. Where in Book III love had been the "most sacred fire ... whence spring all noble deeds and never dying fame" (III.iii.1), by Book V it has become the

> lovely baite, that doth procure
> Great warriors oft their rigour to represse,
> And mighty hands forget their manlinesse.
>
> (V.viii.1)

The love spoken of so disparagingly in these lines is no base concupiscent desire, but rather the noble passion of Artegall and Britomart—"Yet could it not sterne Artegall retaine" (V.viii.3). In Book VI love does retain Calidore (and this is, in

42. On the differing relations of Books V and VI to history, see Michael O'Connell, *Mirror and Veil: The Historical Dimension of Spenser's "Faerie Queene"* (Chapel Hill: Univ. of North Carolina Press, 1977), pp. 125–189.

part, why the books are so different), but it retains him only at the expense of his assigned quest. "Who now does follow the foule Blatant Beast, / Whilest Calidore does follow that faire Mayd" (VI.x.1). For Redcross and Britomart, following their love was part of following their quest. The poem demands of Artegall and Calidore a choice that earlier knights had not been required to make.

The harsher world of the last two books, with its need for a stern renunciation of the amorous passion that for Spenser and his contemporaries had been the *sine qua non* of poetry, proves inhospitable to heroic romance. Even when freed from the distracting influence of love, heroic action is less successful in these last two books, both poetically and practically. This is particularly obvious in Book V, where Lord Grey's Irish exploits resist Spenser's best attempts to transform them into a legend of Justice. But it is true too in Book VI, where, as J.C. Maxwell has remarked, the quest pattern "was little more than an encumbrance" in the way of Spenser's depiction of courtesy.[43] In Book V the heroic action is so brutal, and so unreasoning in its brutality, that we reject Spenser's presentation of it as a model of justice—all the more so because it contradicts his own best truth, the vision of Justice controlled by Equity in Isis Church.[44] And in Book VI the prime virtue of Courtesy seems better exemplified by Calidore's truant pastoral retirement than by his heroic pursuit of the Blatant Beast. These books thus divorce heroic action from virtue as well as from love. They furthermore rob it of its usual practical efficacy. Artegall overcomes Grantorto and begins to deal justice in Irenae's land, "But ere he could reforme it thoroughly, / He through

43. J.C. Maxwell, "The Truancy of Calidore," in *That Soveraine Light: Essays in Honor of Edmund Spenser,* ed. William R. Mueller and Don Cameron Allen (Baltimore: Johns Hopkins Univ. Press, 1952), p. 68.
44. On the Isis Church passage, see Frank Kermode, *Renaissance Essays* (1971; rpt. London: Collins, 1973), pp. 49–59.

occasion called was away, / To Faerie Court . . ." (V.xii.27). His work, like Lord Grey's, is left unfinished, and he himself is calumniated, as Lord Grey was, by envy and detraction. Calidore fares only slightly better. He does capture the Blatant Beast, but by the end of Book VI the Beast is once again at large ("So now he raungeth through the world againe"), his captivity having lasted scarcely two stanzas.[45]

The optimistic faith that had animated the early books, the faith that history was going the right way, seems to have left Spenser in the 1590s. Heroic poetry requires, as Cuddie argued in the October eclogue, an heroic age. By the time he wrote Books V and VI, that age seemed to have passed. And so he begins each of these last books by comparing the "state of present time" with the ideal "image of the antique world" and in each he finds

> Such oddes . . . twixt those, and these which are,
> As that, through long continuance of his course,
> Me seems the world is runne quite out of square,
> From the first point of his appointed sourse,
> And being once amisse growes daily wourse and wourse.
>
> (V.proem.1)[46]

The sentiment is thoroughly conventional, but its prominent expression here contrasts with the equally prominent assertion of divine grace working through history in Books I and II.[47]

---

45. The split "between mythic success and palpable disappointment" in Books V and VI is suggestively explored by Judith H. Anderson in *The Growth of a Personal Voice: "Piers Plowman" and "The Faerie Queene"* (New Haven: Yale Univ. Press, 1976). Anderson's perceptive remark that "personality becomes a more explicit, self-conscious concern in these Books" and that "unity of experience and wholeness of being also become more problematical" (p. 154) might with certain modifications be extended to cover the beginning and the end of Spenser's career generally. Like most of us, Spenser is most intent on himself when he is least sure of himself.

46. Cf. VI.proem.5.

47. See, for example, I.vii.1 and II.viii.1–2. There is a similar passage in Book V (V.xi.1), but it is supported neither by the action of the poem nor by the

And its pessimism is, as we have seen, confirmed by the action of the poem, as was the optimism of the early books. But not only does the heroic action fail to achieve the kind of success that it had won in earlier books; the poet and his poems are among the victims of its failure. In the last stanzas of Book VI, the Blatant Beast turns on Spenser.

> Ne may this homely verse, of many meanest,
>> Hope to escape his venemous despite,
>> More then my former writs, all were they cleanest
>> From blamefull blot, and free from all that wite,
>> With which some wicked tongues did it backbite,
>> And bring into a mighty Peres displeasure,
>> That never so deserved to endite.
>> Therefore do you my rimes keep better measure,
> And seeke to please, that now is counted wisemens threasure.
>
> (VI.xii.41)

As the Blatant Beast reduced Artegall's triumph to defeat, so here it unmakes Spenser's *utile*, leaving him only with the *dulce* with which he had begun. If he were to satisfy through poetry the humanist expectation that learning would be turned to the useful work of the world, he had to command the respect and attention of those in power. By the time he finished Book VI, Spenser evidently felt he had lost both. The result was a renewed self-consciousness about his role as poet and a backward and inward turn toward "the sacred noursery of vertue," which is both garden and mind. In making this turn, Spenser once again opened the breach between the poet of the inner pastoral world and the poet of heroic accomplishment, between the love poet and the laureate.

The center of Spenser's retreat is found in canto x of Book VI, where he and we and Calidore surprise Colin Clout on Mt. Acidale. Calidore and his creator, the epic poet, have wandered

---

historical events the poem mirrors, the English efforts in the Low Countries, France, and Ireland.

far out of the way of duty (the image and the judgment are Spenser's, and he applies them equally to both knight and poet), only to encounter in the secretmost recesses of the pastoral land an image of themselves. For Calidore, that image is the ideal vision of the courtesy which he is meant to embody. For the poet, it is Colin Clout, in whose guise he had formerly masked. Some critics would argue that this meeting merely reunites the pastoral and the epic strains of Spenser's poetry after the arid division of Book V, while others would claim, rather, that it presents once again what has always been united, though now one side and now the other may have predominated.[48] But such arguments neglect the dramatic construction of the episode and indeed of the whole of Book VI. Calidore comes on the scene as an intruder, an outsider whose very presence causes Colin's vision to dissolve. Moreover, the knight of courtesy fails to understand what he has seen and must have it explained to him by the shepherd-poet. And yet, even given the didactic explanation, Calidore's experience on Mt. Acidale, unlike Redcross's in the House of Holiness, seems not to contribute to his formation as a knight. It neither enhances his courtesy, which was innate, nor moves him to heroic action. On the contrary, he remains in seclusion until called forth by the brigands' destruction of his pastoral retreat.[49] Far from enabling Calidore to act, Colin's vision and its earlier

48. See, for example, the readings of Graham Hough, *A Preface to "The Faerie Queene"* (1962; rpt. New York: Norton, 1963), pp. 201–212; Kathleen Williams, *Spenser's World of Glass* (Berkeley: Univ. of California Press, 1966), pp. 189–223; and Maurice Evans, *Spenser's Anatomy of Heroism* (Cambridge: Cambridge Univ. Press, 1970), pp. 209–228.

49. Harry Berger, Jr., "The Prospect of Imagination: Spenser and the Limits of Poetry," *SEL*, 1 (1961), 93, offers a succinct summary of the problems posed by the scene on Mt. Acidale. "It is a digression from a digression. It is unrelated to the main quest, has no effect on it, does not noticeably alter the hero after he leaves Colin." For the opposing argument—i.e., that Calidore does undergo an education in true courtesy on Mt. Acidale—see Humphrey Tonkin, *Spenser's Courteous Pastoral* (Oxford: Clarendon Press, 1972), pp. 111–155.

simulacrum, the scene of Pastorella on a hill "environ'd with a girland, goodly graced, / Of lovely lasses" (VI.ix.8), temporarily disarm and disable him, at least so far as his quest is concerned, thus confirming both Sidney's deathbed conviction that "beauty itself, in all earthly complexions, [is] more apt to allure men to evil than to frame any good in them," and Spenser's own statement in Book V that "beauties lovely baite . . . doth procure / Great warriours oft their rigour to represse, / And mighty hands forget their manlinesse" (V.viii.1). This is not to deny that Calidore accomplishes heroic feats on Pastorella's behalf. Like Pyrocles and Musidorus, the truant knights in Sidney's *Arcadia*, Calidore saves his love both from a savage beast and from lawless men. But—and in this he also resembles Sidney's protagonists—his feats have nothing to do with his public duty, nor has that public duty anything to do with his love. In both Book VI and the *Arcadia*, private affection opposes public obligation.

But for all the similarity between the *Arcadia* and Book VI of *The Faerie Queene*, the mention of Sidney should remind us of our starting point: Spenser's unique sense of himself as a poet. Though both Sidney and Spenser were expressly implicated in the truancy of their characters, Spenser "came into [his] course againe" (as he put it) by continuing his poem,[50] Sidney by breaking his off. For Spenser, duty lay in the accomplishment of his heroic narrative; for Sidney, as for Calidore, it lay, rather, in the accomplishment of some heroic action. But by the time he wrote Book VI, not even Spenser could come into his course again without leaving a part of himself behind. And that, for the laureate, is the significance of the encounter on Mt.

50. "But now I come into my course againe, / To his achievement of the Blatant Beast." Note that Calidore's "achievement" is Spenser's "course." The "I" here is clearly Spenser the epic poet and not Colin the pastoral poet, who has been left behind on Mt. Acidale and whose "course" has nothing to do with heroic "achievement."

Acidale. Like the knight of courtesy, whose presence destroys the vision of courtesy, the epic poet approaches, delights in, but ultimately destroys the world that sustains his pastoral self. Again, as in *The Shepheardes Calender,* Colin breaks his pipe, but here the breakage goes much further, for brigands invade and ravage his homeland. Here once more the contrast with Sidney proves instructive. Like Spenser, Sidney writes himself into his fiction. But his Philisides is just another truant knight masking as a shepherd. The pastoral world is meant to be left behind. Colin Clout belongs to that world, and, when it is destroyed, he must to some extent share its fate.

Though in a more subtle way, the scene on Mt. Acidale bears still further testimony to the disjunction between the two sides of Spenser's poetic identity, for it is here that the union of heroic activity and amorous contemplation breaks down. They had been joined in the figure of the Faerie Queene, "in whose fair eyes," as Harvey wrote, "love linked with virtue sits,"[51] and throughout the poem, devotion to Gloriana had directed and inspired the accomplishment of the epic poet. She had raised his thoughts "too humble and too vile" and provided "the argument of [his] afflicted style." She had been to him, as the various proems proclaim, the "mirror and grace of majesty," the living image of "Faerie lond," the model of rule and chastity, "the Queene of love, and Prince of peace," the "Dread Soveraign Goddesse" whose justice informs his discourse, the source from which "all goodly vertues well." From the April eclogue, where the shepherds' queen, Eliza, figured as a fourth Grace and where Hobbinoll and Thenot lamented that Colin's private love had turned him from the singing of such songs, devotion to the Queen had been Spenser's touchstone of poetic responsibility. What then are we to think when in the midst of *The Faerie Queene* Colin and the Graces reappear in a scene

51. Gabriel Harvey printed in the *Variorum,* III, 186.

closely reminiscent of the April eclogue, with "a country lasse" in the place of the Queen, particularly when Spenser himself calls attention to the substitution? The form of his remark is, naturally enough, an apology. "Pardon thy shepheard," he begs of the great Gloriana, "to make one minime of thy poore handmayd" (VI.x.28). But this self-conscious plea only compounds the fault by breaking the fiction and revealing the historical Spenser behind the pastoral mask of Colin Clout. As in the *Amoretti,* the poet speaks in his own person to associate visionary delight with his private love and wearisome duty with the Faerie Queene.[52] Here the dissociation between his pastoral and his heroic personae is very nearly complete. The conclusion of Book VI makes it still more so. The epic poet ends with the bitter regret that because of the Blatant Beast—the image of the great world's hostility to heroic accomplishment—poetry must be reduced to mere pleasure. "Seeke to please," he tells his verse, "that now is counted wisemens threasure." But for Colin on Mt. Acidale—a place designed "to serve all delight"—pleasure had been sufficient unto itself. As his work on *The Faerie Queene* drew toward a close, the poet, who years before had complained that "the gods made me the gift of delight but not of the useful," found those two Horatian poles of his literary identity once again pulling apart.

Port After Stormy Seas

Whether by accident or design, the final shape of Spenser's career resembles the shape of old Melibee's. Each begins with the pastoral and then, as Melibee says, "When pride of youth forth pricked [his] desire," each attaches himself to the court and its public concerns. But after years "excluded from native

52. Cf. VI.proem.1.

home," each ruefully returns to the pastoral world (VI.ix.24–25). As Isabel MacCaffrey has remarked, "Spenser evidently attached important meanings to this pattern."[53] It recurs, as she notes, in *Colin Clouts Come Home Againe,* and the title of that poem might well serve as the heading to the final chapter of Spenser's creative life. In his last works, in Book VI of *The Faerie Queene,* in the *Amoretti* and the *Epithalamion,* in the hymns of Divine Beauty and Love, and, to an extent, in the two Mutability Cantos, particularly in their setting on Arlo Hill, Spenser does come home, as he did in the last section of *Colin Clout.* He comes home to the pastoral, the personal, and the amorous. That these are also among his most resonant works, among those which engage the cosmic shape of things most confidently, is testimony to the poetic richness of that home. Whatever the laureate's obligations to the public world, it is in this private realm that he finds the source of his inspiration. And though Spenser's turning back to the self and the secret springs of poetry may be in part the result of that unhappy encounter with the world represented by the threatening of the Blatant Beast, it is no repentance. Unlike the other poets of his generation, Spenser responds to such pressure not by renouncing, but rather by reaffirming, the value of poetry. The sometimes hostile active world belongs, he lets us see, to the realm of mutability. Poetry alone has access to the unchanging forms of moral and aesthetic perfection, to "the sacred noursery of vertue" whose ways "none can find, but who has taught them by the Muse" (VI.proem.2–3). Others may have claimed for poetry a similar superiority to those "serving sciences" that depend on nature rather than on the grace of inspiration, but only Spenser turned that claim into a career. He thus gave to the idea

---

53. Isabel MacCaffrey, *Spenser's Allegory: The Anatomy of Imagination* (Princeton: Princeton Univ. Press, 1976), pp. 366–370. The examples of retirement mentioned in my next few paragraphs were suggested by MacCaffrey.

of the laureate poet a local habitation and a name. The "Edmund Spenser" of literary history—"the New Poet," the "first . . . great reformer," "our Virgil"—was for later writers perhaps Spenser's most significant creation. It is in this sense that he particularly deserves to be called "the poets' poet."

If there is any tendency toward repentance at the end of his career, what he repents is not poetry but his engagement with the active world. Melibee may speak for this side of Spenser when he castigates the vanity of the court and regrets that he "spent [his] youth in vaine" seeking public position. As in *Colin Clouts Come Home Againe,* the great world is presented as a place of hollow aspiration and inevitable repentance, a place opposed to the virtuous tranquillity of the pastoral world. But this is only one side of Spenser, and, even at the end, perhaps not the dominant one. Whatever his ultimate disillusionment with the active life, Spenser never unequivocally restricts the poet to private contemplation. The poet's pastoral mask is, after all, a mask. Though he may, by virtue of his gift and his art, present himself as a native resident of the land of poetry, he is by education, if not by birth, a gentleman, a man of whom public service is rightfully expected.

The Hermit, another retired wiseman in Book VI, but one "of gentle race," better represents the doubleness of Spenser's view. He too "from all this worlds incombrance did himselfe assoyle," but only after dutifully spending his youth and strength in the "worlds contentious toyle" (VI.v.37). Thus the undercurrent of irony in the exchange between Melibee and Calidore in praise of the shepherd's life. "Fittest is," as Melibee says, "that all contented rest / With that they hold" (VI.ix.29). The shepherd's life may fit Melibee, but not Calidore, who holds and is held by duty of his knighthood. The laureate is both contemplative shepherd and questing knight. In this he resembles Redcross, the "clownishe younge man," raised as a ploughman, who takes on the armor of heroic endeavor but who will, as Contemplation tells him, one day "wash thy hands from guilt of bloudy field: / For bloud can nought but sin, and war but sorrowes yield" (I.x.60).[54] What kept Spenser from something like the Hermit's open declaration of retirement from "this worlds incombrance" was, I suppose, the fear that such promptings might be only the counsel of Despair, "Sleepe after toyle, port after stormie seas, / Ease after warre, death after life does greatly please" (I.ix.40). In no book of *The Faerie Queene* is the lure of the private world more attractive than in the last, but in none are the warnings against resting in "middest of the race" more pressing.[55] For Spenser, the Christian humanist, the race was never clearly over, so he could never join the Roman Horace in saying of his public poetic duties, *Non eadem est aetas, non mens.*[56] His idea of a literary career thus did not allow for the Irish equivalent of a Sabine farm, though his work does give considerable emphasis to the image of Colin Clout coming home again.

Spenser's idea of a poet was finally an unstable but necessary union of two ideas, embodied in two roles—shepherd and knight, Colin and Calidore—neither of which could be renounced in favor of the other. The first gained him a place in the genus *poetae* as it was understood by his generation. The second defined him as the unique English member of the species of professed national poets. Without the first he would have been no poet at all, however much public verse he had written. Without the second he, like Sidney, Harington, or Lodge, would have been able to make of poetry no more than a diver-

54. Donald Cheney has suggested the connection between the poet and the Redcross Knight in *Spenser's Image of Nature: Wild Man and Shepherd in "The Faerie Queene"* (New Haven: Yale Univ. Press, 1966), pp. 18–22.

55. Berger points out that "the most frequently repeated motif [in Book VI] is . . . that of a character surprised in a moment of diversion" ("Prospect," p. 103).

56. Horace, *Epistle* I.i.4.

sion of youth. But not even Spenser could maintain the precarious equilibrium that had made possible his extraordinary accomplishment of the 1580s, an equilibrium that depended on both roles being subsumed by the poem. Nor could his successors achieve anything approaching that balance. They did not really try. Men like Daniel and Drayton professed themselves poets and stuck to their profession more easily because Spenser had been there first. But while they recognized, praised, and relied on his achievement of a literary career, they neither followed nor dared approve his mixing of the two roles. They wrote in both the pastoral and the heroic guise, but they kept the two nicely separated. *The Faerie Queene* they found "too fabulously mixed," and criticized its "imaginary ground," its want of historical verity.[57] A similar hardening of generic distinctions was in process in Italy and France, and it is not surprising that English poets should have responded to it. What is surprising is that, without denying either the humanist or the romantic sides of his cultural and literary heritage and in a country that had known no major poet for two hundred years, Spenser could have created a body of work sufficient to give form and substance to an ideal that other men entertained only in the realm of hypothetical speculation.Despite the pressures of his generation, Spenser took poetry beyond repentance and, in so doing, gave England its first laureate poet.

57. Daniel and Drayton's remarks are reprinted in *Spenser: The Critical Heritage,* ed. R. M. Cummings (New York: Barnes & Noble, 1971), pp. 75 and 79. The importance of fiction to Spenser's poetic accomplishment is discussed by A. C. Hamilton, *The Structure of Allegory in "The Faerie Queene"* (Oxford: Clarendon Press, 1961), pp. 15–29. See also William Nelson, *Fact or Fiction: The Dilemma of the Renaissance Storyteller* (Cambridge: Harvard Univ. Press, 1973).

3

Self-
Creating
Ben Jonson

———

The title of this chapter comes from Dekker's *Satiromastix,*
one of the last shots fired in the famous War of the Theaters—
and one of the best aimed. The hyphenated adjective scored a
direct hit. More than that of any other poet of his generation,
more perhaps than that of any other poet of the English Renaissance, Ben Jonson's self-creation drew immediate attention to
itself. "True poets," Dekker wrote, "are with Art and Nature
crowned."[1] It is the passive construction, the "are ...
crowned," that particularly condemns Jonson. Unlike Dekker,
Jonson obtruded himself on his work, manifestly seeking to
make it an index of his laureate standing. As Owen Felltham
was to charge some thirty years later, Jonson could never "forbear [his] crown / Till the world put it on."[2] What Dekker,
Felltham, and Jonson's many other critics fail to acknowledge
is that given the poetic forms available to his generation he
could attain the laurel only by reaching for it.

1. *Satiromastix, or the Untrussing of the Humorous Poet,* in *The Dramatic Works of Thomas Dekker,* ed. Fredson Bowers, 4 vols. (Cambridge:
Cambridge Univ. Press, 1953–1961), I, 377.
2. Owen Felltham quoted in *Ben Jonson,* ed. C. H. Herford, Percy Simpson, and Evelyn Simpson, 11 vols. (Oxford: Clarendon Press, 1925–1952), XI,
340. Subsequent references to this edition will be included in the text.

At their most successful, the various signs that make known a poet's laureate identity appear rather the products of nature than of arbitrary convention. Ideally we read them not as the author's way of saying something about himself—such obtrusiveness inevitably detracts from their effect—but rather as clues that lead us to reality. We discover his identity inductively without his having to proclaim it. So it is with the most prominent signs that mark Spenser's career, particularly his passage from pastoral to epic. Thanks to this choice of genres, he seems a "natural" laureate.

That this should be so is a bit odd. There is no reason in nature why the laureate self—a virtuous, centered, serious self, characterized by its knowledge of and fidelity to itself and the governing ethos of the age—should be expressed in long poems rather than short, in pastoral rather than epigram, epistle, or ode—no reason, for that matter, why it should use poems at all. But such was the force of the Virgilian model (strengthened in Spenser's case by a Virgilian concern for history, a Virgilian placement of the ruler, and a goodly number of specifically Virgilian echoes) that its arbitrariness was not felt. It seemed to signify "laureate" naturally. And though the subsequent careers of Milton, Pope, Wordsworth, and Joyce have modified both the self and the model, each has nevertheless enforced the association of role-type and genre and with it the impression of naturalness.

What does a great public poet do? He first writes some small works in which his poetic identity is both questioned and established. Then he writes an epic, forging in the smithy of his soul the uncreated conscience of his race. Given the status of the connection between genre and role, a poet who wrote epic (or some recognizable version of it) could in other aspects of his self-presentation make large concessions to the literary expectations of his age, as Spenser did, without abandoning his laureate identity.

But what of a poet like Jonson? A bare list of his works would surely not move one to proclaim him a "natural" laureate, produced by the purely organic generation of diachrony. Here was no Virgil. Jonson's pastoral was the last of his works, and it was never finished. His epic, the *Heroologia*, was perhaps never started. And even if we accept, as Jonson wants us to, Horace as a substitute model, what we notice most is the poor fit. Pope is the English Horace (a Horace with Virgilian coloring) and as such he, like Spenser, is a "natural" laureate. Jonson is not even close. None of the genres in which he wrote most—comedy, epigram, or masque—possessed a conventional laureate association, whether Horatian or Virgilian. Jonson was close not to the laureate patterns of antiquity but to the literature of his own generation, to the literary avant-garde at the inns of court and the new literary market in the public and private theaters. Within that closeness, he undertook to open a space sufficient to distinguish himself as laureate from the inns-of-court amateurs and from the theatrical professionals. But his lack of the usual genre markings did make that undertaking difficult. Jonson was attempting, as he said in the epigraph to *The Alchemist,*

> petere inde coronam,
> Unde prius nulli velarint tempora,

"to seek a crown thence, whence the Muses have never yet veiled anyone's temples."[3] No wonder Dekker thought him self-created. If Jonson is far more insistent in his laureate self-presentation than either Spenser or Milton, so insistent that sometimes the poet overwhelms the poem, it is because the most readily comprehensible signs of a laureate identity were denied him.

3. *Collation of the Ben Jonson Folios, 1616–31–1640,* trans. H. L. Ford. (Oxford: Oxford Univ. Press, 1932), p. 11.

Relocating Poetry

Why that denial? Why couldn't Jonson have begun with pastoral and then worked up to a long heroic poem, as Spenser did? The answer, we instinctively suppose, is to be found in Jonson's temperament, in the nature of his "genius." Jonson was not like that. But how do we know what Jonson was like if not from the poems and plays he actually wrote and from the role he actually played? The argument from individual temperament attributes to the author the character of his works so that their character can then be derived from his—a tightly circular argument, irrefutable but tautological. By looking outside Jonson to the literary world of which he was a part, we can significantly enlarge the circle of explanation, though perhaps not eliminate its circularity. Not Jonson's temperament, but the temperament of his generation, a temperament shaped in large part by the generation's need to find for itself a voice and manner distinct from those of its predecessor, caused that denial.

Jonson and his immediate contemporaries could not do what Spenser had done because Spenser had so recently done it. Spenser's deliberate accomplishment of a laureate career and Sidney's posthumous emergence as a laureate poet, despite his own adoption of the amateur mask of literary rebellion and repentance, demonstrated the possibility of a major public poetic career in English but, at the same time, made it impossible for anyone else to achieve such a career by working in a similar vein. Where Sidney and Spenser had begun in a near void, at least so far as English models of a laureate career were concerned, men born two decades later discovered a surplus. The pastoral, the sonnet sequence, the chivalric, Arcadian, and amorous romance, the long nationalistic poem, perhaps even the epic had been exhausted, and with them the mellifluous, ornamented style and the aureate attitudes that had been their body

and soul. Even Daniel and Drayton, born only a decade after
Sidney and Spenser, came late enough to fall under this ban,
though early enough not to know it. Possessed by a new concern for literal truth, they did move in a new direction. They
wrote their long poems about English history and topography
rather than about shepherd princes or faerie knights. But they
did not move far enough. Each created a vast *oeuvre* that, for
all its touches of individuality, could be no more than a vast
ombre. They were poets in the laureate sense, but shadow
poets.

But if Daniel and Drayton did not realize that an independent poetic career could no longer be made with the materials
that had served Spenser and Sidney, men younger than they,
men who came of age after the publication of *The Faerie
Queene* and the *Arcadia,* did. Joseph Hall, born in 1574,
eleven years after Daniel and Drayton and twenty-two years
after Spenser, clearly has both Daniel and Drayton in mind in
his portrayal of the foolish poetaster Labeo. The career pattern
he mocks is, however, the half-Petrarchan, half-Virgilian amal-
gam associated with Sidney and Spenser. Speaking of Labeo's
Muse, Hall says that

> Her *arma virum* goes by two degrees,
> The sheepcote first hath been her nursery,
> Where she hath worn her idle infancy . . .
> As did whilere the homely Carmelite
> Following Virgil, and he Theocrite;
> Or else hath been in Venus chamber trained
> To play with Cupid, till she had attained
> To comment well upon a beauteous face,
> Then was she fit for an heroic place.[4]

If for Hall the two great Elizabethans were beyond direct reproach (though lines five and six of the passage above, with

4. *The Collected Poems of Joseph Hall,* ed. A. Davenport (Liverpool:
Liverpool Univ. Press, 1949), p. 95.

their close echo of E. K.'s preface to *The Shepheardes Calender,* come dangerously close to reproaching Spenser), they were, to all but fools like Labeo, equally beyond imitation—figures, as Hall said, "whom no earthly wight / Dares once to emulate, much less dares despite."[5] The new poets of Hall's generation thus needed new models.

Hall was not the first to question the generic and stylistic traits that had characterized the generation of Sidney and Spenser. Thomas Nashe, whose *Anatomy of Absurdity* had anatomized particularly the absurdity of romance, whose *Choice of Valentines* had mocked the Petrarchan-Platonic ideal of love, whose *Unfortunate Traveler* had ridiculed chivalric romance (and a good deal else besides), whose contributions to the Marprelate Controversy and to the Nashe-Harvey quarrel had (in Guilpin's phrase) "taught the Muse to scold," and whose *Isle of Dogs* (written in collaboration with Ben Jonson) had brought satiric scolding to the stage, was the great precursor— a precursor whose imaginative vigor Hall could not hope to match. But Hall did provide the most thoroughgoing and systematic repudiation of the aureate Elizabethans. In the first book of his *Virgidemiae,* he surveyed all the kinds then current—romance, sonnet, elegy, tragedy, doleful legend, panegyric, pastoral, and even religious poetry—and found them all wanting. All these "meal-mouthed poesies" flatter vice by "prank[ing] base men in proud superlatives." Only satire escapes this charge. Soon, however, one comes to feel that Hall objects less to flattery than to the sheer quantity of this stuff. It left nothing for him and his generation to do. As he says of romance, "What needs it? Are there not enow beside?"[6]

Hall's strictures were not universally accepted, not even by those of his own age. So hotly were they debated that among the many literary tiffs of the 1590s historians have found a

5. Hall, p. 16.   6. Hall, p. 94.

place for a "Hall-Marston Controversy," which in some accounts swells into the "Hall-Marston-Guilpin-Jonson-Weever-
Breton Quarrels." But though they did dispute (Marston most
fully) some of Hall's charges, the fundamental source of contention seems to have been rather some real or imagined personal affront than any basic disagreement with the substance
of his argument. Like Hall, his opponents confine their own
work very largely to satire and, as in his, the attack on "meal-
mouthed poesies" figures largely in their verse. More significant still, the pressure for novelty that marks Hall is equally
evident in them.

Nashe had already claimed that in writing *The Choice of
Valentines* he was "only induced by variety. / Complaints and
praises everyone can write," but his, he tells us, is a subject on
which "none did ever write / That hath succeeded in these latter
times."[7] Others announce similar motives. In 1598, the year in
which the second three books of the *Virgidemiae* appeared,
Everard Guilpin described his as an age of decline after "the
first beginners" of English poetry had already "mounted the
full." But far from imitating the triumphs of those first beginners, Guilpin can make room for himself only by dismissing
their "whining love song[s]."

> The satire only and epigrammatist
> (Concise epigram and sharp satirist)
> Keep diet from this surfeit of excess.[8]

Even a writer as little a part of the avant-garde as Richard
Barnfield realized the need for novelty. "Being determined to
write of something, and yet not resolved of anything, I consid-

7. *The Works of Thomas Nashe,* ed. Ronald B. McKerrow, rev. ed., 5 vols.
(Oxford: Blackwell, 1958), III, 403.

8. Everard Guilpin, *Skialethia or A Shadowe of Truth, in Certaine Epigrams and Satyres,* ed. D. Allen Carroll (Chapel Hill: Univ. of North Carolina
Press, 1974), pp. 39 and 61–62.

ered with myself, if one should write of love, they will say, 'Why everyone writes of love. . . .' To be short, I could think of nothing, but either it was common, or not at all in request."[9] So, in 1598, three years after having made his literary debut as an imitator of Spenser, Barnfield tried his hand at a mild and dotty sort of satire and produced *The Encomium of Lady Pecunia*. The pretense of doing "things unattempted yet in prose or rime" is, of course, among the most familiar of poetic conventions. Milton translated his version of it almost verbatim from Ariosto, who got it from Boiardo, Horace, and Lucretius. But the convention persists because of each new literary generation's need for a space of its own—particularly when it follows an age of great and recognized accomplishment. And that was precisely the situation in which Hall, Guilpin, Barnfield, and their coevals found themselves. By the mid-1590s, it was clear to all but the most obtuse that the golden poetry of Sidney and Spenser was played out and could no longer serve as an inspiration for new writers.

But neither the men I have mentioned so far nor the many others like them, including John Weever, Thomas Bastard, Sir John Davies, Edward Sharpham, and John Donne, were seriously inconvenienced by the unavailability of the Elizabethan *cursus poetarum*. It mattered little to them that one could no longer climb the ladder from pastoral to epic, for none of them aspired to a laureate career. They wrote elegy, satire, and epigram in a clipped and acerbic style, in part because Sidney and Spenser had not done so before them, but they had no concern for the problem of how to make the voice of this new generation into a vehicle for a major public literary career. Though differing in subject and form from their sonnet-writing predecessors, they shared the short literary careers and the gentle-

9. Richard Barnfield, *Poems, 1595–1598,* ed. Edward Arber (Westminster: A. Constable, 1896), p. 83.

manly disdain for literature that had characterized the Elizabethan amateurs. Nashe referred to his work as "a mere toy, not
deserving any judicial man's view"; Davies talked of having
"misspent" fifteen days in the making of his first book; Marston allowed the printer to present his collected works as "juvenilia and youthful recreations"; Hall spoke of his poetry, only
nine years after its publication, as "long sithence out of date"
having "yielded her place to graver studies"; and Donne, who
kept most of his poems out of print, was reportedly embarrassed by their continued circulation in manuscript.[10] However
well or badly these men wrote and however much or little
energy they devoted to their literary labors, none wished to be
known primarily as a poet, and so none had to forge for himself
a literary identity consonant at once with the poetic practice of
his generation and with the ideal of a laureate self.

This was, however, precisely the problem that faced Ben
Jonson. From all we can tell, Jonson's was never to be a brief
literary career that would in time yield to the graver demands
of church or state. For him, any graver demand would have to
be answered by poetry itself. But Jonson did resemble Hall,
Marston, Donne, and the others in age and taste. Like most of
them, he was born in the early 1570s, and, also like them, he
began writing in the mid-1590s. And if he differed from them in
having been a student of neither the universities nor the inns of
court, he did identify himself with those centers of intellectual

10. Nashe, I, 153; *The Poems of Sir John Davies,* ed. Robert Krueger (Oxford: Clarendon Press, 1975), p. 89; *The Workes of Mr. John Marston* (1633),
sig. A3ᵛ; Hall, p. 127. For Donne, see John Carey, *John Donne: Life, Mind and
Art* (New York: Oxford Univ. Press, 1981), pp. 69–70. According to Carey,
"Donne is singular among English poets in that he never refers to his poetry
except disparagingly." The other passages cited in this note and many other
similar passages cited elsewhere in this book are only a small part of the
enormous mass of evidence that might be opposed to Carey's statement. Far
from being singular, Donne's disparagement of his verse is thoroughly conventional.

fashion in much the way that Spenser, twenty years earlier, had identified himself with the Sidney circle. For the bricklayer's stepson, as for the "shepherd"-sizar, literary respectability, and with it the hope of patronage, lay in association with the social and intellectual élite of his generation. And in Jonson's generation, as we have seen, that association was likely to involve the exclusion of much that had characterized both the individual works and the careers of Sidney and Spenser.

Such exclusion decisively marks Jonson's first twenty years as a professed poet. In that time, he wrote no sonnet, no pastoral, no romance, and no long poem—the longest being "The Famous Voyage," a 196-line scatological mock epic. *The Forest,* the collection of poems that Jonson prepared for the 1616 folio *Works,* begins by explaining "Why I Write Not of Love," and the nine plays presented in that volume do not contain a single serious love scene. The volume does, however, include many poems and many dramatic scenes that satirize both lovers and love poets.

It has not, I think, been noticed that Jonson's "explanation" of why he did not write of love is modeled on Ovid, whose *Amores* begins with a very similar passage explaining "how Cupid forced him to write of love rather than war" *(Quemadmodum a Cupidine pro bellis amoris scribere coactus sit).* Cupid thwarts Jonson's plan to write of love just as he had upset Ovid's epic intention. That Jonson should base his poem of self-presentation on Ovid's is a curiously appropriate gesture, for Ovid, more than any other ancient poet, had been the prime mover of Jonson's generation. First in Marlowe's undergraduate translations of the *Amores* and then in the succeeding flood of Ovidian elegy and epyllion, the new generation and its immediate precursors offered, as William Keach has recently put it, their "alternatives to the Spenserian synthesis"—as, in his own time, Ovid had offered his alternative to the Virgilian synthesis.[11] The Ovidian flood was, of course, soon topped by the still more voluminous current of satire, a current that caught in its flow even the Ovidian poems of Nashe, Donne, Marston, Weever, and Beaumont. But, as Keach has pointed out, satire was already shadowed in the cynicism of the *Amores*. So both as amorist and as satirist, Ovid functioned as the first teacher to the new age. In echoing him, Jonson thus recalled, though many years after the Ovidian fashion of the 1590s had subsided, his association with the generation that had given it birth.

But Jonson did not only imitate Ovid. He reversed him. Where Ovid had been forced to write of love, Jonson is kept from doing so. In this reversal Jonson distinguished himself both from Ovid and from the Ovidian poets of his generation and of the generation that preceded it—poets who had, almost without exception, fallen silent by the time *The Forest* appeared in 1616. Jonson may have grown old, as he ruefully admits in the poem's last words, but he, unlike the amateurs who had followed Ovid, was still writing.

Our knowledge of Jonson's attitude toward Ovid and the Ovidian idea of the poet does not, however, depend on this one, oblique allusion. In *Poetaster* Ovid is a major character, as are Horace and Virgil. By identifying himself with Horace and positioning himself with respect to the other two, Jonson performs perhaps his most elaborate act of self-presentation. It is here that he most fully defines his relation to the two prime models of a poetic career, the amateur and the laureate, the first represented by Ovid, the second by Virgil.

Ovid has first say in *Poetaster*. Initially he, and he alone, represents and defends poetry. If Jonson, as poet, has a spokes-

11. William Keach, *Elizabethan Erotic Narratives: Irony and Pathos in the Ovidian Poetry of Shakespeare, Marlowe, and Their Contemporaries* (New Brunswick: Rutgers Univ. Press, 1971), pp. 219 ff.

man in this play, it would seem, so far as one can tell from the first act, to be Ovid. And, indeed, in the opening encounter with his father, Ovid firmly retains our approval. Set against the mean and narrow materialism of his father and the sycophancy of his father's supporters, even Ovid's "poetical fancies and furies" show to advantage. But while approving him, the play reveals Ovid to be a poet of a quite particular and readily recognizable sort. Like Peele, Marlowe, Lyly, Lodge, and Greene (who called himself "a second Ovid"),[12] he is a prodigal poet. The scene of paternal admonition has its counterpart in many of the autobiographical fictions written by these Elizabethan prodigals, as does the later scene of judgment. Ovid is, moreover, both an amateur and a lover, a poet in rebellion not only against his blinkered father but also against the fundamental values of the state and its religion. We do not, of course, know all this in the opening scene. The blasphemy for which Ovid is banished occurs only later and even then we are not sure how rigorously Jonson means us to blame it. Are we to accept the full severity of Augustus' condemnation or rather to believe with Horace that Ovid's have been "harmless pleasures, bred of noble wit"? The uncertainty is itself significant. Jonson does not himself reprehend such amateur license, but he does show that it is liable to virtuous reprehension. Though he no doubt admired Ovid and many of his Elizabethan followers, Jonson detaches himself from both and from the tradition they represent, a tradition that he reduces to absurdity in Ovid's last lines:

> The truest wisdom silly men can have,
> Is dotage on the follies of their flesh.   (IV, 289)

On such idolatrous dotage the brief autonomy of the Elizabethan amateur was based. Jonson clearly did not intend to be such a poet.

12. *The Life and Complete Works of Robert Greene,* ed. Alexander B. Grosart, 15 vols. (1881–1883; rpt. New York: Russell, 1964), XII, 274.

His attitude toward Virgil is considerably more complex. Unlike Ovid, Virgil is unquestionably an ideal poet, an archetypal laureate, a man

> refined
> From all the tartarous moods of common men,
> Bearing the nature and similitude
> Of a right heavenly body; most severe
> In fashion and collection of himself;
> And, then, as clear and confident as Jove.
>
> (IV, 292–293)

But this praise of Virgil's godlike moral perfection leaves his poetry unregarded. The poet is prior and superior to the poem, whose excellence derives in any case from his. There is no question of his writing better than he knows; he can only strive to paint "his mind's peace" with whatever inevitable loss results from his dependence on "fleshly pencils." More specifically literary commendation ("And for his poesy . . . ") thus rightly comes in as an afterthought.

This deflection of regard from the product to the producer had one obvious advantage and at least one unintended disadvantage. It made it possible to base a laureate claim on one's character rather than on one's choice of genres. Virgil is not a laureate because he wrote an epic poem. He is a laureate because he is a good man. For Jonson, in a generation deprived of the epic, this was a readjustment of considerable significance. But it created new difficulties.

Virgil's very perfection put him out of reach. He is in his way as distant from Horace, and thus from Jonson, as was Ovid. He appears only in the fifth act and then almost as a *deus ex machina*—a figure wholly removed from the world of poetasters and fools to which Horace by his poverty, his urbanity, and his satire so inextricably belongs. "He is come out of Campania" where no Crispinus, Demetrius, or Tucca—the tormentors of Horace—has ever dared accost or accuse him. Accord-

ing to the "Apologetical Dialogue" appended to *Poetaster,*
Jonson chose

> Augustus Caesar's times,
> When wit and arts were at their height in Rome,
> To show that Virgil, Horace, and the rest
> Of those great master-spirits did not want
> Detractors then or practisers against them.
>
> (IV, 320)

But in the play Virgil is subject to no detraction. If Jonson's
intention was, as he goes on to say, to liken his own situation to
that of Virgil and Horace and thus to put his enemies to shame,
he only half succeeded.

The action of *Poetaster* further distinguishes Horace from
Virgil, even as it brings them together. It represents, after the
initial exposure of Ovid, the elevation of Horace into the
rarefied company of Augustus and Virgil and the exclusion
from that company of his detractors. This movement was fundamental to Jonson's sense of himself—to his sense both of his
actual situation and of his ideal destiny. Trapped in a vulgar
and degrading world of mimics and hacks, he belonged with
kings. Adumbrated in *Every Man Out of His Humor,* the pattern of release and recognition found its first full expression in
Cynthia's Revels and recurred in the two odes to himself and in
the "Apologetical Dialogue." In all but the last of these, the
monarch represents the point of destination. For Virgil no such
passage was needed. At his first entry, he is hailed by Augustus
as an equal:

> Welcome to Caesar, Virgil! Caesar and Virgil
> Shall differ but in sound; to Caesar, Virgil,
> Of his expressed greatness, shall be made
> A second surname, and to Virgil, Caesar.
>
> (IV, 294)

Virgil belongs by nature to the realm of absolute and achieved being; Horace to the realm of mere becoming. Virgil possesses his laureate identity as a given; Horace must create his.

Even in his praise of Virgil, that praise which defines the laureate ideal, Horace must prove himself. No free offering, it is the successful completion of a test. "What think you . . . of Virgil?" Augustus asks, and he calls first on Horace, for Horace is "the poorest / And likeliest to envy or to detract" (IV, 292). Virgil's worth is known. It is fixed and unassailable. Only Horace's is in doubt. Can this man—soon to be accused of self-love, arrogance, impudence, and railing—say good of anyone? That he does succeed in praising Virgil "argues," as Augustus remarks, "a truth of merit in you"—and presumably in Jonson, for whom Horace stood. It says nothing of Virgil.

A similar ambivalence marks Jonson's choice of a text for Virgil to read. On one level that choice links Virgil and Horace; on another it further distinguishes them. The passage, from Book IV of the *Aeneid,* describes the sexual union of Dido and Aeneas and its rumorous aftermath. The usual inclination of critics has been to regard as significant only its second half, the personification of Rumor, and to confine its reference to the attack on Horace. That attack does clearly provide the passage its most immediate context. Virgil's reading is interrupted by the noisy arrival of Horace's accusers. But though dramatic contiguity makes this reference primary, the poorness of fit leads us to look elsewhere as well. For the rumor about Horace is false; that about Dido and Aeneas is true. Nor is there any similarity in the rumored events. Horace is accused of treasonous libel, Dido and Aeneas of sexual license. Much more similar is the discovery of Ovid and Julia, where the rumor is both true and about licentiousness. That earlier scene shares with Virgil's poem even an equivocal distribution of blame, finding fault with both the lovers and the rumor that exposes them. And though strenuously moral, the passage may by its very subject serve to associate Ovid and Virgil as poets. There existed Elizabethan precedent for such association, precedent that depended on this particular passage. In his *School of Abuse*, Stephen Gosson called both Virgil and Ovid "amorous poets": "the one shows his art in the lust of Dido, the other his cunning in the incest of Myrrha."[13]

Jonson would surely have rejected Gosson's jingling equation of Virgil and Ovid, but he might have agreed that both were amorous poets. Despite the great differences in its treatment, their subject linked them. It also differentiated them from satirical Horace. Virgil occupies a place in Jonson's play a little like that occupied by Sidney and Spenser in his literary milieu. And indeed, the Dido episode, the story of a warrior detained by love from the pursuit of his heroic duty, finds its likeness in both *Arcadia* and *The Faerie Queene*. Like Sidney and Spenser, Virgil is a laureate poet of undoubted accomplishment. But the nature of his accomplishment, the subjects he treated and the forms he used, removes him from the direct emulation of Horace, just as Sidney and Spenser were removed from that of Jonson. In *Poetaster* the difference is not between generations, nor could it be if historical credibility were to be maintained. But though Virgil and Horace are of an age, the distance between them is no less great and is similar in kind to that which separated Jonson from his great Elizabethan predecessors.

The new emphasis that one observes in *Poetaster* on the nature of the poet as opposed to the nature of his poems—an emphasis that put a particular strain on Jonson's laureate self-presentation—derives only in part from the loss of the usual genre markings. A further casualty of the passage from one

13. Stephen Gosson, *The School of Abuse* (1841; rpt. New York: AMS Press, 1970), p. 10.

generation to another was the notion of inspiration, and with it went a certain naive enthusiasm for poetry itself. Typical of that earlier attitude is Lorenzo Junior's impassioned blank-verse defense of poetry in *Every Man In His Humor* as "blessed, eternal, and most true divine," fed with "sacred invention," "attired in the majesty of art," and freed of "any relish of an earthly thought" (III, 285). But such flight soared beyond the earthly prose of even the first version of *Every Man In,* and when Jonson revised the play for inclusion in the 1616 folio the whole speech was cut. In its place he put Justice Clement's homely observation that poets "are not born every year, as an alderman. There goes more to the making of a good poet, than a sheriff"—to which young Lorenzo, now anglicized into Edward Knowell, drily remarks, "Sir, you have saved me the labor of a defense" (III, 400). By this substitution, Jonson not only replaced verse with prose, passion with reason, and rebellious youth with judicial age. He also shifted the burden of defense from poetry to the poet. The poet's birth and breeding, rather than the sacred character of poetry itself, serve to answer those who think it an "idle, . . . fruitless, and unprofitable art."

The claim to divine inspiration could not survive the new, astringent realism of the 1590s. Such stilt-walking stuff had become the exclusive prop of fools like Hall's Labeo.

> Labeo reaches right (who can deny?)
> The true strains of heroic poesy:
> For he can tell how fury reft his sense
> And Phoebus filled him with intelligence.
> He can implore the heathen deities
> To guide his bold and busy enterprise.[14]

Jonson's invocation to his epode on the Phoenix and the Turtle suggests his sensitivity to this emerging fashion. He humorously surveys the "poets' heaven" in search of a "great name"

14. Hall, p. 94.

to countenance his "active muse," rejecting in turn Hercules, Phoebus, Bacchus, Pallas, Venus, Cupid, Hermes, and all the ladies of the Thespian lake, only to conclude with a firm self-assertion: "No, I bring/My own true fire" (VIII, 108). Jonson's muse, as a great many other passages in his verse confirm, was himself, and on that self his poetic undertaking depended.

But even Jonson's own true fire was habitually banked. Many critics observing this have concluded that the fire never burned very brightly, that Jonson was an ambitious and hardworking drudge. No one who has paid much heed to Asper, Volpone, Sir Epicure Mammon, Truewit, or Tom Quarlous could long persist in this view. Surely their creator did not lack fire. Gabriele Jackson has found enough material to fill a book on *Vision and Judgment in Ben Jonson,* and others have talked plausibly of his Dionysian qualities.[15] Nor should one give much credence to Edmund Wilson's notion that Jonson suffered from psychic constipation.[16] Whatever the inhibition, it belonged less to him individually than to his generation. In the 1590s even a satirist had to avoid letting himself be too obviously carried away. Marston failed to heed this rule and was mockingly dubbed "Furor Poeticus" by a Cambridge wit.[17]

15. Gabriele Jackson, *Vision and Judgment* (New Haven: Yale Univ. Press, 1968). *Dionysian* comes from Arthur F. Marotti, "All About Jonson's Poetry," *ELH,* 39 (1972), 208–237. Thomas M. Greene uses the terms *Protean* and *centrifugal* to get at some of the same qualities in "Ben Jonson and the Centered Self," *SEL,* 10 (1970), 325–348.

16. Edmund Wilson, "Morose Ben Jonson," in *The Triple Thinkers* (London: Lehman, 1952), pp. 203–220.

17. *The Three Parnassus Plays (1598–1601),* ed. J.B. Leishman (London: Nicholson, 1949), pp. 82–92. In his *Scourge of Villainy,* Marston had himself called attention to the indecorum of his aspiring verse:

> O how on tiptoes proudly mounts my Muse,
> Stalking a loftier gate than satyr's use.
> Methinks some sacred rage warms all my veins,
> Making my spright mount up to higher strains
> Than well beseems a rough-tongued satyr's part.

And when in *Every Man Out* Asper, one of Jonson's own self-projections, shows excessive satiric zeal, another Jonsonian persona breaks in to remark,

> Why, this is right furor poeticus!
> Kind gentlemen, we hope your patience
> Will yet conceive the best, or entertain
> This supposition: that a madman speaks. (III, 433)

Mockery here, as in the Cambridge response to Marston, is coupled with admiration. The intellectual élite of Jonson's generation delighted in fustian, and even demanded it, but was not much inclined to take it seriously. To an amateur like Marston being taken seriously might not matter. To Jonson it was essential.

Jonson did not of course do without inspiration. If our usual notions of the creative process are at all right, he could not have done. Nor did he wholly eliminate the claim to inspiration from his self-presentation. But inspiration, enthusiasm, poetic fury, and the aureate style that most often expresses them are circumscribed and judged in his work. Gabriele Jackson had, after all, to talk of vision *and* judgment in Ben Jonson; the other critics, of the Dionysian *and* the Apollonian.[18] Even in conversation Jonson humorously "placed" his visionary experience. "He hath consumed a whole night," or so he told Drummond, "in lying looking to his great toe, about which he

---

The Poems of John Marston, ed. Arnold Davenport (Liverpool: Liverpool Univ. Press, 1961), p. 158. The word that I have modernized as *satyr's* in the second and fifth lines above is written *Satyres* in the original and may also be rendered as *satire's*.

18. The pressure toward judgment is among the most frequently remarked characteristics of Jonson's work. A. Richard Dutton has, for example, argued that "the act of creation for Jonson is also an act of judgment. There is a paradox in all his plays . . . between the patient effort which goes towards the solid depiction of his characters, and the structural logic of his drama, which is invariably reductive, bent on questioning and often destroying what he has created." "The Significance of Jonson's Revision of *Every Man In His Hu-*

hath seen Tartars and Turks, Romans and Carthaginians fight in his imagination" (I, 141). Jonson admits to having a hyperactive imagination, but he keeps it at a safely ironic distance in the vicinity of his great toe. Drummond was less impressed by the distance than by the imagination. In his opinion, Jonson was "oppressed with fantasy, which hath ever mastered his reason, a general disease in many poets" (I, 151). If so, this was one of those "ill parts" that Jonson was careful to dissemble. In his generation, a reputation for excessive imagination could no longer serve as the basis for a laureate poet's self-presentation.

Nearly one hundred years ago, J. A. Symonds objected that "the fixed idea that scholarship and sturdy labor could supply the place of inspiration ... weighed heavily upon [Jonson's] genius."[19] Whether or not we agree with Symond's implication that the weight damaged both the genius and its products, we can, I think, accept and even extend the remainder of his statement. Jonson did use scholarship and labor to fill the place that in the previous generation had been occupied by inspiration. Learning and hard, slow work became his sign, as inspiration had been Spenser's. Where Spenser presented himself as Colin Clout piping to the Graces and a visionary company of naked damsels on Mt. Acidale, Jonson is the Author in his study spending

> half my nights, and all my days,
> Here in a cell, to get a dark, pale face,
> To come forth worth the ivy or the bays.
>
> (IV, 324)

---

mour," *MLR,* 69 (1974), 246. More common is the view set forth in Jonas A. Barish's *Ben Jonson and the Language of Prose Comedy* (1960; rpt. New York: Norton, 1970) that the demand for judgment gradually diminishes in the course of Jonson's career. See also Barish's article "Feasting and Judging in Jonsonian Comedy," *Renaissance Drama,* 5 (1972), 3–35.

19. Quoted by J. G. Nichols, *The Poetry of Ben Jonson* (New York: Barnes and Noble, 1969), p. 16.

He advertised his connection with antiquaries and scholars, freighted the margins of his work with learned citations, bragged to Drummond that "he was better versed and knew more Greek and Latin than all the poets in England," and had his portrait painted with a band declaring him DOCTISSIM[US] POETARUM ANGLORUM.

If we can trust E. K.'s report, Spenser's *English Poet* had argued that poetry was "no art, but a divine gift and heavenly instinct, not to be gotten by labor and learning, but adorned with both, and poured into the wit by a certain *enthousiasmos* and celestial inspiration." Jonson in that section of *Discoveries* titled *De poetica* reversed Spenser's emphases. He does talk of *ingenium,* "divine instinct," and "poetical rapture." But even these seem rather matters of birth than of subsequent mystic intervention. He ends the discussion of *ingenium* with another version of the sentence he gave Justice Clement in *Every Man In*: "Every beggarly corporation affords the state a mayor or two baliffs yearly, but *solus rex aut poeta non quotannis nascitur*" (VIII, 637). The power that distinguishes the poet is not poured into him. It is part of him. Though the more usual formulae do occasionally come to his pen (as in the late poems on the death of Lady Venetia Digby), Jonson makes no consistent appeal to any inspiring figure outside himself. No Gloriana, no Stella elevates his verse. The good man is himself the star and the planet of the age wherein he lives. Unlike Spenser, Jonson is not lifted above himself by poetry. On the contrary, he hopes to lift poetry up to his level, to "raise the despised head of poetry again" (V, 21). And in this extraordinary undertaking, labor and learning were, as the remaining portions of his *de poetica* can testify, no mere ornaments: "Indeed, things wrote with labor deserve to be so read and will last their age. ... But that which we especially require in [the poet] is an exactness of study and multiplicity of reading.... And [let him] not think he can leap forth suddenly a poet by dreaming he hath been in Parnassus or having washed his lips (as they say) in Helicon. There goes more to his making than so" (VIII, 638–639).

By this claim to inspiration and by his progression from pastoral to epic, Spenser had been a "natural" laureate. Jonson, who knew that "without nature, art can claim no being," was obliged by Spenser's preemption of those familiar signs of a laureate nature to emphasize in his own self-presentation exercise, imitation, study, art, and, above all, moral goodness. "For," as he insisted in the preface to *Volpone,* "if men will impartially, and not asquint, look toward the offices and function of a poet, they will easily conclude to themselves the impossibility of any man's being the good poet without first being a good man" (V, 17).[20] But could such goodness be made manifest in the poetic kinds available to Jonson and his generation?

A *Laureate Satirist*

So far I have talked only of what was denied Jonson by the accident of his having come of age in the mid-1590s. But surely there was more than denial. What did the literary milieu of those years give him? A full answer would have to include the epigrammatic form that he practiced and the theatrical market that he exploited, and of these I shall wish to speak later. But

20. Jonson's desire to be thought a good man, his concern about the moral implications of self-presentation, and his nervousness about his own laureate title are suggested by three contiguous sentences in Drummond. I quote them in Drummond's spelling:

> of all stiles he loved most to be named honest, and hath of that ane hundreth letters so naming him
> he had this oft
>> thy flattering Picture Phrenee is lyke the
>> only jn this that ye both painted be.
> In his merry humor, he was wont to name himself the Poet (I, 150)

the most obvious gift of the 1590s was satire. Of the notable English writers who were of an age with Jonson, only the two professional dramatists—Dekker and Heywood—escaped being deeply involved in the satiric movement, and even they were clearly marked by it. The others—Donne, Hall, Marston, Tourneur, Webster, and Jonson himself, as well as the less notable Rowlands, Barnfield, Guilpin, Weever, and Sharpham—all made satire a central part of their literary production. For them Juvenal's sentence, *difficile est saturam non scribere,* had a particular appropriateness. It was indeed difficult for a writer born in the 1570s to resist the lure of satire—not because the world had suddenly become so provokingly wicked or foolish, but because everyone his age was writing it. Satire was the sign of their generation.

Why this should have been so is relatively easy to see, even if one ignores both the actual abuses that in the Elizabethan *fin de régime* deserved castigation and the high rate of unemployment among university and inns-of-court men that prompted them to do the castigating. The historical dynamic that opposes generation to generation and the literary system that sets genre against genre sufficiently explain their choice.

In an essay on the generational pattern of American literature, Malcolm Cowley has perceived a regular ebb and flow of moods, "an immensely slow heart-beat rhythm," as he calls it, "of diastole and systole."

Writers of any new age group . . . try to avoid the mistakes and enthusiasms of the group that preceded them. As the groups follow each other at intervals of ten or fifteen years, there seems to be an alternation of expansive and contractive moods, of interests turned outward

---

That these sentences stand next to one another without being aware of one another enforces our sense that, though Jonson often approaches self-knowledge, he generally turns away from it. The notion of the "good man" is, incidentally, among the topics that recur most obsessively in *Timber*. See, for example, VII, 563, 566, 597, 604–605, and 608.

to social problems and of those turned inward to dilemmas of the author.[21]

Some such pattern can be found in the history of English as well as American literature, though it could perhaps not be related unerringly to the succession of generations. The heart may at times beat even more slowly than Cowley suggests, with several successive age groups contributing to one long expansion or contraction. Thus the whole of the early seventeenth century may seem a period of contraction, of essentially private poetry, and the eighty years or so following the Restoration a period of expansion. But even within these longer, larger waves of successive groups carried forward by the work of one another, we find smaller movements that do seem to confirm Cowley's scheme. The writers born in the 1590s—Carew, Herbert, and Herrick most prominent among them—provide one such example. Though these men owe a quite obvious and freely acknowledged debt to Donne and Jonson, they borrowed not from the outward-turned satire that had been the initial sign of the Donne-Jonson age group but rather from the later more inward-turned lyrical works.

In the relation of Donne, Jonson, Hall, Marston, and their immediate contemporaries to the age group of Sidney and Spenser, one need, however, be concerned with no such subtlety. Satire, with its at least pretended attention to "social problems," stood in clear opposition to the solipsism of love poetry, the satirist's *speculum consuetudinis* providing fit antidote to the lover's picture of the mistress in his heart. How ever much we may feel that the spiritual breadth of the earlier writers makes them more truly expansive, theirs was for the most part an internal expansion, stretched to and perhaps beyond its limits by Spenser's visionary engagement with history.

21. Malcolm Cowley, —And I Worked at the Writer's Trade: Chapters of Literary History, 1918–1978 (New York: Viking, 1978), p. 14.

The antiromantic literary identity of the new generation looked outward by nature and demanded satire as its natural guise.

Already in earlier generations satire had served to mark the abandonment of love poetry. Readers of *The Steel Glass* (1576), one of the works of Gascoigne's well-advertised repentance, got the sign interpreted this way by Nicholas Bowyer:

> From lays of love to satires sad and sage,
> Our poet turns the travail of his time,
> And as he pleased the vein of youthful age,
> With pleasant pen employed in loving rime,
> So now he seeks the gravest to delight,
> With works of worth much better than they show.[22]

The pattern had been shadowed twenty years earlier in the Tottle arrangement of Wyatt's poems, the satirical "My John Poins" following the Petrarchan sonnets, and it found several notable imitators in the years after the publication of Gascoigne's poem, including Thomas Lodge and Robert Greene—if, that is, cony-catching pamphlets can be counted as a form of satire. One way (and there were a variety of others) to atone for the licentious indulgence of youth was to expose the abuses of city and court, to renounce private pleasure in favor of the public use associated with satire. Even Euphues, the most renowned fictional representative of amorous prodigality, marked his reformation with didactic treatises of sometimes sharply satirical flavor, beginning with "A Cooling Card for Philautus and All Fond Lovers." But in the 1590s what had hitherto been one way of marking the final stage of an amateur literary career became the principal differentiating mark of the newest age group. What more suitable way of rejecting the work of their predecessors than the way some of those prede-

---

22. *The Complete Works of George Gascoigne*, ed. John W. Cunliffe, 2 vols. (Cambridge: Cambridge Univ. Press, 1910), II, 139.

cessors had themselves used in their moments of repentance? If for the young writers of the 1590s theirs was an age of satire, it was in part because satire had already served as a pill to purge romance.

So pervasive was the sense of enmity between the satiric and the erotic that one of the young writers, one rather out of sympathy with the taste of his age but caught by it nevertheless, felt called upon to furnish a mythological explanation. Venus-hating Diana was, according to John Weever, at fault. Through her intervention, the child of Weever's Ovidian lovers, Faunus and Melliflora, is transformed into a satyr, who in turn begets the line of satyr-satirists from which Weever's poet coevals descend.

> This boon Diana then did ask of Jove,
> (More to be venged on the Queen of Love),
> That Faunus' late-transformed son's satires,
> (So called because they satisfied her ires)
> Should evermore be utter enemies
> To lovers' pastimes, sportful veneries.
> Jove granted her this lawful, just demand,
> As we may see within our faerie land:
> The satyrs' jerking, sharp-fanged poesy,
> Lashing and biting Venus' luxury.[23]

It is "our faerie land," Spenser's England, that has fallen under the sway of this new "jerking, sharp-fanged poesy." According to Weever's myth, faeries and satyrs are direct rivals. Unlike the goatlike satyrs,

> The faeries proved full stout, hardy knights,
> In jousts, in tilts, in tournaments, and fights,
> As Spenser shows. But Spenser now is gone,
> You faerie knights, your greatest loss bemoan.[24]

23. John Weever, *Faunus and Melliflora,* ed. A. Davenport (Liverpool: Liverpool Univ. Press, 1948), pp. 42–43.
24. Weever, p. 42.

Though the satirists' primary target was love, they had, Weever intimates, struck down the heroic as well.

Marston, whose "censuring vein" Weever says he "was born to hate," provides an illustration of this casual and indirect displacement of the heroic. "I that even now lisped like an amorist," Marston proclaims in the opening lines of one of his *Certain Satires*, "Am turned into a snapchance satirist." The primary opposition is, of course, between amorist and satirist. But Marston's editor is, I think, right to hear in these lines an echo—a mocking, parodic echo—of "the pseudo-Virgilian four-line introduction to the *Aeneid*," which Spenser had borrowed to introduce *The Faerie Queene*.[25] The satirist, who makes many of his most telling points by parodying all idealistic pretension, can allow the heroic no place. And indeed, according to the prescription of Renaissance theorists, snapchance satire was as much the stylistic opposite of the heroic as of the erotic. "Satires do not begin with invocations," wrote the Italian critic Sansovino in his influential *Discorso sopra la materia della satira*. "The subject of satire suits neither the ornamentation, nor the grace, nor the fire, nor the sweetness of speech that a high and heroic subject requires."[26] The particular fitness of satire as the distinguishing mark of an age group that followed writers who had triumphed in both love poetry and heroic romance was thus powerfully enforced.

But here again the question of Jonson's peculiar vocation arises. If satire provided a uniquely appropriate distinguishing mark for his amateur contemporaries, could it work equally well for him? Could satire serve as a vehicle for the self-presentation of a laureate poet?

25. Marston, *Poems*, pp. 72 and 228.
26. "Alla materia Satirica non si convien l'ornamento ne la gratia, ne i fuchi, ne la soavità del dire che vuol la materia Heroica & alta." Quoted by Louis Lecocq, *La satire en Angleterre de 1588 à 1603* (Paris: Didier, 1969), p. 256, n. 64.

In some ways it obviously could. It might, in fact, have been seen as solving many of the problems Spenser had faced as an aspiring laureate in a generation of love poets. Unlike love poetry, satire is determinedly moral in its intent. It seeks to correct abuses, among them the very abuses that love poetry perpetrates. Far from losing itself in solipsistic and idolatrous contemplation, satire engages the world of action directly. Its values are public, its point of view firmly located near the social, religious, and even political center of its culture. Reasons like these no doubt motivated Gascoigne's choice of satire as a means of signaling his moral regeneration, and they may have given comfort to Jonson as well. But the adjectives that Bowyer applies to satires like Gascoigne's, "sad and sage," hardly fit the satiric mode of Jonson's generation. Gascoigne's solemn didacticism had long since given way to a new manner inspired by Persius and Juvenal and best figured in the much-used images of satyr and dog—a rough, snapping satire, the envious barking of a scruffy outsider. Such work could bring honor neither to its creators nor to their age. On the contrary, it revealed the corruption of both—or so, at least, some observers were ready to suggest.

Indeed, nothing is of more credit or request now than a petulant paper or scoffing verses; and it is but convenient to the times and manners we live with to have then the worst writings and studies flourish when the best begin to be despised. Ill arts begin where good end.
The time was when men would learn and study good things, not envy those that had them. Then men were had in price for learning. Now letters only make men vile. He is upbraidingly called a poet, as if it were a most contemptable nick-name. But the professors, indeed, have made learning cheap. Railing and tinkling rimers, whose writings the vulgar more greedily read as being taken with the scurrility and petulancy of such wits. He shall not have a reader now unless he jeer and lie. It is the food of men's natures, the diet of the times! (VIII, 571– 572).

This vigorous condemnation of the scurrilous, railing manner that so characterized late Elizabethan satire was, as it happens, intended to have no such reference at all. Its author was himself one of the foremost of those Elizabethan satirists, one never much given to self-reproach. The passage appears in Jonson's own *Discoveries,* where it does have a quite explicit topical reference. The topic is not, however, the satirical verses of Jonson himself or even those of other writers of the 1590s. On the contrary, Jonson's own writings are firmly identified as those "best" which have begun to be despised. Written late in his life, in response perhaps to poems like Owen Felltham's on *The New Inn* or Alexander Gill's on *The Magnetic Lady,* these paragraphs of apparently disinterested, if violently expressed, judgment are preceded and followed by others in which Jonson shamelessly exposes the raw wound that set him off. "It is a barbarous envy to take from those men's virtues which, because thou canst not arrive at, thou impotently despairest to imitate. Is it a crime in me that I know that which others had not yet known but from me? Or that I am the author of many things which never would have come in thy thought but that I taught them? . . . But they are rather enemies of my fame than me, these barkers" (VIII, 571 and 573). But who, we may ask, taught them to bark? By his own account Jonson did. His was the generation that gave satire its great currency, his the generation to which the central core of his attack seems most naturally to apply.

The application is not, I think, unfair. Which generation after all, that of Jonson's coevals or that of his younger detractors, better fits his description? Do we find more petulant, scoffing papers in 1620 or in 1600, in the generation of Wither, Browne, Herrick, King, Herbert, and Carew or in the generation of Donne, Hall, Marston, and Jonson? If one group or the other must be condemned, shouldn't it be the earlier? But we are under no obligation to condemn either. What matters to us in our effort to understand Jonson's laureate self-fashioning is less the accuracy of his judgment that its terms, his equation of railing with the decline of art and learning. Without necessarily accepting this argument ourselves, we should observe how readily Jonson could do so, when properly provoked. It was an argument that made sense to him.

And if it made sense to him in the 1620s or 1630s, it would probably have made sense to him on some level, however unwilling he may have been to acknowledge it, a quarter of a century earlier. Even then the idea would not have been new. J. J. Scaliger's *Confutatio Stultissimae Burdonum Fabulae,* from which Jonson translated the substance of the passage I have quoted, dates from the first years of the seventeenth century. And had the words been Jonson's own and written out fresh in the final decade of his life, we would still have plentiful evidence that the attitude they express lurked near the center of his consciousness in the late 1590s, as he strove to establish for himself a position that would at once satisfy the demands of his satire-writing generation and the demands of his own laureate ambition.

For all its moral attractiveness as corrector of manners, satire, and particularly the Juvenalian satire of the 1590s, was marred by a perversity that laid it open to moral reproach—a perversity identified most often with the satirist himself. By his passionate fixation on evil, the satirist came to seem more reprehensible than any but the most vile of his victims, his destructive zeal more dangerous than their merely eccentric folly. What could provoke such bitter fury? Virtuous indignation seemed an insufficient and perhaps morally inappropriate cause. Envy, the very fault Jonson discovered in his scurrilous detractors, provided a satiric mainspring more credible both psychologically and morally. Usually presented as "well-parted, a sufficient scholar," yet "wanting that place in the world's account which he thinks his merit capable of," the

Elizabethan satirist habitually "falls into such an envious apoplexy, with which his judgement is so dazzled and distasted, that he grows violently impatient of any opposite happiness in another" (III, 423). With minor alterations, this description, originally applied by Jonson himself to Macilente, the central character in *Every Man Out of His Humor,* could be made to fit not only the satiric characters in a number of other late sixteenth- and early seventeenth-century plays—Lampathio Doria, Malevole, Vendici, Bosola, Ingenioso, Furor Poeticus, Jacques, and Thersites—but also the railing personae adopted in prose and verse satires by Nashe, Hall, Marston, and many of their lesser coevals.

"When we speak of ambivalence," René Girard has remarked, "we are only pointing out a problem that remains to be solved."[27] For Jonson, satire and, more particularly, his own role as satirist were such problems. In *Every Man Out* he made both his first attempt to solve them and his first presentation of himself to the young wits of the inns of court as a man of their generation who shared their tastes. Seventeen years later, in dedicating the folio reprinting of the play, Jonson still emphasizes that connection. "When I wrote this poem," he tells the young gentlemen who now inhabit the inns of court, "I had friendship with divers in your societies, who, as they were great names in learning, so they were no less examples of living. Of them and then (that I say no more) it was not despised" (III, 421). *Every Man Out* was also Jonson's first presentation of himself to the reading public, his first published work. And even in the 1616 folio it is preceded only by *Every Man In,* which, by its dedication to his schoolmaster, William Camden, announces itself as prefatory and perhaps immature. "First fruits," Jonson calls it. In its depiction of the poet as an aureate

27. René Girard, *Violence and the Sacred,* trans. Patrick Gregory (Baltimore: Johns Hopkins Univ. Press, 1977), p. 1.

enthusiast, *Every Man In* had been, as we have noticed, something of a false start—a false start whose tracks Jonson partially erased from the folio version. As poet, Lorenzo Junior fit neither Jonson's generation nor Jonson himself. In *Every Man Out* Jonson stepped onto what must have seemed to him, as a young writer eager to associate himself with the intellectual and literary avant-garde of his generation, native soil. But this too, he discovered, was a step clouded by ambivalence.

Was this satiric home ground indeed any firmer? Was it firm enough to support Jonson's laureate ambition? Macilente certainly lives up to his billing as apoplectically envious and, in doing so, he accomplishes the satirist's work with exemplary zeal. If not the scourge of villainy, he is a most active scourge of folly. "'Ware how you offend him," warns Carlo Buffone. "He carries oil and fire in his pen, will scald where it drops" (III, 451). Typical of both his scalding style and his motivation is his response to the clownish mushroom-gentleman, Sogliardo:

> S'blood, why should such a prick-eared hind as this
> Be rich, ha? a fool! such a transparent gull
> That may be seen through! wherefore should he have land,
> Houses, and lordships? O, I could eat my entrails
> And sink my soul into the earth with sorrow.   (III, 444–445)

A passage like this alerts us to the reason for Jonson's ambivalence. Eating one's own entrails with envy may appropriately suggest satiric despite and thus suit the gnawing humor of the times, as, in the previous generation, a heart consumed with desire suitably expressed amorous passion. But neither the one nor the other could easily be made to body forth laureate rectitude.

Envy is not, however, the only source of satire in *Every Man Out of His Humor,* nor is Macilente the play's only satirist. He shares that role with the play's putative author, Asper. Unlike Macilente, Asper "is of an ingenious and free spirit . . . one whom no servile hope of gain or frosty apprehension of danger can make to be a parasite, either to time, place, or opinion"—characteristics that moved Herford and Simpson to declare that, "in Asper, Jonson for the first, but by no means for the last, time drew his ideal poet" (III, 423, and I, 388). Asper's satiric fury is no less eager than Macilente's. Both are bent on violence. Where Macilente wishes that

> the engine of my grief could cast
> Mine eyeballs, like two globes of wildfire, forth
> To melt this unproportioned frame of nature,

Asper vows to

> strip the ragged follies of the time
> Naked as at their birth
> . . . and with a whip of steel
> Print wounding lashes in their iron ribs.   (III, 443 and 428–429)

The difference between them lies rather in that crucial matter of motivation. Not envy, but a righteous and disinterested impatience with "this impious world" drives Asper. But his virtue finds little occasion to display itself directly, for he appears in his own person only in the induction. During the five acts that constitute the play proper, he is caught in the role of Macilente, which as actor he plays and which as author he is said to have written.

Why did Jonson make this division between satiric author and satiric character? For Alvin Kernan, writing in the 1950s under the sway of the New Critical theory of the persona and the New Critical prohibitions against fallacies biographical and intentional, the answer was clear. In separating Macilente from Asper, Jonson was showing the independence of "the sane, reasonable author interested in the correction of vice" from "the unbalanced, intemperate railer who inevitably becomes his theatrical persona." He was, in short, demonstrating to his audience just what the New Critics, Kernan among them, demonstrated to theirs: "that the character of the satirist is a mask which an author assumes for the purpose of making some lasting impression on the world he is attacking."[28] As this suggests, a major purpose of Kernan's influential book was to correct the naive biographical assumption that a perverse satiric spokesman reflects a perverse author. Kernan thus hoped to take Elizabethan satire out of the hands of the amateur psychologists and return it to the literary critics. Far from being marks of authorial perversity, the grotesque twists in the satiric character are, he argues, conventional devices consciously adopted to achieve a particular end, "the successful attack on foolishness and vice." Just as Asper is not Macilente, so Nashe, Marston, Donne, Hall, and Jonson are not to be identified with their satiric personae. Looking for the poet in his poem is looking for the wrong thing in the wrong place. And lest one think this only a modern critical shibboleth, *Every Man Out of His Humor* proves otherwise. Jonson was a New Critical theorist *avant la lettre*.

We can, I think, safely go along with Kernan in rejecting the naive biographical explanation of Elizabethan satire without, however, accepting his total removal of the author from his work. It would indeed be strange, as Kernan points out, "if every author of formal satire from Nashe to George Wither was sadistic, rough, frank, lascivious, fired by envy, subject to melancholy, guilty of the same sins he castigated, and so stupid that he was unable to conceal any of these weaknesses."[29] But is it so strange for men, who are of about the same age, who share many of the same opportunities and frustrations, and who live and work in close proximity to one another, to present themselves in a similar way, even if the identity they claim is an odd one? Can't we find many equally bizarre examples among the youth, including the literary youth, of our own century,

28. Alvin Kernan, *The Cankered Muse: Satire of the English Renaissance* (New Haven: Yale Univ. Press, 1959), pp. 158 and 137.
29. Kernan, p. 135.

from the Dandies and Dadaists to the Beatniks and Hippies? Whatever the men who wrote Elizabethan satire were "really" like, they chose to be seen as possessed of some combination of the characteristics Kernan lists. The role of snarling satirist was the basis of their self-presentation, the prime element in their literary identity.

Take, for example, the "case" of John Marston. His name appears on the title page of neither *Certain Satires* nor the *Scourge of Villainy*. Instead these works are attributed to a certain W. Kinsayder, who is presumably their speaker. Kernan seizes on this as evidence of Marston's independence from his persona, and so it might seem. But each book contains numerous hints as to the true identity of its author, not the least of which is the name *Kinsayder* itself. As those readers with a smattering of Greek would have realized, it translates into "mar stone." Kinsayder and Marston may not have been identical; they may not even have been very much alike. But Marston did for a time wish to be taken for Kinsayder—and, to judge from the remarks of his contemporaries, he was successful. Kinsayder was not merely a version of the conventional mask of satire; it was Marston's own mask, his instrument of self-presentation. Between Nashe, Hall, or Donne and their satiric spokesmen a similar relationship existed. They were thus present in their poems in the same way (if not always to the same degree) that any one of us is present in the gestures that declare our identity.

But, as always, Jonson's laureate intentions distinguish him from the other writers of his generation—not, however, to loosen the knot joining him to his work, but rather to tie it more firmly. As amateur poets, Marston, Hall, and Donne played in their writings roles that they could eventually discard. Like the part of lover-prodigal enacted by the amateurs of the preceding literary generation, their satiric role represented only a limited part of their identity, not the central ethical core of their being. For Jonson, bound by the stipulation that if he were to be a good poet he must first be a good man, there could be no such easy escape from his literary persona.

What then of the separation between Asper and Macilente? As Jackson Cope has suggested, "a closer look shows that Jonson does less to split than to fuse the pair."[30] Not only does Asper play the part of Macilente, but, as we have already had occasion to notice, he very much resembles him in his passionately destructive satiric manner. Even their names suggest complementary aspects of a single persona, the rough and bitter nature of Asper fittingly embodied in the emaciated form of Macilente. Furthermore, both bear an unmistakable likeness to their common creator, Ben Jonson, who, when he wrote this play, was himself a "lean ... hollow-cheeked scrag."[31] Like Asper, Jonson wrote a play called *Every Man Out of His Humor* and, like Macilente, he was both soldier and scholar.

This Jonsonian presence is further complicated by Carlo Buffone, who describes the author in terms that evoke the historical Ben Jonson but that, in doing so, associate him with Buffone himself. Drinking to the health of the audience, Buffone declares,

This is that our poet calls Castalian liquor, when he comes abroad now and then, once in a fortnight, and makes a good meal among players, where he has *caninum appetitum*; marry, at home he keeps a good philosophical diet, beans and buttermilk; an honest pure rogue, he will take you off three, four, five of these, one after another, and look villainously when he has done, like a one-headed Cerberus. He do' not hear me, I hope. And then, when his belly is well ballasted, and his brain rigged a little, he sails away withal, as though he would work wonders when he comes home. (III, 440)

"Here," Cope observes, "is the familiar, unmistakable portrait of ugly, hard-drinking Ben; Ben of the Mermaid; chief wit and

---

30. Jackson I. Cope, *The Theatre and the Dream: From Metaphor to Form in Renaissance Drama* (Baltimore: Johns Hopkins Univ. Press, 1973), p. 229.
31. Dekker, *Satiromastix*, p. 381.

belly of the Tribe of Ben."[32] But here too is a near portrait of
Buffone himself, who shares the author's *caninum appetitum*
and who stands before us with a cup of Ben's favorite Canary in
his hand. What is more, Buffone wields, along with Macilente,
the satirist's whip. He is, as "the author's friend" Cordatus
remarks, "an impudent common jester, a violent railer," one
who will "profane even the most holy things to excite laughter;
no honorable or reverend personage whatsoever can come
within the reach of his eye, but is turned into all manner of
variety by his adulterate similes" (III, 441). To accomplish the
ends of satire and, perhaps more important, to establish on
stage a version of the satiric mode that was the signature style
of his generation, Jonson needed not only the righteously indig-
nant Asper but also the envious Macilente and even the scurrilous Buffone. And he needed too the suggestion that these
various personae have some likeness both to one another and
to him.

Much can thus be said for Cope's position. His conclusion
is nevertheless enough overstated to send us back in the direction of Kernan. "Far from separating author from satirist,"
Cope argues, "Jonson . . . saw that the point of satire is engagement and not only provided an angry observer but shaped him
into the very image of the author who walks the streets outside
the poem."[33] It may well be that the point of satire is, or at least
depends on, engagement. If I am right, the point of any laureate
work depends on engagement. But whatever occasional
glimpses of Jonson we get in Asper, Macilente, or Carlo Buffone and whatever significance we attribute to those glimpses,
surely none of the three can be properly called "the very image
of the author." The truth lies rather between this position and
Kernan's. Jonson undoubtedly did much to fuse Asper, Macilente, Buffone, and himself, but he did still more to separate
them. He clearly wanted to put some distance between his

upright, his envious, and his profane satiric personae, between himself and all three. Yet, as Cope helps us to see, the distance continually threatens to disappear. Jonson could not stand back from his work. He felt compelled, whether because of the nature of Elizabethan satire or because of his own laureate ambition, to assert his responsibility and to reveal his presence.

Presence was perhaps implied in the phonetic likeness between the words "author" and "actor" that Jonson used to name the two sides of Asper-Macilente. That likeness had already caught the fancy of the Romans, who linked the words in phrases like *auctor, actor illarum fuit* (Cicero, *Pro P. Sestio*) or *auctorem actoremque habere aliquem* (Cornelius Nepos, *Atticus*). For "the author," Asper, to realize his satiric intention, he must, as he says, "turn an actor," play Macilente. His authorial presence, his authority, makes itself effective through the actions which, as actor, he performs. The author is an actor, a role-player, whose various parts depend on and refer back to his moral authority. There can thus be no complete divorce of the writer from his work. The work may in some ways resemble a dramatic part. But it is a part that the writer has authored and that he enacts, a part for which he bears the responsibility.

Jonson does, however, intimate that, if successful in the role that *Every Man Out of His Humor* embodies, he will not have to play it again. He too will be put out of his humor. The reason is, of course, that the humor of this play cannot satisfactorily suit his laureate pretension. Asper does have clear marks of the laureate. One could hardly ask a higher standard of evaluation than he does: "Let me be censured by the austerest brow, / Where I want art or judgment, tax me freely" (III, 430). Neither an amateur nor a professional would make such a demand for his work. But, as we have seen, Asper quickly gives way to Macilente and Carlo Buffone, and on them no laureate career could be based. Indeed, Buffone might have been named for his inappropriateness. In *The Art of English Poesy,* Puttenham says of Skelton that he was "a sharp satirist, but with more railing and scoffery than became a Poet Laureate; such among the Greeks were called 'pantomimi,' with us 'buffoons,' altogether applying their wits to scurrilities and other ridiculous matters."[34] And the envious Macilente is only marginally better. So in the end both are put out of their humor. Carlo's lips are sealed and Macilente is freed of his envy.

Given Jonson's involvement with these characters, the play's closing gestures can, I think, be read as his own renunciation of certain of the satiric traits most characteristic of his generation. As such, the conclusion of *Every Man Out* resembles the conclusions of many amateur works, in which the author or his semifictional surrogate promises not to offend in like sort again. Despite their great surface dissimilarity, a still closer resemblance links *Every Man Out* to *The Shepheardes Calender*. What A. C. Hamilton said of Spenser's poem, that in it Spenser "cast off his shepherd's weeds [to] emerge as England's heroic poet,"[35] could easily be paraphrased to fit Jonson's. In *Every Man Out of His Humor* Jonson casts off the satiric weeds fashioned by Marston, Hall, and company to emerge as England's next laureate poet. In these two poems of literary self-presentation, each published when its author was in his mid-twenties and each proclaiming by its dedication, Spenser's to Sidney and Jonson's to the Inns of Court, its author's alliance with the amateur élite of his generation, Spenser and Jonson adopt the fashionable mode of their time only to criticize and partially detach themselves from it. They thus establish themselves as poets but let it be known that they are poets of an unusual sort. And for each, the aspiration that sets him apart from his contemporaries also directs him toward the monarch, who is central to the higher and truer poetic identity

34. Quoted by Oscar James Campbell, *Comicall Satyre and Shakespeare's "Troilus and Cressida"* (San Marino, Calif.: Huntington Library, 1938), p. 30.
35. See above p. 72.

that he seeks. In *The Shepheardes Calender* the April eclogue, with its lay in praise of the shepherds' queen Eliza, provided a touchstone of the true poetic accomplishment from which Colin has been diverted by love. And in *Every Man Out* the sight of Queen Elizabeth cures Macilente of his envious humor.

> Never till now did object greet mine eyes
> With any light content, but in her graces
> All my malicious powers have lost their stings.
> Envy is fled my soul at sight of her,
> And she hath chased all black thoughts from my bosom,
> Like as the sun doth darkness from the world.
> My stream of humor is run out of me.
>
> (III, 599)

But applied to Jonson, Hamilton's phrase must be qualified in just the way we qualified it in discussing Spenser. There is some casting off of one literary costume (though more putting it on and wearing it), but there is no unequivocal emergence of the poet in any other. Both *The Shepheardes Calender* and *Every Man Out of His Humor* make large claims for their authors, but neither discovers a role for him to play that would either bring him closer to the monarch or allow him to express more fully his laureate nature. For both, the amateur "weeds" are unsuitable, but no other guise seems available.

Fashioning another guise is the work of Jonson's next two plays, *Cynthia's Revels* and the *Poetaster*. Crites and Horace, Jonson's self-projections in these plays, are still satirists, but satirists in retreat, more concerned with keeping their own virtues intact than with righting the ills of the world. Where, as regards Jonson's self-presentation, the function of *Every Man Out* had been to associate him with the literary manner of his generation, the function of these is to establish his laureate standing as a good man worthy of the monarch's patronage. A juxtaposition of the first speech of *Every Man Out* with the last of *Poetaster* reveals the distance between them. Asper's aggressive assertion of satiric engagement,

> Who is so patient of this impious world,
> That he can check his spirit or rein his tongue?
> ... Not I!   (III, 428)

gives way to the counsel of Olympian detachment that Augustus directs at Virgil and Horace:

> But let not your high thoughts descend so low
> As these despised objects; let them fall
> With their flat, grovelling souls. Be you yourselves,
> And as with our best favors you stand crowned,
> So let your mutual loves be still renowned.
>
> (IV, 316)

Instead of transforming the world, the Juvenalian satirist has himself been transformed. From an impatient castigator of vice and folly, he has become a self-congratulating stoic.

The tension between the two roles is perhaps most acute in the second of the three plays where Crites is forced to ask himself how his satiric interest in folly can be reconciled with his goodness of nature.

> O, how despised and base a thing is man
> If he not strive t'erect his grovelling thoughts
> Above the strain of flesh! But how more cheap,
> When even his best and understanding part,
> The crown and strength of all his faculties,
> Floats, like a dead drowned body, on the stream
> Of vulgar humor, mixed with commonest dregs!
> I suffer for their guilt now, and my soul,
> Like one that looks on ill-affected eyes,
> Is hurt with mere intention on their follies.
> Why will I view them then, my sense might ask me?
>
> (IV, 62)

To this question neither Crites himself nor the play as a whole provides any answer. Yet neither acknowledges this lack. The question is asked not to be answered—Crites has no real doubt concerning his own moral superiority—but to be forestalled. The play thus denies the tension at its center. It approves Crites no less resoundingly than its author approved it, "By———, 'tis good, and if you like it, you may" (IV, 183).

No admirer of Jonson can discuss *Cynthia's Revels* with much pleasure, so embarrassingly does he "open himself," as he put it in the prologue with unconsciously ironic accuracy. Yet we cannot ignore his self-exposure, for, though Jonson badly miscalculated its effect, it forms an essential and quite deliberate part of his public self-presentation. He was, as he said, trying "new ways to come to learned ears" (IV, 43). He addressed his play to the court, wrote it in the manner of Lyly's court comedies, and had it played by the troupe most patronized by courtiers, the Children of the Chapel. His aim, like that of Crites, was clearly "to lift [his] state / Above a vulgar height." He wrote with the same intention that inspires Arete to have Crites prepare a masque for Cynthia's revels,

> That from the merit of it we may take
> Desired occasion to prefer your worth,
> And make your service known to Cynthia.
> (IV, 92)

Both seek to be noticed. Jonson's play is thus a quite explicit advertisement of its author, an advertisement that contains within itself an example of the success that should crown such advertising. Jonson not only compliments the Queen and the courtiers; he shows how well he does it and how such skill should be rewarded. But the effect is awkward rather than accomplished, reminding one of Gabriel Harvey's presentation at court or of Malvolio in yellow cross-garters. Jonson's eagerness to please conflicts with his posture of dignified self-sufficiency. Neither as satirist nor as laureate can he accept the role of mere court entertainer, yet that is the only role he is likely to be offered. The rest seems as much a fanciful, foolish, and self-aggrandizing daydream as do the imaginings of Phantaste, Moria, and Philautia, satirized ladies of Cynthia's court who "put case" that they "had the grant of Juno to wish ourselves into what happy state we could" (IV, 103). Jonson too puts case. The result is *Cynthia's Revels*. The difference is that the three ladies know their daydream for what it is. Jonson seems not to.

In neither *Cynthia's Revels* nor *Poetaster* does Jonson discover a language of self-presentation that would allow him to be both satirist and laureate. As he defines them, the two positions are mutually exclusive. "A creature," like Crites (of whom this commendation is spoken) or like Horace, "of most perfect and divine temper, one in whom the humors and elements are peaceably met" (IV, 74), may be fit companion for a monarch, but he is too sublimely removed from any particular humor to be a very active satirist. At best the good man serves as foil to show off vice and folly. But he must remain a passive and unconscious foil, for once he takes notice of his role and advertises it with satiric intent he loses the self-sufficiency that is the basis of his perfection and thus ceases to be himself. Others of equally divine temper, Arete and Cynthia in *Cynthia's Revels* or Virgil and Augustus in *Poetaster,* may justly claim his attention and he theirs. Like concentric circles, these figures of moral, aesthetic, and political virtue fit together. But let the thoughts of any one of them wander so far as to regard the eccentric humorists jostling around them and the circle of perfection is broken, their own goodness laid open to question. "Why will I view them then?" Crites asks himself. Having no answer either for Crites or for himself, Jonson makes the retreat that leads from Asper to Crites to Horace and that ends in the "Apologetical Dialogue" with the Author—Jonson himself—alone in his study soaring "high and aloof, / Safe from the wolf's black jaw and the dull ass's hoof" (IV, 324).

But the very intensity of Jonson's imagery belies his claim to imperturbable superiority. If his detractors are wolfish and asinine, he himself is nevertheless still biting and kicking. He can neither reconcile his two roles nor abandon one in favor of the other. "We have the feeling," as Robert Jones has written, "that the lashing satirist is trying to look over the fools' heads toward the best, or that the aloof poet is ignoring his elect audience to shout at the world of fools."[36] Ultimately the effort of self-presentation destroys the object for which it is being expended. The more Jonson labors to purify his satiric motives, the less effective the satire becomes. The more he struggles to assert his laureate nature, the less natural his claim appears. And as a matter of historical fact, far from making his enemies "sit down and blush," his identification of himself with Crites and Horace only "provoked the angry wasps" (IV, 320).

Every Man Out, Cynthia's Revels, and *Poetaster* stand alone on the threshold of Jonson's career. Never again would he write a play in which a character so clearly represented his own sense of himself. Like Spenser after *The Shepheardes Calender,* Jonson subsequently recedes into his work, emerging only in truculently un-Spenserian prologues and prefaces. But one has only to think of the ambivalence of *Volpone, Epicoene, The Alchemist,* or *Bartholomew Fair*—or rather of the ambivalence with which we are likely to greet their goings out—to realize that the conflict between laureate self-righteousness and satiric excess remained central to Jonson's work as a dramatist and that, even freed from the immediate pressure of authorial self-presentation, the conflict yielded to no ready solution.

A Laureate Dramatist

Not only Jonson's laureate ambition distinguished him from the other most notable satirists of his generation. He also ar-

36. Robert C. Jones, "The Satirist's Retirement in Jonson's 'Apological Dialogue,'" *ELH,* 34 (1967), 447–467.

rived at literature by a quite different path. The years that Donne, Marston, and Hall passed at the university and the inns of court were spent by Jonson first as an apprentice bricklayer, then as a soldier in Flanders, and finally (and most significantly) as a common player and play-patcher. He began writing not as a university wit descending from Parnassus, but as a Paris-Garden ham, a denizen of the literary hill's lowest reaches. Dekker remembers him there, clothed in the degrading garb of an actor: "in a player's old cast cloak," in the borrowed "gown of Roscius the Stager," "in leather pilch by a play wagon."[37] And when a very few years later Jonson boasts that he will "raise the despised head of poetry again and, stripping her out of those rotten and base rags wherewith the times have adulterated her form, restore her to her primitive habit, feature, and majesty" (V, 21), we in turn remember that he himself wore the basest rags of poetry. As Jonson made himself a laureate satirist by opposing the satiric manner of his generation, so he attempts to make himself a laureate dramatist by combating drama.

A laureate dramatist—to the Elizabethan mind there was something improbable about the very idea. As late as 1639, Jasper Mayne's publisher could still write that Mayne had no ambition to publish his *City Match,* "holding works of this light nature to be things which need an apology for being written at all, not esteeming otherwise of them, whose abilities in this kind are most passable, than of masquers who spangle and glitter for the time, but 'tis thorough tinsel."[38] Jonson alone met this amateur prejudice head-on. Of the Elizabethan and Jacobean poets who aspired to a laureate career, he alone strove to make stage plays—which for the purpose he

37. Dekker, *Satiromastix,* pp. 326 and 351.
38. Quoted by Gerald Eades Bentley, *The Profession of Dramatist in Shakespeare's Time, 1590–1642* (Princeton: Princeton Univ. Press, 1971), p. 38. Bentley's chapter on "The Status of Dramatists, Plays, Actors, and Theatres" provides the best introduction available to its subject.

redefined as "comical satires," "dramatic poems," and finally "works"—count as signs of his literary eminence.[39] Though Spenser is reported to have written (or perhaps only to have thought of writing) "nine English comedies," neither the playhouse nor the printshop saw any of them. Likewise, Drayton, who had a hand in some two dozen plays, kept all but one from publication and even that one appeared anonymously. Daniel took play writing a bit more seriously, as did his patrons, Fulke Greville and the Countess of Pembroke, but his plays, like theirs, were of the neoclassical, closet sort. For the one that was played, he felt he must apologize: "My necessity, I confess, hath driven me to do a thing unworthy of me and against my heart in making the stage the speaker of my lines."[40] Even Chapman, who wrote for both stage and print, made for his plays none of the large claims that puffed his nondramatic works. On the contrary, he concluded the rare dedication of *The Widow's Tears* with this shamefaced valediction: "And so, till some work more worthy I can select and perfect out of my other studies, that may better express me, and more fit the gravity of your ripe inclination, I rest. . . ."[41] Apparently none of these poets felt that stage plays well expressed them and so, though occasionally drawn to write them, they were more inclined to conceal than to publicize the fact.

That they wrote for the stage at all is, however, of great significance for our understanding of Jonson. In the last two decades of the sixteenth century, the theater became a power-

39. W. David Kay has written interestingly of Jonson's attempt "to win a genuine literary reputation based in large part on writing for the theater" in "The Shaping of Ben Jonson's Career: A Reexamination of Facts and Problems," *MP*, 67 (1969/70), 224–237. Though my discussion differs from Kay's in its emphases and its evidence, we agree in our understanding of Jonson's ambition and the problems he encountered in trying to fulfill it.

40. Samuel Daniel, *The Tragedy of Philotis*, ed. Laurence Michel (New Haven: Yale Univ. Press, 1949), p. 37.

41. George Chapman, *The Widow's Tears*, ed. Ethel M. Smeak (Lincoln: Univ. of Nebraska Press, 1966), p. 3.

ful literary magnet, drawing to itself all but a few writers—
Harington, Donne, or Hall—whose gentlemanly standing for-
bid such license, and even these few holdouts were likely to be,
as Donne was, "great frequenter[s] of plays." More numerous
were those who succumbed and wrote: Gosson, Lyly, Lodge,
Kyd, Greene, Marlowe, Nashe, Webster, Tourneur, Marston,
Shakespeare, Dekker, and Heywood, to name only the best
known. With the exception of the last three, all of these men
were amateurs, though some maintained only a tenuous hold
on that distinction. And, as amateurs, they were often inclined
to resent the theater even as it attracted them. Gosson became
one of the most vociferous enemies of players and playing; Lyly
thought "it folly that, one foot being in the grave, I should have
the other on the stage"; Nashe and Greene complained of their
dependence on mere "taffety fools," on "those puppets . . . that
speak from our mouths"; and Marston feared that his good
fortune in "these stage-pleasings" would keep him from calling
his eyes into himself.[42] But though they claimed to find their
contact with the theater morally dangerous and socially degrading, they nevertheless wrote for it.

The appeal was at least twofold. Both financial advantage
and "pride of wit," as Drayton termed it, drew them. In the few
years since the building of the first permanent London theater,
the stage had become the largest and most lucrative literary
market in England. Indeed, Francis Meres could lament that
"for lack of patrons (O ingrateful and damned age) our poets
are solely or chiefly maintained, countenanced, and patronized [by] our witty comedians and stately tragedians."[43]
Henslowe's *Diary* provides much concrete evidence of this

42. *The Complete Works of John Lyly,* ed. R. Warwick Bond, 3 vols. (Oxford: Clarendon Press, 1902), I, 69; Nashe, III, 324; Greene, XII, 144; and *The
Plays of John Marston,* ed. H. Harvey Wood, 3 vols. (Edinburgh: Oliver and
Boyd, 1938), II, 143.
43. Francis Meres, *Palladis Tamia,* ed. Arthur Freeman (New York: Garland, 1973), pp. 278–278ᵛ.

theatrical patronage. It shows the demand for plays to have been constant and the price good. At the usual rate of £6 per play, one needed only to write two plays a year to pass the ordinary income of a schoolmaster, curate, or lecturer, the positions most readily available to a university graduate.[44] And play writing kept a man in London where something better might turn up. No wonder then that the unemployed scholars in *The Second Return from Parnassus,* like the prodigal gentleman in Greene's *Never Too Late,* fall back on the theater. Though in their pride they might rebelliously ask,

> And must the basest trade yield us relief?
> Must we be practiced to those leaden spouts,
> That nought do vent but what they do receive?[45]

their real-life counterparts proved ready to take this dose of humiliation with their fee. And what the gentlemen amateurs could not resist must have appeared far less resistable to Ben Jonson, for whom there was no other practical way of living as a writer or of escaping the still baser trade of his bricklaying stepfather.

Money was not, however, the theater's only attraction, nor was pride ranged solely on the opposing side. There was also that "pride of wit." The London theaters were charged with an extraordinary vitality—a vitality to which even the fulminations of the Puritan preachers and city magistrates testify. "By no one thing is [the politic state and government of this city] so greatly annoyed and disquieted as by players and plays and the disorders which follow thereupon," the Lord Mayor wrote to the Archbishop of Canterbury.[46] Public enemy number one in the eyes of the city fathers, the turbulent energy of

44. See Bentley's chapter on "Dramatists' Pay."
45. *Three Parnassus Plays,* pp. 343–345.
46. Quoted by Bentley, p. 44.

the theater deeply stirred their witty sons—as Drayton's sonnet reminds us.

> In pride of wit, when high desire of fame
> Gave life and courage to my lab'ring pen,
> And first the sound and virtue of my name
> Won grace and credit in the ears of men,
> With those the thronged theaters that press,
> I in the circuit for the laurel strove,
> Where the full praise, I freely must confess,
> In heat of blood a modest mind might move.
> With shouts and claps at every little pause,
> When the proud round on every side hath rung. . . .[47]

We encounter the same excitement everywhere. The proud round and the vulgar show that animated it—the brave struttings, the towering bombast, the gorgeous trappings, the crowds, the applause—could be dismissed only at the price of cutting oneself off from all that was most alive in the literary culture of the age. Yet given the unsavory reputation of the stage and the low status of playwrights, how could a poet of laureate ambition help but feel it his duty to attempt such dismissal?

Not, of course, that drama was an exile from the critically defined realm of poetry. In the Renaissance hierarchy of literary forms, its major genres each held an honored place. Tragedy rivaled epic for the title of generic preeminence, and even comedy, with its laudable aim of reforming manners and morals, might in humanist eyes seem the appropriate labor of a great poet. Indeed, it was with the express purpose of getting Spenser to shift his efforts from *The Faerie Queene* to his nine comedies that Harvey addressed his friend. For, he argued, "it hath been the usual practice of the most exquisite and odd wits

---

47. *The Works of Michael Drayton*, ed. J. William Hebel, 5 vols. (Oxford: Blackwell, 1932), II, 334.

in all nations, and specially in Italy, rather to show and advance themselves that way [i.e., by writing comedy] than any other."[48] He then goes on to cite as examples Bibiena, Machiavelli, Aretino, Ariosto, Bembo, Aristophanes, Menander, Plautus, and Terence. Such distinguished precedents beg emulation. But when Harvey wrote, there existed only the foreign precedents. The dream of what might be was as yet clouded by no experience of what was. In 1579 the London theater was still in its infancy and Harvey, writing from Cambridge, perhaps knew little of even that beginning. Sidney, who knew far more, certainly did not approve. Far from confirming the nobility of its lineage, English drama caused "her mother Poesy's honesty to be called in question."[49] And the taint Sidney noticed became increasingly evident with the theater's growing prosperity. By the 1590s, only an observer as shallow and chauvinist as Francis Meres would have been likely to declare the popular London playwrights trueborn descendants of Sophocles, Seneca, Menander, and Terence.

Though a quarter of a century later Jonson would elevate Shakespeare to the rank of the ancients, he did not share Meres's early optimism. Not even the plays that won Jonson himself a place in Meres's book among "our best for tragedy" were in their author's opinion worth saving. None was ever printed. And it is hard to believe that Jonson thought better of the work of those other English playwrights whose names Meres jumbled together with so little discrimination. No, to Jonson, as to Sidney and to most other Elizabethans who thought seriously on the question, English drama was a bastard child of poetry, an unmistakably illegitimate offspring. Success in such a debased kind could never establish one as a true poet.

48. *The Works of Edmund Spenser: A Variorum Edition,* ed. Edwin Greenlaw, C. G. Osgood, et al., 11 vols. (Baltimore: Johns Hopkins Univ. Press, 1932–1957), X, 471–472.

49. Sidney, *An Apology for Poetry,* ed. Geoffrey Shepherd (1965; rpt. Manchester: Manchester Univ. Press, 1973), p. 137.

Yet, given his social and financial position and the structure of the literary world he inhabited, how could Jonson survive as a writer without writing plays? He had somehow to rise above the drama, but he could not do without it.

Jonson's solution to this problem is well known, better known than the problem itself. He became, as Drummond sourly remarked, "a great lover and praiser of himself, a condemner and scorner of others" (I, 151). What other strategy was available? How else could he have made stage plays—those semianonymous, rarely respected by-products of the Elizabethan entertainment industry—a sign of their author's laureate identity? His audience needed instruction; he ventured to supply it. He knew he would be thought "arrogant" and "peremptory," and he attempted to qualify that inevitable reaction by associating it in advance with the "common spawn of ignorance, / Our fry of writers," and by redefining his apparent immodesty as the "constant firmness" of "one that knows the strength of his own muse" (IV, 205–206). But whatever the risks, he felt that the plays could not be left to speak for themselves. If their laureate meaning was to be understood, it needed an interpreter.

And so he puts himself before us, in prologue and epilogue, in dedicatory preface, induction, and chorus, defining the true office of the poet, rehearsing the needful rules of art, anticipating objections from both the ignorant and the learned. But more frequent even than such careful instruction is bare, repeated assertion: "Music worth your ears . . . quick comedy refined . . . a legitimate poem . . . the best of this race . . . one such as other plays should be . . . if this play do not like, the devil is in't . . . by———, 'tis good!"[50] And often the assertion is accompanied by a suggestion that disagreement can only be a sign of folly.

50. III, 430; V, 24; V, 431; III, 303; VI, 163; and IV, 183.

If that not like you, that he sends tonight,
'Tis you have left to judge, not he to write.
(VI, 282)

"Careless of all vulgar censure, as not depending on common approbation, he is confident it shall super-please judicious spectators" (VI, 511). His carelessness and confidence were not, however, so great that he could leave even the judicious unprompted. The danger that, seeing his work on the stage, they might mistake the category to which it belonged and thus judge both it and its author wrongly was too great.

It is for this reason too that self-praise was not enough. Jonson had not only to assimilate his work to the learned canons of merit. He had also to distinguish it from the common run of Elizabethan drama. And in doing so, more energetically perhaps than even the occasion demanded, he won that reputation as a scorner of other men that has cost him dearly ever since—particularly because the most conspicuous of those other men was Shakespeare. Posterity has found it hard to forgive Jonson's slighting allusions to the "mouldy tale" of *Pericles,* to the faulty logic of *Julius Caesar* and the erring geography of *The Winter's Tale,* to "York and Lancaster's long jars," to the "creaking throne," the "tempestuous drum," and the chorus that "wafts you o'er the seas."[51] These remarks and a handful of others like them have regularly been thought the expression of discreditable envy—the jealousy a pedantic and laborious toad of London felt for the gentle Swan of Avon. But to personalize Jonson's remarks this way is, I think, to miss their essential meaning. For Jonson, Shakespeare had, in the phrase of T. J. B. Spencer, a "typological significance."[52] Shakespeare was the leading representative of that professional the-

51. VI, 492; VI, 280, and VIII, 584; I, 138; and III, 303.
52. T. J. B. Spencer, "Ben Jonson on His Beloved, the Author Mr. William Shakespeare," in *The Elizabethan Theatre IV,* ed. George R. Hibbard (To-

atrical world from which Jonson was trying to distinguish himself and was thus a foil against which Jonson's particular virtue could better shine, a passive figure in the system of differences by which Jonson made his laureate standing manifest.

It is in this light that we should read passages like the famous one from the Induction to *Bartholomew Fair,* where, with obvious reference to *The Winter's Tale* and *The Tempest,* a scrivener relates "the author's" view of his play.

> If there be never a servant-monster i' the fair, who can help it, he says, nor a nest of antics? He is loth to make nature afraid in his plays, like those that beget tales, tempests, and such-like drolleries, to mix his head with other men's heels. Let the concupiscence of jigs and dances reign as strong as it will amongst you.   (IV, 16)

The same constellation of terms recurs, with no specifically Shakespearean reference, in the preface to *The Alchemist.* There Jonson advises the reader, "Thou wert never more fair in the way to be cozened than in this age, in poetry, especially in plays, wherein now the concupiscence of dances and of antics so reigneth as to run away from nature and be afraid of her" (V, 291). Taken together neither passage seems particularly personal. Each describes rather the realm of contemporary drama in which, by popular choice, concupiscence reigns. And, had we more of the context of the second, it would be clear that

---

ronto: Macmillan, 1974), pp. 22–40. Lawrence Lipking has recently written on Jonson's attitude toward Shakespeare in *The Life of the Poet: Beginning and Ending Poetic Careers* (Chicago: Univ. of Chicago Press, 1981), pp. 138–146. Lipking's book, which I saw only after mine was in the hands of its publisher, is concerned with many of the same issues (though not, for the most part, with the same texts) that interest me here. Lipking, too, writes of what he calls "great careers," careers of the laureate sort. But where I direct my attention to the outer workings of both careers and texts—that is, to the system of differences by which a poet might make his status known—Lipking directs his to the inner development of both. He emphasizes the individual poetic utterence, the *parole*; I emphasize the literary system, the *langue.* The books are thus complementary accounts of the same phenomenon.

both are essentially exercises in self-presentation. There is, both assert, one implicitly and the other explicitly, a great difference between Jonson and the other dramatists of his age. On the recognition of that difference, Jonson's public identity depended.

His identity did not, however, depend on any settled enmity toward Shakespeare, though as long as both remained active in the theater the reality of Shakespeare's position forbade any denial of their difference. But when Shakespeare had been for some time safely dead and when his plays were being brought out in a handsome folio edition, Jonson, whose own *Works* had by then been given the folio treatment and who had himself retired from the theater, generously welcomed his erstwhile rival over to the laureate side of the fence. "To the Memory of my Beloved, the Author, Mr. William Shakespeare," maintains all the old distinctions. Only Shakespeare's position with respect to them has changed. The poet who wanted art is now praised for art; the poet who made Nature afraid now makes "Nature herself . . . proud of his designs"; the poet who wrote too quickly and too carelessly is now acclaimed for having sweated and struck "the second heat"; the poet who was most firmly bound to the concupiscence of the age now emerges "not of an age, but for all time!" (VIII, 390–392). Neither set of judgments tells us anything of Jonson's personal feelings toward Shakespeare. Both do, however, tell us a great deal, as they were meant to do, of Jonson himself and of the poetic dignity toward which he aspired. At first the insistence on difference served that end; later it was the admission of likeness. But the end remained the same, as did the general cultural determinants that made Jonson present himself in the way he did.

Readers have often noticed that Jonson demands a quite particular response to his work. He wants his audience to judge as well as to enjoy, to regard sense above spectacle, to use its ears before its eyes, to remain detached and observant, not allowing itself to be caught up, carried away, or taken in. Where Shakespeare and the other professional dramatists agree in seeking "a loving audience," Jonson prefers "an understanding one." I have borrowed these last terms from L.A. Beaurline, who elaborates on the distinction. "Shakespeare," he writes, "conceived of a harmony of poet, actors, and audience, in a bond of hearts that ties with more than words. Jonson felt a threatening tension between himself, the stage, and his audience, with the consequent need to control them, to subordinate them, in the service of his art."[53] Though it is not part of Beaurline's argument to say so, this peculiarity too is a function of Jonson's laureate self-presentation. The tension Beaurline identifies derives from the conflict we have already examined between the accepted status of plays and playwrights and the very different status Jonson sought for himself, while the demand for understanding comes from Jonson's sense that the self-presentational language in which he addressed his audience might be intelligible only to a few. He was afraid that without constant prodding his theatergoing contemporaries would be unable to read the signs of his greatness, would be unable to distinguish between a legitimate poem and a bastard stage play, between a true poet and a mere poetaster. Hence, to mention only the most obvious example, the extraordinary devices of induction and chorus. Unlike the Shakespearean chorus of *Henry V* that "wafts you o'er the seas," lulling the audience into passively benign acceptance, Jonson's metatheatrical interventions awaken critical awareness. He wants us to think before we feel.

Put this way Jonson comes out sounding remarkably like Bertolt Brecht, who fully shared his disdain for the "magic" of

---

53. L. A. Beaurline, *Jonson and Elizabethan Comedy: Essays in Dramatic Rhetoric* (San Marino, Calif.: Huntington Library, 1978), p. 10.

the theater, for plays that cast a spell. Both distance their spectators. But where Brecht wants his audience to reflect on the issues raised by the play, Jonson asks his to consider rather the aesthetic qualities of the play itself and what these tell us of the moral quality of the man who made it. Jonson directs attention not to the world and what the play says about it, but to the poet and what the play says about him. It is for this reason that the satire of the Comical Satires has so little bite. In becoming second-order signifiers (to make a raid on the jargon of Roland Barthes's *Mythologies*), the first-order signs are drained of their original meaning. The ostensible satire is attenuated, distorted, alienated from us by the secondary motive that seizes on it. Like a ham actor, the author who refuses to disappear into the work distracts his audience from what should presumably be its object.

Only in the great middle plays from *Volpone* to *Bartholomew Fair* does the pressure of self-presentation ease off. But through these there runs a still deeper current of that antitheatricalism that elsewhere is an obvious reflex of Jonson's laureate self-presentation. Jonson belongs, as Jonas Barish has argued in one of the several brilliant studies that have made him Jonson's leading modern interpreter,

in a Christian-Platonic-Stoic tradition that finds value embodied in what is immutable and unchanging, and tends to dismiss as unreal whatever is past and passing and to come. What endures, for him, has substance; what changes reveals itself thereby as illusory. . . . The bias against change, the allegiance to silence, stasis, and immobility carry with them an implied bias against the theater.[54]

Barish finds evidence of this bias not only in a great many explicit statements but also in Jonson's strained relations with

54. Jonas A. Barish, "Jonson and the Loathèd Stage," in *A Celebration of Ben Jonson*, ed. William Blissett et al. (Toronto: Univ. of Toronto Press, 1973), pp. 38 and 41. This article reappears as a chapter of Barish's important new book, *The Antitheatrical Prejudice* (Berkeley: Univ. of California Press, 1981).

his audiences, in his opposition to the stage practices of the day, and in his preference for print over theatrical production—in, that is, the whole system of gestures that served to differentiate Jonson from the other playwrights of his age.

Jonson's hostility to dramatic action itself—to plot—provides a still more radical illustration of the antitheatricalism forced on him both by the moral tradition, which as laureate he sought to embody, and by his self-defining opposition to the professional dramatists. "Words above action," he wrote in the Prologue to *Cynthia's Revels,* "matter above words." And, as the context makes clear, it is in recompense for this double subordination of action to the more static and less theatrical words and matter that Jonson expects the understanding part of his audience to honor him. His muse, he says, "shuns the print of any beaten path,"

> Pied ignorance she neither loves nor fears,
> Nor hunts she after popular applause,
> Or foamy praise that drops from common jaws.
> The garland that she wears their hands must twine,
> Who can both censure, understand, define
> What merit is, then cast those piercing rays,
> Round as a crown, instead of honored bays,
> About his poesy, which, he knows, affords
> Words above action, matter above words.   (IV, 43)

In direct contrast to this laureate posture is the attitude of Antonio Balladino (*alias* Anthony Munday), the popular professional dramatist parodied in *The Case Is Altered.* "Tut, give me the penny," Balladino is made to say. "Give me the penny. I care not for the gentlemen, I. Let me have good ground. No matter for the pen. The plot shall carry it" (III, 108). But, as its title suggests, *The Case Is Altered* did not itself sufficiently avoid this contemptible dependence on plot, and so was denied entry into Jonson's folio *Works.*

Not even Jonson could do without action in his plays. Late

in his career he admitted that "the fable . . . is (as it were) the form and soul of any poetical work or poem" (VIII, 635), and he had a good deal to say about the fable's proper management, its confinement in time and place and its division into *protasis, epitasis, catastasis,* and *catastrophe,* as though firm government might prevail against the anarchy of plot. But earlier he had done what he could to eliminate it. In the Comical Satires remarkably little happens, and what does happen is more a frenzied agitation in place than the kind of overarching development that "carries" the play in the work of Jonson's professional contemporaries. When, halfway through *Every Man Out,* Mitis protests that "the argument of his comedy might have been of some other nature, as of a duke to be in love with a countess, and that countess to be in love with the duke's son, and the son to love the lady's waitingmaid; some such cross-wooing, with a clown for their servingman," Cordatus responds on behalf of the author with a Ciceronian definition that envisions no particular action at all. Comedy should, he says, "be *imitatio vitae, speculum consuetudinis, imago veritatis*" (III, 515). Though this does not exclude action, it does, given Jonson's predilections, make it improbable. Unlike the romantic plots that Jonson mocked, with their familiar patterns of loss and recovery, separation and reunion, love and marriage, Jonson's satiric specula offer no beginning, middle, or end. Thus the aimless movement of the Comical Satires and their imposed conclusions. Without some larger concession to plot, Jonson could hardly hope to succeed as a dramatist, not even as a laureate dramatist.

He made the concession in his next two plays but did so in such a way as to concede little more than his own surrogate presence at the center. *Sejanus* and *Volpone* abandon nothing of the radical antitheatricalism of the Comical Satires, but they achieve a dramatic effectiveness (I would make this claim for both, though the verdict of the ages grants it only to *Volpone*) that puts them in a quite different class. Where the others are staged satires, these are plays. They have the continued action of plays, the essential element of plot that in his laureate purity Jonson had earlier disdained. He still disdains it. But by a brilliant *tour de force* he manages to have his plot without its having him. He dissociates himself from it and makes it rather the responsibility of characters whom he can ultimately repudiate, characters whose inveterate theatricality keeps the play going until that very theatricality brings about the destruction of those who practice it.

As *Hamlet* is the English Renaissance's greatest tribute to theatrical man, so *Volpone* is the finest attack. The power of each comes in part from an openness to the appeal of the other. Hamlet struggles against mere playing; Volpone makes us delight in it. If we think not of the quality of their performance but of its relation to any external system of value, "mere playing" fairly describes the activity of Volpone and Mosca. Both are master actors and master plotters whose playing has no end greater than itself. Though they talk of wealth and accumulate a vast heap of it, gold is never more than a prop and a pretext— an excuse to ignore the terrifying truth that only the continuing masquerade sustains their existence. It is not having but getting that matters. In this they resemble Sejanus, who finds in the expected moment of triumph a sudden lack:

> Is there not something more than to be Caesar?
> Must we rest there? It irks t'have come so far,
> To be so near a stay.   (IV, 437)

So for Volpone and Mosca the word that drives them on to overreach and finally to undo themselves is the word of apparently ultimate victory:

> We must here be fixed;
> Here we must rest; this is our masterpiece;
> We cannot think to go beyond this.   (V, 109)

Stasis—the fundamental distinguishing characteristic of the good man and thus of the laureate—is what Sejanus, Volpone, and Mosca can least bear. In the unmoving quiet of success, their masks fall away exposing the emptiness of a self without limits.

This moment in *Volpone,* the moment at the beginning of Act V, after the brilliant success of the first trial scene, opens, as Stephen Greenblatt has written, an abyss.

In the flatness of these scenes . . . we fully understand for the first time the meaning of Volpone's extraordinary energy, as we glimpse the void which that energy has been struggling to fill. What we perceive . . . are those vast spaces that opened up on both a physical and a psychological plane in the Renaissance. . . . Volpone is consummately a man who has created his own identity, fashioned parts for himself which he proceeds to play with all the technical skill of a fine actor. Liberated from any hierarchy in the universe which would impose limits on his being, dependent only upon his own powerful imagination, he seems freer than anyone in his world. Indeed, with his ready disguises, he is liberated even from himself, uncommitted to a single, fixed role. He has the energy of a Proteus. Yet in the lull following the false ending, we perceive the converse, as it were, of this splendid energy, a yawning emptiness which at once permits its flowering and swallows it up.[55]

Such argument by analogy is always perilous. In his leap from the structure of Jonson's play to the structure of the Renaissance psyche, Greenblatt is, however, upheld by our sense of both the play and the age. *Volpone* does touch on the deepest anxieties of its time—anxieties that persist, as Greenblatt argues, into ours. Both the excitement of Volpone's newfound freedom of the self and the fear of it are essential constituents of Renaissance and post-Renaissance man.[56] And so, too, is the revived awareness of life as a play.

55. Stephen Greenblatt, "The False Ending in *Volpone,*" *JEGP,* 75 (1976), 93–96.
56. See Thomas M. Greene, "The Flexibility of the Self in Renaissance Literature," in *The Disciplines of Criticism: Essays in Literary Theory, Inter-*

Given his laureate conception of the good man as one "placed high on the top of all virtue," one who "looked down on the stage of the world and condemned the play of fortune," Jonson could only oppose this new histrionic flexibility of self—all the more vigorously because it was so much the basis of his own self-creation. To Jonson the flexibility of the self necessarily meant having no self at all. Thus in *Volpone* he rejects, as Greenblatt observes, "not the abuse of playing but playing itself."[57] But to reject playing was to reject the very stuff of the theatrical medium in which he worked. So long as the pressure to define himself remained strong, so long, that is, as the accurate construal of his status remained in doubt, he could be a laureate poet in the theater only by opposing the theater, by unmasking the moral emptiness of its mimicry, its metamorphoses, and its plotting. Unless he held fast to the good man's station as unmoved spectator, the poet risked being implicated in the madness of the "turning world" that

> studies spectacles and shows,
> And after varied as fresh objects goes,
> Giddy with change, and therefore cannot see
> Right, the right way.   (VIII, 118)

Seeing right the right way (and being seen to do so) remained the distinguishing characteristic of both the good man and the good poet.

Readers have, however, often noticed a softening of attitude in Jonson's next several comedies. *Epicoene, The Alchemist,* and *Bartholomew Fair* reprove the reprovers of drama and reward the masquerading plotters. These were good years for Jonson—though even their success had, as I shall argue in the next section, its own shadow. But whatever his continuing difficulties, Jonson had by 1609 (the year of *Epicoene*) achieved

---

pretation, and History, ed. Peter Demetz et al. (New Haven: Yale Univ. Press, 1968), pp. 241–264.

57. Greenblatt, p. 103.

much of the recognition he had so determinedly sought. Noble patronage had eased his financial dependence on the stage. His talent as a writer of masques was in demand at court. And *Volpone* had received a triumphant reception at both universities. Jonson now moved with confidence in the exclusive circle of the rich, the wellborn, the powerful, and the learned—a circle that a decade earlier might have seemed forever closed to him by his base association with the theater. The Paris-Garden Zulziman had become (in fact, if not in official title) the King's Poet.

The laureate distinction had been made and understood. It no longer required the same insistence. Like Lovewit, who at the end of *The Alchemist* forgives Face his histrionic transgression, Jonson could now in gratitude express some tolerance for the art that had so well served him. "That master," says Lovewit, speaking as well for his author,

> That had received such happiness by a servant . . .
> Were very ungrateful, if he would not be
> A little indulgent to that servant's wit,
> And help his fortune, though with some small strain
> Of his own candor. (V, 407)

For Jonson such tolerance marks a significant change. But two of these plays go even further. *Epicoene* and *Bartholomew Fair* not only allow what Jonson had formerly condemned; they turn a critical regard on the values he had formerly supported, the values on which his laureate self-presentation had been based. In *The Silent Woman,* Morose's pathological aversion to noise reduces to absurdity the stoic teaching (which was Jonson's own) that "I should always collect and contain my mind, not suffering it to flow loosely, that I should look to what things were necessary to the carriage of my life, and what not, embracing the one and eschewing the other. In short, that I should endear myself to rest and avoid turmoil" (V, 258). And in *Bartholomew Fair* the blindness of Adam Overdo calls into question the efficacy of classical learning as an instrument for the reform of the world. Adam is forced to acknowledge that despite his intimacy with Horace and Persius (favorites of Jonson's as well) he is but fallible "flesh and blood." Feasting in these plays takes the place that judgment fills in the Comical Satires and in *Sejanus, Volpone,* and *Cataline.*[58]

The presence of *Cataline* in this list reminds us of the great lumps of unyielding stuff in Jonson that not even success could soften. Written in 1611, between *The Alchemist* and *Bartholomew Fair,* this second Roman tragedy is as uncompromisingly antitheatrical as the first—as antitheatrical, for that matter, as any of Jonson's plays. But even the new tolerance of the comedies breaks on rocky chunks of the same composition. After watching for five acts the "alchemical" operations of Face and his collaborators, we are, I suspect, less ready than Lovewit to forgive him. Face is, after all, no innocent Brainworm but a schemer whose conniving self-interest rivals Mosca's or Volpone's. Still more strained is likely to be our response to the conclusion of *Epicoene.* The treatment of Morose, who is guilty of no fault greater than extreme eccentricity, is so sadistically savage that we end sympathizing rather with him than with his victorious tormentors. If their actions exemplify the world's turmoil, Morose did well to avoid it.

And what of *Bartholomew Fair?* Often seen as the richest, fullest, most humane of Jonson's plays, it leads rather to a rueful admission of frailty than to a joyous affirmation of life. The "enormity" of the fair is no less enormous because Adam Overdo cannot find it out, the "abomination" of the puppet show no less abominable because Zeal-of-the-Land Busy becomes a beholder. When Jonson puts the defense of drama into the wooden hands of the Puppet Dionysius, whose most telling argument is to lift his skirts, the strain on his candor is too great to be ignored. How are we to take the puppet show? Does

58. See Jonas A. Barish, "Feasting and Judging in Jonsonian Comedy," *Renaissance Drama,* 5 (1972), 3–35.

Jonson really accept and intend us to accept this smutty and stupid reduction of love and friendship, this grotesque violation of every critical precept that he ever enunciated, as the ultimate answer to the antitheatrical objections of its critics? So Jonas Barish supposes: "Only, it would appear, by acknowledging his kinship with the puppets can a man transcend his own grossness, vaporessness, and automatism."[59] Perhaps so. But it is an acknowledgment that Jonson could finally not force from himself. His play too effectively shows how indefensible that which it purports to defend really is. Its celebration threatens to end in disgust. Judgment fails, yes—but look how desperately we need it! In *Bartholomew Fair,* the play of Jonson's that most persistently questions the bases of his laureate self-presentation—stoic self-sufficiency, learning, reforming zeal, and the claim to judgment—we thus unexpectedly discover our need of the laureate.

Self-presentation is not central to *Bartholomew Fair.* It contains no Asper, no Crites, no Horace. After settling certain articles of agreement between himself and his audience, Jonson retires and lets the world of his play unfold in his absence. But that very removal of himself allows him to examine and even reverse the system of oppositions in terms of which he had presented himself for over fifteen years. "How much of my laureate claim can I abandon?" he seems to ask. "How much of the popular drama can I embrace?" And here, as in *Epicoene* or *The Alchemist,* he pushes so far that he provokes a movement of revulsion. Better to leave the loathèd stage at once than to be the darling of Bartholomew Cokes, the colleague of Littlewit and Leatherhead. This revulsion finds no direct expression in *Bartholomew Fair.*[60] On the contrary, the play ends on the

59. Barish, "*Bartholomew Fair* and Its Puppets," *MLQ,* 20 (1959), 16.
60. Revulsion may be expressed by the play and provoked in the audience when Mistress Overdo begins vomiting in the final scene. I owe this suggestion to Michael O'Connell who reports having attended a production in which the scene had precisely this effect.

benign note of reconciliation that has so impressed the critics. "I invite you home with me to my house, to supper. I will have none fear to go along, for my intents are *ad correctionem, non ad destructionem; ad aedificandum, non ad diruendum*"(IV, 140). For the moment, abomination and enormity are forgotten. The mild and good-naturedly satirical spirit of Horace, Adam's friend and Jonson's, reigns. But founded, as it is, on the acceptance of what Jonson had always found least acceptable, the reign of mildness could only be of short duration. For all its good humor, *Bartholomew Fair* made it no easier to be either a laureate or a dramatist.

Patronage and Its Perils

Return for a moment to the threshold of Jonson's career, to the Comical Satires. Satiric poems written for theatrical production, they nevertheless envision for the poet a position independent of both satire and the stage. *Cynthia's Revels* and *Poetaster* describe their ideal poets as the objects of noble patronage and as the companions of kings. Arete "prefers" the worth of Crites and Cynthia accepts and honors him; Maecenas and Augustus do the same for Horace. Clearly Jonson hoped that these lessons in the proper treatment of poets would take hold and make a similar fate his.

Perhaps they did. As we have already noticed, the first decade of the seventeenth century was a period of remarkable success for Jonson. In February of 1602, just a few months after the production of *Poetaster,* John Manningham, then a student of the Middle Temple, noted in his diary that "Ben Jonson, the poet, now lives upon one Townshend and scorns the world."[61] A year or so later, Jonson shifted his lodgings to

61. *The Diary of John Manningham*, ed. Robert Parker Sorlien (Hanover, N.H.: Univ. Press of New England, 1976), p. 187.

the house of Esmé Stuart, Lord of Aubigny, and records for succeeding years connect him in various ways with Sir Robert Cotton, the Earl of Suffolk, Sir John and Sir William Roe, Sir William Cornwallis, the Earl of Salisbury, the Countess of Bedford, Sir Walter Raleigh, the Earl of Pembroke, the Countess of Rutland, Sir Robert Sidney, Sir Robert and Lady Mary Wroth, the Countess of Montgomery, Sir Henry Goodyere, Sir Robert Aytoun, Sir Henry Cary, Sir Thomas Edgerton, and many others. The former itinerant actor and piecework play-patcher had, it seems, found an escape from dependence on the loathèd stage. Years later he was to tell Drummond that "of all his plays he never gained two hundred pounds" (I, 148). From patronage he gained far more. A poem written late in his life to the Earl of Portland was said to have netted him £40; a masque produced for Buckingham brought £100; other verses, masques, and dedications won further bequests of a similarly munificent sort. In addition to such occasional largesse, he was granted a royal pension of 100 marks (later increased to £100), the reversion of the office of Master of Revels (which he did not live to enjoy), the post of City Chronologer, and a lectureship in rhetoric at Gresham College—all of which depended, as did any official position or public income, on patronage.

But patronage meant far more to Jonson than money, more even than the hospitality and protection he so frequently acknowledges. Entry into the system of patronage was a sign of his poetic elevation, testimony to his attainment of that laureate status for which he strove. Patronage associated him with the gentlemen amateurs, whose nonliterary advancement depended equally on the assistance of the wealthy and well-placed, and it dissociated him from the mere professionals, particularly the play-writing professionals. As the Lord Chamberlain's men, The Lord Admiral's men, or the King's men, actors held a marginal place in the system of patronage. Dramatic authors had none at all. Not until 1611, when the most active part of his career as dramatist was behind him, did Jonson first dedicate a published play, the quarto of *Cataline His Conspiracy*, to a particular patron, and then it was because the play's utter failure in the theater proved it belonged elsewhere.[62] Only in the more select regard of a "reader extraordinary" could its worth be known. "Against the noise of opinion," Jonson wrote to the Earl of Pembroke, "I appeal to the great and singular faculty of judgment in your lordship, able to vindicate truth from error. It is the first of this race that ever I dedicated to any person; and had I not thought it the best, it should have been taught a less ambition" (V, 431).

The failure of *Cataline* was symptomatic of Jonson's failure, a failure we have examined at some length, to find in drama a suitable vehicle for his laureate undertaking. In *Cataline* Jonson attempted, as he had not done since the Comical Satires a decade earlier, to present on stage an image of that ideal rectitude which it was the laureate's job to embody and convey. Cicero stands in the direct line of Crites and Horace and is, if anything, still less stage-worthy than they. In his marmoreal quietude and confidence, he brings an unmoving and unmovable denial of action fatal to drama. *Cataline* was thus not merely ejected from the theater, it was self-ejected, though it went out protesting the audience's ignorance. "In this jig-given times," it had the temerity to present itself as "a legitimate poem"—which, whatever Jonson meant, meant to most theatergoers that it was no play. But clearly all was not failure. Not only did Jonson write plays that did please their audiences (at whatever strain to his own candor), but he developed in

62. Jonson had previously dedicated the 1607 quarto of *Volpone* to the universities of Cambridge and Oxford, and he was later to provide dedications, most of them to particular individuals, for all the plays reprinted in the 1616 folio. This in itself is a sign of the transformation of these plays into "works" and their entry into the realm of patronage. A quick look through the published plays of Jonson's most prominent contemporaries—Greene, Marlowe, Peele,

nondramatic verse and the masque a mastery of forms better suited to express the social, literary, and moral identity he claimed for himself.

The great bulk of the nondramatic verse Jonson printed in the 1616 folio ranges itself in the collection he called *Epigrams*. The title first suggests Jonson's generational location. Partisans of the new poetry proclaimed that "the satirist only and the epigrammatist keep diet from [the] surfeit" of love poetry, while its enemies singled out for attack the satirist, the humorist, and the epigrammatist. But if the epigram was a generational marker, it was one that Jonson transformed, in much the way Spenser had transformed the love poetry of his generation, so as to say something about his particular laureate identity. The fruit of other men's idleness, epigrams were, Jonson said, "the ripest of my studies" (VIII, 25). And the difference this declaration suggests appears plainly in the poems themselves. Though many wittily whip and scourge vice and folly in the manner of Bastard, Davies, Guilpin, Weever, and Donne, others (and these the most memorable) celebrate virtue in a style that was Jonson's own. These panegyric epigrams were, as Jonson himself pointed out in an epistle to Sidney's daughter, the Countess of Rutland, "strange poems, which as yet / Had not their form touched by an English wit." Poems of praise, they were also poems of patronage, poems where "all that have but done my Muse least grace / Shall thronging come and boast [their] happy place" (VIII, 115).

These poems are as finely crafted as they are strange. In them the Christian-Platonic-Stoic values that Jonson had for so

---

Chapman, Shakespeare, Dekker, Heywood, Marston, Middleton, Beaumont, and Fletcher—suggests that the dedication of *Cataline* was a new departure not only for Jonson, but also for playwrights generally. Only two plays published before 1611, Chapman's *All Fools* (1605) and Fletcher's *Faithful Shepherdess* (ca. 1609), carry individual dedications, and both present themselves as exceptions. After 1611, such dedications become relatively frequent.

long and with such indifferent success tried to represent on stage at last found full and effective expression. Their manly simplicity, their air of achieved being, bespeaks the goodness of both the poet and his subjects. Take, for example, the second of the two epigrams to William Roe. In it we encounter not the dramatic gropings of *homo histricus,* striving to discover himself in the parts he plays, but rather the laureate's art of completion and full presence.

> Roe (and my joy to name) th'art now to go
>   Countries and climes, manners and men to know,
> T'extract and choose the best of all these known
>   And those to turn to blood and make thine own.
> May winds as soft as breath of kissing friends
>   Attend thee hence; and there, may all thy ends,
> As the beginnings here, prove purely sweet,
>   And perfect in a circle always meet.
> So, when we, blest with thy return, shall see
>   Thyself, with thy first thoughts, brought home by thee,
> We each to other may this voice inspire:
>   "This is that good Aeneas, past through fire,
> Through seas, storms, tempest, and embarked for hell,
> Come back untouched. This man hath traveled well."
>
> (VIII, 80–81)

Here Jonson achieves massive stillness in a small point. He earns the right to judge. "This man hath traveled well." Style and structure together signal the self, as the movement of the verse imitates the movement of Roe's imagined voyage. Each turns in a closed circle on its own firm center. The first line announces Roe's departure; the last congratulates him on his return. Both departure and return can occur in a single moment because, like the poem, Roe travels without traveling. He makes his own the best of manners, yet comes back untouched.

The quality of active stillness characterizes many of Jonson's poems of praise. To the learned antiquary John Selden he writes,

> you that have been
> Ever at home, yet have all countries seen
> And like a compass keeping one foot still
> Upon your center do your circle fill
> Of general knowledge. . . .   (VIII, 159)

Circle, center, still, home. In Jonson's poetry these words and others related to them—*straight, upright, round, stand,* and *dwell*—gather through repetition a solemn and steadying weight of moral significance.[63] Thomas Edgerton is praised for being "*still* . . . present to the better cause" (VIII, 52); the Earl of Pembroke, for keeping "one stature *still,* / And one true posture" (VIII, 66); and Sir Edward Herbert, for "Thy *standing upright* to thyself, thy ends / Like *straight*" (VIII, 68). "Then *stand* unto thyself," Jonson advises Alphonso Ferrabosco, "not seek without / For fame" (VIII, 83). And to Sir Thomas Roe he writes:

> Thou hast begun well, Roe, which *stand* well too,
> And I know nothing more thou hast to do.
> He that is *round* within himself, and *straight,*
> Need seek no other strength, no other height.
> . . . .
> Be always to thy gathered self the same,
> And study conscience more than thou wouldst fame.
>   (VIII, 63)

In *The Forest* this moral centeredness takes on an even more powerfully domestic resonance. The glory of Penshurst in contrast to other stately homes is that "their lords have built, but thy lord *dwells*" (VIII, 96). The particular virtue of Sir Robert Wroth is of a similarly settled sort,

> Thy peace is made; and when a man's state is well
> 'Tis better if he here can *dwell.*   (VIII, 99)

---

63. See Greene, "Ben Jonson and the Centered Self."

as is that of the "virtuous gentlewoman" who speaks the next poem:

> Nor for my peace will I go far,
>   As wanderers do, that still do roam,
> But make my strengths, such as they are,
>   Here in my bosom, and at *home*.   (VIII, 102)

Firmly rooted in an unchanging self, these men and women, like the poet who extols them and who himself professes to "live to that point . . . for which I am a man, / And *dwell* as in my *center* as I can" (VIII, 219), know themselves and can thus resist the mad mimicry of the world, the theatrical shifts of face that characterize the welter of mere antic pretenders to greatness and fashion.

One feels in these poems both the power of exclusion and the presence of the great excluder. Definition is by difference, and Jonson is always there heroically drawing the line. The good are few; the bad, many—so many that, "'tis grown almost a danger to speak true." Yet, as Jonson writes to Lady Aubigny,

> For others' ill, ought none their good forget.
> I, therefore, who profess myself in love
>   With every virtue, wheresoere it move,
> And howsoever, as I am at feud
>   With sin and vice, though with a throne endued,
> And, in this name, am given out dangerous
>   By arts and practice of the vicious,
> Such as suspect themselves and think it fit
>   For their own capital crimes t'indite my wit;
> I, that have suffered this; and, though forsook
>   Of Fortune, have not altered yet my look,
> Or so myself abandoned, as because
>   Men are not just or keep no holy laws
> Of nature and society, I should faint,
>   Or fear to draw true lines, 'cause others paint;
> I, Madam, am become your praiser.   (VIII, 117)

The poems Jonson chose to print in the 1616 folio fall, with few exceptions, into two discrete generic categories: satire and encomium. What a passage like the one to Lady Aubigny suggests is that the satirist and the encomiast, the scorner and the praiser, are one. Each role is a necessary function of the other. Together they express the single and unalterable laureate self. In the dramatic medium of the Comical Satires, his attempts to join the two proved self-defeating. Here, though he may still seem to protest too much, he is more successful. But whether successful or not, the attempt could not be avoided. Satire and encomium could not be left as separate literary kinds, each requiring its own, quite distinct speaker. Jonson's moral profession, the profession of a laureate, stands behind all his poems, whatever their genre. They are as they are because he is as he is—and because the world is as it is.

But, whatever its accomplishment, the epigram must yield to the masque as the supreme vehicle of Jonson's laureate self-realization. For the masque gave Jonson the chance to play Crites to a real-life Cynthia, Horace to an English Augustus. The masque made him in fact what he had long dreamt of being, the King's Poet. His "feud with sin and vice" might, were those qualities "with a throne endued," require him to attack the king. His willingness to do so is a powerful sign of his satiric rectitude. Ideally, however, praise rather than blame would be the monarch's just desert, and his poet would be able to add the prestige and even the coercive power of the state to the moral strength of his own isolated virtue. This is the triumphant end toward which the Comical Satires point, and it is still, some thirty years later, the consummation Jonson envisions for himself in the angry ode he appended to *The New Inn*. In the theater, he charges, pride and impudence have usurped his chair, "the chair of wit," and damned his play. But he'll have his revenge

> when they hear thee sing
>   The glories of thy King,
> His zeal to God and his just awe o'er men,
>   They may, blood-shaken, then
> Feel such a flesh-quake to possess their powers,
>   As they shall cry, like ours,
>   In sound of peace or wars,
>   No harp ere hit the stars,
> In tuning forth the acts of his sweet reign
> And raising Charles his chariot 'bove his Wain.
>
> (VI, 494)

Singing the glories of his king is precisely the task of the masque writer. No literary form focuses more narrowly on the monarch, who is both chief spectator and central figure of the spectacle. As the epigrams testify to an essentially private moral order centering on the good man, so the masque celebrates the cosmic order that on earth finds its chief representative in the king,

> That in his own true circle still doth run
> And holds his course as certain as the sun.
>
> (VII, 353)

In this superimposition of figures—the circle of the state on the circle of the self—Jonson found, as Spenser had before him, a sign of his laureate identity whose meaning was confirmed both by the "natural" hierarchy of society and by the historical example of Augustus and Virgil.

The names of Spenser and Virgil recall, however, the central problem Jonson faced as a laureate poet—the inadequacy of the genres in which he worked. Could any collection of epigrams and masques, however closely they associated the poet with the king and his chief courtiers and however convincingly they identified poet, king, and courtiers with an ideal moral order, be read as the equivalent of an epic poem? Jonson might praise William Roe as another Aeneas or apostrophize James as Jove, Hesperus, Pan, or Neptune, but could the epigrams and masques themselves be made to equal in weight and substance of accomplishment the ancient and modern narrative accounts of heroes and gods? Jonson's contemporaries seem never to have thought so. In listing the evidence of Jonson's literary greatness, as many of them did, they often refer to his *Fox, Alchemist, Silent Woman,* and *Sejanus* but only rarely to his nondramatic poetry and masques. The former they seem to have considered a comparatively minor accomplishment, and the latter they were scarcely willing to regard as literature at all.

So much of Jonson's time, talent, and ambition were invested in the masque that his difficulties with it are particularly significant. When in 1629 he wrote his violent ode to himself, he had, after all, been chief contriver of court entertainments for over twenty years. If a flesh-quake had not yet possessed his detractors, new masques were unlikely to bring it on. Samuel Daniel, Jonson's earliest competitor in the form, was quick to realize its insufficiency and careful to avoid any similar investment of his authorial identity in so ephemeral a genre. In perhaps intentional opposition to Jonson, Daniel talks of masque-makers as "poor engineers for shadows" and gladly gives the greatest credit "in these things wherein the only life consists in show" to the architect. In his opinion, "whoever strives"—as Jonson did—"to show most wit about these punctillos of dreams and shows are sure sick of a disease they cannot hide." As for himself, Daniel publishes his masques through no "forwardness to show my invention therein, for, I thank God, I labor not with that ostentation nor affect to be known to be the man *digitoque monstrarier hic est*."[64] His reticence seems genuine, as well it might. A younger member of the Spenser-Sidney generation, with a lengthy historical epic to his credit, Daniel felt no need to make the masque a sign of his laureate nature.

64. *The Complete Works in Verse and Prose of Samuel Daniel,* ed. A.B. Grosart, 4 vols. (London: Privately Printed, 1885), III, 196 and 305–307.

Jonson, uncomfortable both as satirist and dramatist, did feel that need and was thus bold to answer those who "squeamishly cry out that all endeavor of learning and sharpness in these transitory devices . . . is superfluous" (VII, 209). The text, not the show, was, he insisted, the soul of the masque, and the poet its chief inventor. But as had so often been the case before, the effort of self-assertion threatened to defeat its end. Rather than appearing great by the very nature of the thing he had done, Jonson seemed to be laboring with ostentation to establish an unnatural claim. And worst of all, the ostentation went for naught. His masques were preferred as long as James lived, and Jonson himself was pensioned and employed. But the general estimate of the masque as a literary form remained close to Daniel's opinion. Costumes and scenery, the spectacle and the machine, are most often remembered, by those who left any record of their impression, with only an occasional reference to the "device," which is liable to damnation as "long and tedious . . . more like a play than a masque" if it threatens to outgrow its subordinate place.[65] Even the King appears to have been more concerned with the show than the poetry. "Why don't they dance?" he angrily shouted at the Whitehall performance of *Pleasure Reconciled to Virtue.* "What did you make me come here for? Devil take all of you, dance!" (X, 583).

Unable to overcome this prevailing prejudice, Jonson eventually succumbed to it—first with self-depreciating humor and then with brutal disdain. In *Neptune's Triumph,* one of the last of his Jacobean masques, he has the Poet introduce himself as "the most unprofitable of [the King's] servants. . . . A kind of a Christmas engine, one that is used at least once a year for a trifling instrument of wit, or so" (VII, 683). And of the anti-masque, which in response to James's taste for the noisy and

65. This remark was made of Campion's *Lords' Masque* and is quoted in *Inigo Jones: The Theatre of the Stuart Court,* ed. Stephen Orgel and Roy Strong, 2 vols. (London: Sotheby, 1973), I, 242.

the boisterous had gradually come to occupy a larger and larger place in Jonson's masques, he has the Poet say,

> We have none!
> . . . neither do I think them
> A worthy part of presentation,
> Being things so heterogene to all device,
> Mere by-works, and at best outlandish nothings.
>
> (VII, 688)

It is possible that these remarks and the extended reduction of poetry to cooking that accompanies them reflect Jonson's sense of security, his confidence that his courtly auditors, knowing his true position, would take them ironically. But I don't think so. They agree too well with the facts to be so easily reversed. Turning out an annual Christmas entertainment *had* become Jonson's primary literary activity. His antimasques *were* increasingly "heterogene to all device." And, like the Master Cook, he *did* find himself constrained rather to please the royal palate than to satisfy the rules of art. So long, however, as his talent remained in demand, he could regard these indignities with wry equanimity. The advent of Charles cost him this good humor along with his position. Inigo Jones, his former collaborator, now became "the main dominus do-all i'the work," and Jonson angrily reversed the proud claim he had made twenty-five years earlier in the preface to *Hymenaei.* "Painting and carpentry," he now admits with wounded sarcasm, "are the soul of masque!" (VIII, 404). Clearly a form dominated by the arts of the scene decorator could not serve to mark a laureate poet.

But epigram and masque suffered from more than generic insufficiency. Their very relation to the system of patronage—the relation that made them so useful to Jonson as signs of his social elevation—rendered their author liable to the familiar charge of flattery. To Jonson, whose laureate self-presentation depended on a reputation for honesty, this was a matter of intense concern. Again and again he insists that his love is "not bought," that he has "no ends," that his work is "free / From servile flattery (common poets' shame)" (VIII, 384 and 41). Yet this freedom obviously had limits. He confessed to Drummond that "he hath a mind to be a churchman, and so he might have favor to make one sermon to the King, he careth not what thereafter should befall him, for he would not flatter though he saw Death" (I, 141). Apparently the dozen and a half masques, the several panegyric addresses, and the handful of epigrams he had by then written for James had not permitted him to speak without flattery. And, indeed, in the poems themselves he regrets his flattery almost as often as he denies it. He begs forgiveness for praising "anyone that doth not deserve" (VIII, 26); he admits having "too oft preferred / Men past their terms and praised some names too much" (VIII, 159); and he castigates his muse for making him "commit most fierce idolatry / To a great image through thy luxury" (VIII, 48). And though he resolves henceforth to "write / Things manly, and not smelling parasite," it was, as he knew, difficult for a court poet to rid himself of that odor.

Commendatory poems and masques share a referential function that distinguishes them from other literary forms. They mirror a quite particular reality, and, as Jonson wrote in *Hymenaei*,

> Mirrors though decked with diamonds are naught worth
> If the life forms of things they set not forth.
>
> (VII, 235)

The life form might be an ideal, a Platonic image of the way things should be rather than the way they are. This is the usual modern defense of the masque, and Jonson himself seems to have had some such idea in mind when he apologized for having praised some names too much: "'Twas with purpose to have made them such" (VIII, 159). But he knew that when the names of specific people—people whose favor he had solicited—were linked with particular virtues such an excuse would not save him from the charge of flattery. So he assures us "I now / Mean what I speak, and still will keep that vow" (VIII, 159). But could he keep it? Not without resorting to such indirection as to render his meaning unintelligible. We have recently been shown that he may have meant *The Gypsies Metamorphosed* satirically.[66] According to this reading, the masque reveals Buckingham and his family to be little better than a pack of successfully ambitious gypsies. But apparently Buckingham, who commissioned the piece, who paid Jonson handsomely for it, and who acted in it, did not notice the satire, nor did his doting sovereign who happily sat through it three times. Had they noticed, they would no doubt have behaved differently. Far less daring thrusts in his plays got Jonson in legal trouble on at least four different occasions. Whatever satiric meaning he may have buried in *The Gypsies Metamorphosed,* his patrons were clearly flattered. Is it unfair to turn Pope's sentence on its head: Scandal in disguise is praise undeserved?

There is no question here of assigning blame. I wish rather to make clear the dilemma Jonson faced. The sign that read "laureate" might, unfortunately, also read "flatterer"—a second meaning that cancelled the first. Jonson himself explained the situation, both the need and the risk, in the first of several epigrams he dedicated to the Earl of Salisbury.

> 'Tofore great men were glad of poets. Now
> I, not the worst, am covetous of thee.
> Yet dare not to my thought least hope allow
> Of adding to thy fame; thine may to me,
> When in my book men read but Cecil's name.
>
> (VIII, 40–41)

66. Dale B. J. Randall, *Jonson's Gypsies Unmasked* (Durham, N.C.: Duke Univ. Press, 1975).

But then he hastens to add that for Cecil's name to have its desired effect men must also find "what I write thereof . . . free/ From servile flattery." The problem is endemic to court poets. Spenser faced it too. But the narrative genre that signaled Spenser's poetic eminence allowed a greater removal from "present occasions" than did either epigram or masque. And the court for which Spenser wrote had in its own time, as it still has today, a better reputation than did the one Jonson addressed. The decline, which began in the 1590s, coincided with the emergence of Jonson's generation and profoundly affected its social and literary sensibility. But not even that decline, though precipitous in the early decades of the seventeenth century, could erase the idea—fixed for Spenser and for Jonson by the illustrious example of Virgil, Horace, Ariosto, and Ronsard— that a laureate career depended on the close association of poet and ruler. Given the persistence and the social implications of that idea, the poet of laureate ambition inevitably found himself caught up in a system of courtly patronage of which flattery was an integral and inalienable part.

The Body and Soul of Ben Jonson

The terms of opposition set forth in Jonson's preface to *Hymenaei* reveal the structure of differences on which his self-presentation had depended from the beginning of his career. He opposes "body" to "soul," "show" to "invention," "outward celebration" to "inward parts," "present occasions" to "removed mysteries." Where the first member of each pair is "objected to sense," "momentary," "merely taking," and then "utterly forgotten," the second is "subjected to understanding," "lasting," "impressing," and thus destined to "live" (VII, 209– 210). For Jonson the problem had always been that the latter set could not exist without the former. He would gladly have declared the body of art the exclusive province of the poetasters, mimics, and jig-makers, reserving only the soul for himself. But without the body, his satire would have lacked an object, his plays would have remained unperformed, and his masques and epigrams would have lost both occasion and support. To deny the body, as in his more aggressively self-righteous moods he was inclined to do, was to starve the soul—to leave "sense" without "voice." By this reckoning, the perfect poet would be he who never deigned to write a poem, who never sullied an idea with the imperfection of sound. Jonson was not such a one. But he did find the signifiers available to him, "the loathèd stage and the more loathsome age," inadequate to the laureate meaning with which he labored to charge them.

In his last works, this problem assumes a new and more intimate aspect. The body against which he protests is his own. The poet who had so long lacked a "natural" sign of his literary eminence, now finds himself misspoken even by his own physical nature. Age, illness, and fat impede not only the production but also the reception of his work. "Absurdity on him," Expection cries out in *The Staple of News,* "for a huge, overgrown playmaker!" (VI, 362), and elsewhere Jonson speaks of himself as "a bed-rid wit," "an ancient bard," "the tun of Heidelberg . . . one great blot,"

> as Virgil cold,
> As Horace fat, or as Anacreon old.
> (VIII, 248, 274, 227, and 199)

Nor do these distinguished ancient names much alter the reading of the physical signs. Though he protests that

> it is not always face,
> Clothes, or fortune gives the grace,
> Or the feature, or the youth,
> But the language and the truth, (VIII, 131)

his own "hundred of grey hairs," his "mountain belly," and his "rocky face" (VIII, 150) continually intrude to block the right apprehension of his language and truth. In the theater, he had hoped for an audience capable of disregarding the "show," an audience of "men that have more of ears / Than eyes to judge us" (VI, 491). But here he has himself become the distracting show and so regrets that the visible deformities of his person have stopped his addressee's ears to the beauty of his verse.

The body and soul of Ben Jonson can, however, no more be known independently of one another than could be the body and soul of a play or a masque. Get one, he writes in an epistle to Lady Covell, and you get the other. "You won not verses, Madam, you won me."

> So have you gained a servant and a muse,
>   The first of which I fear you will refuse;
> And you may justly, being tardy, cold,
>   Unprofitable chattel, fat and old,
> Laden with belly, and doth hardly approach
>   His friends but to break chairs or crack a coach.
> His weight is twenty stone within two pounds;
>   And that's made up as doth the purse abound.
>   (VIII, 230)

The tone is humorous, but the humor is unstable, threatening to slide into servile self-pity (as in the original epilogue to *The New Inn*) or to explode in angry defiance (as in the "Ode to Himself"). Jonson's humor had always lacked sympathy. Neither as satirist nor as self-righteous laureate could he easily afford to accept imperfection. Even the vaunted toleration of *Bartholomew Fair*, the acknowledgment of "flesh and blood," was, as we have remarked, strained. So here, where his humor turns on himself, disgust mingles with the laughter.

But why does he so insistently force his obese, pockmarked, wine-drenched person on our attention? Why does he write as though—the words are John Lemly's—"the poetry itself cannot stand alone without the author's grotesque presence"?[67] The answer is quite simply that, for a laureate, the poetry could not stand alone. The playwright who placed himself conspicuously in the gallery when his comedies were acted, the masquemaker who visibly turned "the globe of the earth" (X, 466) at the performance of *Hymenaei,* the poet who put his name at the center of his verse had to be there. He could not stay away. His work was himself and he could not avoid saying so. But like the other signs of his laureate identity—like the satiric mask he had worn with his generation, like the dramatic genres in which he had worked, like the patronage he had eagerly cultivated and advertised—his physical presence was ambiguous, more likely to be read awry than aright. And so he defined himself as a poet in opposition to it, as he defined himself in opposition to the conventional understanding of satire, stage plays, and patronage. In the man, a mistress might "read so much waste as she cannot embrace," but his language

> was as sweet
> And every close did meet
> In sentence of as subtle feet
>   As hath the youngest he,
> That sit in shadow of Apollo's tree. (VIII, 149–150)

And though the man might be "unprofitable chattel, fat and old,"

> the muse is one can tread the air,
> And stroke the water, nimble, chaste, and fair.
> (VIII, 230)

In himself Jonson found the conflict of body and soul that had served as the governing metaphor in his self-defining war with the world. He does not always make us feel that he liked what he found.

---

67. John Lemly, "Masks and Self-Portraits in Jonson's Late Poetry," *ELH,* 44 (1977), 249.

Jonson yearned for transcendence. He longed to "sing high and aloof, / Safe from the wolf's black jaw and the dull ass's hoof" (IV, 324, and VIII, 175). But the fierce ambition that lifted him above his fellow poets and playwrights and made him a laureate was, as we have noticed, itself armed with the wolf's jaw and ass's hoof, with the snapping, kicking spirit of satiric negation. In him, Saussure's famous sentence finds all too obvious an application. "Dans la langue il n'y a que des différences sans termes positifs." The paradoxical force of Saussure's dictum derives from our usual sense that words are in themselves meaningful. We are not aware of their achieving meaning by fending off neighboring signifiers and neighboring signifieds. So among poets, Spenser and Milton appear to possess their laureate identity as an inherent, positive attribute. Not so Jonson. His most obvious positive attribute is rather the constant, sweaty effort to mark a difference. Though he hoped that, "whene'er the carcass dies, this art will live" (VI, 490), he had so contrived things that the art and the carcass from which it strove to distinguish itself were inseparable. Like Sir Henry Morrison in the great ode, his poems, masques, and plays live, if they live at all, "with memory *and Ben*" (VIII, 246).

No other English Renaissance poet so intrudes on his work. No other makes so much of his physical appearance, of his illnesses and poverty, of his quarrels, friendships, defeats, triumphs, likes, and dislikes, of his very name. Next to Jonson even Milton assumes the rarefied form of a symbolic presence, and Spenser pales to mere shadow. Jonson persists, as it were, in the flesh—all twenty stone of him—and so does the despised "body" of his work. The "painting and carpentry," the "brave plush and velvet men," the "stagers and the stage-writes too" defy the oblivion to which he consigned them and live on in his attacks. We know so much of the performances of his plays precisely because he was so displeased with them; we pay great attention to the spectacle of the masque in part at least because he so violently spurned it; and we delight in the Jacobean world of mimicry and fraud because his satire invested it with such energy.

The poet who insisted most vehemently that he could by art and nature rise triumphant above the vulgar morass is thus paradoxically the poet most firmly fixed in it—fixed because of his very insistence. The poet who yearned for transcendence is the poet who never soars. Instead of a flight, his work is an agon, an unresolved struggle of the self against the very conditions of its expression. But that struggle gives Jonson's plays, poems, and masques much of their troubling power—and it has made Jonson himself one of the most enduring presences in our literature. In the labor of self-presentation, rather than in a transcendently achieved laureate self, *The Works of Ben Jonson* find their true, though unacknowledged, center.

4

Milton and the Sons of Orpheus

———

In moving from Spenser's generation and Jonson's to the generation of poets born early in the seventeenth century, we move from the founders of a literary tradition to the followers, from aggressive lead generations to a more complacent, belated one. During the thirty years when the poets we have so far considered were most active, the years from 1580 to 1610, literature was England's most dynamic growth industry. New forms, new genres, new markets were opened, exploited, and often exhausted with a vertiginous rapidity. For a while poetry, fiction, and drama attracted the brightest and most energetic young Englishmen, just as humanism had done in the generation of More and Colet, or government service in that of Burghley and Walsingham, or sea exploration in that of Frobisher and Drake. But as the seventeenth century wore on and new groups of young men emerged, the vitality ebbed away. By the 1630s and 1640s, energy was more likely to flow toward religious and political controversy. The crises of the late 1620s—the Petition of Right, the proroguing of Parliament, the rise of Laud— polarized the nation as it had never been polarized before and focused attention on issues that had little to do with literature.

Much verse was still written and perhaps its average quality was as high as it had ever been. The Caroline poets could not help profitting from the example of their Elizabethan and Jacobean predecessors. But the skills those predecessors had accumulated with great effort, the Caroline poets expended with ease.

Such radically changed circumstances inevitably affected the way poets presented themselves. The self-presentation of Spenser, Jonson, and their coevals had taken clarity of outline from a structure of sharply opposed forces. Humanist expectation played against amateur prodigality; amateur prodigality, against laureate seriousness; laureate seriousness, against professional anonymity. But by the time the Caroline poets began to make themselves known, the tension had gone out of this system of oppositions and had not yet redistributed itself to create a new pattern of authorial roles. The old building still stood, but nothing was holding it up. Though humanist pedagogues and humanist parents continued to talk about service to king and country, the urgency had drained from their talk. And if the pressure to turn one's education to the immediate service of the state had diminished, so too had the impediments to such service. The poets of the 1630s found ecclesiastical, academic, and courtly preferment to match their ambitions (their somewhat reduced ambitions, it is true) far more readily than had those of the 1580s or 1590s. Their literary work was thus not the product of frustration, nor did frustration stamp its features on the amateur mask that most of them still wore. Absent too was the other chief source of the intense self-consciousness we discovered in Spenser's generation—the sense of doing what in England had not been done before, what perhaps could not or should not be done even then. The Caroline poets had little reason to construct, as Sidney had done, an elaborate defense of their poetic vocation or to announce with great fanfare, in the manner of E. K., the emergence of still another

New Poet. Poetry had lost all novelty and all but the faintest whiff of prodigality. Instead, it had become an ordinary and unexceptional part of every young gentleman's social equipment. Nor in the 1630s was there a recurrence of the open conflict of generations that had given such dramatic vigor to the self-presentation of Nashe, Donne, Jonson, Marston, Hall, and their literary coevals. On the contrary, the later poets were, for the most part, content to remain admiring Sons of Ben, dutiful pupils in the School of Donne.

Who were these Caroline poets? Mildmay Fane, Edward Benlowes, Thomas Randolph, William Habington, Sir William Davenant, Edmund Waller, Sir Richard Fanshawe, Sir John Suckling, Sidney Godolphin, Lucius Cary, William Cartwright, Richard Crashaw, Thomas Killigrew, John Cleveland, John Denham, Richard Lovelace, and Abraham Cowley are among the better known names. All these men were born between 1600 and 1618, all but Fane, Benlowes, Lovelace, and Cowley between 1605 and 1615. Two among them, Davenant and Cowley, clearly strove, in the peculiar manner of their generation, to achieve a laureate career. Their failure to impose themselves and their work, as Spenser and Jonson succeeded in doing, on the imagination of posterity is at once the sign and the product of their belatedness. Something of the same failure marks the generation as a whole. Together the Caroline poets made a distinguishable contribution to our literature, but neither individually nor collectively are they illuminated by an aura of greatness—not, that is, so long as we continue to omit the name of their greatest coeval.

By date of birth, John Milton also belongs on this list. Yet I do not imagine his absence will have bothered many readers. Leave Milton's name off a list of the great professed poets of English literature, or even of world literature, and the omission is immediately apparent. Leave his name off a list of his own literary coevals and one scarcely notices. Milton did not keep such company in life, nor has he kept it in the afterlife of literary history. To suggest at this late date that he should begin doing so may seem the height of perversity. Yet I can hardly avoid making such a suggestion, for my contention throughout this book has been that a laureate's self-presentation will be couched in the language of his own generation.

Now there may of course be variations in the application of this principle. In a belated generation, a generation that has lost its sense of a specifically literary mission and identity, a great poet may be able to distinguish himself only by ignoring, or feigning to ignore, the practice of his coevals. For him, solitariness becomes a sign of greatness. So it has been for Milton. And in Milton's case, there is another, more particular reason for isolation. The political and religious polarization of England divided him from his literary contemporaries. They were royalist Anglicans or Catholics; he was an antimonarchical Puritan. As a number of recent studies have argued, this division did much to determine his self-presentation, particularly the presentation of his prophetic vocation.[1] There remain, nevertheless, delays in Milton's laureate emergence, hesitations in his development, that seem to me best understood in the light of his generation's literary belatedness. Milton had something quite different to say than did the cavalier poets, but, to a far greater extent than has usually been acknowledged, the gestural language he used was one he shared with them. Its possibilities and

1. See, for example, Hugh M. Richmond, *The Christian Revolutionary: John Milton* (Berkeley: Univ. of California Press, 1974); William Kerrigan, *The Prophetic Milton* (Charlottesville: Univ. Press of Virginia, 1974); Christopher Hill, *Milton and the English Revolution* (New York: Viking, 1977); John Spencer Hill, *John Milton: Poet, Priest and Prophet* (London: Macmillan, 1979); Joseph Anthony Wittreich, *Visionary Poetics: Milton's Tradition and His Legacy* (San Marino, Calif.: Huntington Library, 1979); and the earlier books of William Haller, *The Rise of Puritanism* (New York: Columbia Univ. Press, 1938) and *Liberty and Reformation in the Puritan Revolution* (New York: Columbia Univ. Press, 1955). Though I am far from agreeing with

its limitations affected him as they did them. Or so I hope to demonstrate. But before doing so, I wish to consider the cavalier poets without Milton—first as a group and then, concentrating on the two cavaliers of laureate ambition, individually. How did the cavaliers respond to their belatedness? And what were the leading terms of their literary self-presentation?

The Mob of Gentlemen

Begin at maximum distance from Milton, with Cowley's "Ode: Sitting and Drinking in the Chair Made Out of the Relics of Sir Francis Drake's Ship." "Cheer up, my mates," Cowley sings out in hearty imitation of the departed sea dogs,

> the wind does fairly blow,
> Clap on more sail and never spare;
> Farewell all lands, for now we are
> In the wide sea of drink, and merrily we go.[2]

As Cowley plays in the relics of the *Golden Hind,* so he and his contemporaries reveled comfortably in the refitted remnants of their more venturesome literary predecessors. The planks that had carried Spenser, Sidney, Shakespeare, Donne, and Jonson into hitherto unknown waters of poetic accomplishment were gotten up as easy chairs for cavalier successors afloat in a wide sea of drink. The high-spirited, even tipsy, air of Cowley's

---

everything in all of these books (they do not always agree with one another), I do recognize the importance of the general position they argue. Milton's authorial self-presentation, particularly in the prose works and in *Paradise Lost,* is strongly marked by his religious convictions and by his revolutionary experience. I would, however, add that his prophetic stance also responded to a crisis in the literary tradition itself, one that can be best appreciated by examining the works of his cavalier coevals.

2. Abraham Cowley, *Poems,* ed. A.R. Waller (Cambridge: Cambridge Univ. Press, 1905), p. 411.

poem, its sophisticated self-mockery, its attachment to a social world of masculine good fellowship, its ease, grace, and metrical freedom, its lack of apparent seriousness (though it takes a more serious turn as it proceeds) are among the most familiar marks of cavalier verse.

So too is Cowley's homage to a more heroic past. *Jonsonus Virbius,* the volume assembled to honor the memory of Father Ben, served as a general gathering place for the choicer wits of the new generation, as had the Mermaid, the Sun, the Dog, and the Triple Tun in Ben's lifetime. A similar, if smaller, sheaf of poems bemoaned the passing of wit's universal monarch, Dr. Donne. Not only was a remarkable amount of commendatory verse produced by the cavaliers, but such verse held a far higher place compared to the general literary output than it had in previous generations. Cartwright's poem on Jonson is his longest and one of his best, and the two he wrote on John Fletcher come not far behind. Likewise, Carew devoted two of his best poems, poems that have earned him a place among the most discriminating of English critics, to the merits of Donne and Jonson. And Randolph, in his "Gratulatory to Mr. Ben Jonson for His Adopting of Him To Be His Son," not only wrote his best poem but also achieved a major assessment both of his author and of himself: "I am akin to heroes, being thine."[3] A strong sense of generational belatedness runs through these poems. Like Randolph, their authors seem poets by adoption rather than by birth. "'Tis a sad truth," Carew writes, "[Donne] didst . . . dispense / Through all our language both the words and sense." Poets will still write, parsons will still preach,

> but the flame
> Of thy brave soul, that shot such heat and light,

3. *Poetical and Dramatic Works of Thomas Randolph,* ed. W. Carew Hazlitt, 2 vols. (London: Reeves and Turner, 1875), II, 537.

As burnt our earth, and made our darkness bright,
Committed holy rapes upon our will,
Did through the eye the melting heart distill,
And the deep knowledge of dark truths so teach,
As sense might judge what fancy could not reach,
Must be desired forever.[4]

One expects such sentiments in a funeral elegy. Donne's own *Anniversaries* provide the most obvious and extended example. But a specificity of reference—a specificity the *Anniversaries* lack—distinguishes Carew's poem and suggests a conviction beyond convention. And similar attitudes find expression in contexts free from the pressure of generic expectation. Thus Waller in "At Penshurst" can talk of Sidney as one who

could so far exalt the name
Of love, and warm our nation with his flame,
That all we can of love or high desire
Seems but the smoke of amorous Sidney's fire.[5]

Whether the relation is of smoke to fire, of subject to monarch, or of adopted son to foster father, it never much flatters the latecomer.

In cavalier verse, homage takes other forms than that of open eulogy. Many of the poems we have been considering—Carew's most brilliantly—imitate their chosen predecessors even as they praise them. Such imitation is, in fact, a leading characteristic of cavalier verse in all genres. Again and again, a title, a turn of phrase, a choice of word or image, a pattern of thought will recall Donne, Jonson, or some other Elizabethan or Jacobean poet. And most often the later poet stands to his model as Cowley stood (or rather sat) to Sir Francis Drake: he

4. *The Poems of Thomas Carew,* ed. Rhodes Dunlap (Oxford: Clarendon Press, 1949), pp. 71–72.
5. Edmund Waller, *Poems 1645* (Menston, Yorkshire: Scolar Press, 1971), p. 21.

plays in the relics but escapes the risk. So it is with Cowley himself in *The Mistress,* with Habington in *Castara,* or with Cleveland in his nonsatiric poems—all of whom echo the abrupt and conceited manner of Donne but lack the fiercely egocentric obsession of his matter. So too Waller smooths and refines the familiar devices of both Donne and Jonson, making agreeably conversational what had been awkwardly intense. Jonson no doubt led the way toward the achievement of social grace. In this the cavaliers are properly his sons. But one has only to compare Jonson's *Penshurst* to Waller's two poems of similar title to recognize the difference. Nowhere in Waller is there an ungainly intrusion to match Jonson's portrait of himself hard at work on his dinner.

> Here no man tells my cups; nor, standing by,
> A waiter doth my gluttony envy,
> But gives me what I call and lets me eat.
> He knows, below, he shall find plenty of meat.[6]

Instead, Waller's lines flow with a liquid smoothness suggestive rather of Pope's youthful *Pastorals,* which they may have helped inspire.

Suckling was particularly adept at the kind of poetic reprise that served to locate and identify the cavaliers. In *The Heirs of Donne and Jonson,* Joseph Summers cites several telling examples, including the parody of Jonson's "Celebration of Charis" in Suckling's "Song to a Lute" ("Hast thou seen the down i' th' air") and the imitation of Donne's "Love's Deity" in Suckling's "Sonnet III" ("Oh! for some honest lover's ghost").[7] The "deliberate lowering of tension" that Summers notices in these poems marks Suckling's borrowings from Shakespeare as well, both in his plays and in a poem like "To My Lady E. C. at Her

6. *Ben Jonson,* ed. C. H. Herford, Percy Simpson, and Evelyn Simpson, 11 vols. (Oxford: Clarendon Press, 1925–1952), VIII, 95.
7. Joseph Summers, *The Heirs of Donne and Jonson* (New York: Oxford Univ. Press, 1970), pp. 42–51.

Going Out of England," whose opening lines are shot through with Hamletic attitudes.

> I must confess, when I did part from you,
> I could not force an artificial dew
> Upon my cheeks, nor with a gilded phrase
> Express how many hundred several ways
> My heart was tortured, nor with arms across
> In discontented garbs set forth my loss:
> Such loud expressions many times do come
> From lightest hearts, great griefs are always dumb.[8]

The effect is startling. Through the politely conventional "tortures" of this valediction (or postvaliction), one hears the unmistakable echo of language that once expressed near-madness and despair. In Suckling's poem, Hamlet dwindles back to what he was said to have been before his father's death, to what Suckling himself aspired to be: "The glass of fashion and the mold of form." And yet, as the famous story of his debate with Jonson bears witness, Suckling was a warmly professed admirer of Shakespeare. In fact he, like Davenant who hinted he was Shakespeare's bastard son, made of admiration a self-presentational role. In the fine Van Dyck portrait, Suckling holds a copy of the Shakespeare folio open to *Hamlet*. That he seems also to be wearing a costume from his own *Aglaura* suggests his intention of acknowledging its literary descent. But here again descent is also decline. In *Aglaura,* as in "To My Lady E. C.," the Shakespearean model is broken up, like another Drake's ship, to provide elegant furnishings for dilettantish amusement.[9]

The likeness between the various cavalier acts of literary appropriation is striking enough to require some more general definition. Clearly Suckling and Waller, Randolph, Cartwright,

8. *The Works of John Suckling,* ed. Thomas Clayton and L. A. Beaurline, 2 vols. (Oxford: Clarendon Press, 1971), I, 29.

9. See Clayton's discussion of this portrait in Suckling, I, lxii–lxiv.

Carew, Cowley, and Cleveland were engaged in a common enterprise, one that distinguished them from English poets of earlier generations. Louis Martz has applied the term *mannerist* to some examples of this enterprise. If we do not let the word draw us too far from the specific concerns of seventeenth-century English poetry, it can, I think, advance our understanding of the cavalier stance. Remarking that "'Mannerism' is derived from the Italian word *maniera*, meaning simply *style*," Martz describes the use of the term in art history. "A Mannerist painter is a painter with high style. . . . A Mannerist painter has learned all that can be learned from the earlier great masters and he now proceeds to turn their art and craft towards other ends, creating a different kind of art in which the high style stands at the front, taking the eye with its elegance and its sophistication."[10] The mannerist is thus by definition an inheritor, a latecomer. The polish and virtuosity of his work, its seemingly effortless savoir faire, depends on the supreme accomplishment of his predecessors. Unable to say more than they, he playfully embroiders and misapplies their way of saying, often decorating the smaller concerns of life in a style forged to express the greater, bidding temporary farewell to a court amour with the gestures of a Hamlet, sitting and drinking with the bravado of a Drake.

Martz introduces the term *mannerist* in a discussion of Carew and later applies it, though in a somewhat broader sense, to Marvell. The stylish refinement of these two poets, as well as their shared dependence on the heritage of Donne and Jonson, makes both likely candidates for the mannerist label. Poems like Carew's "A Rapture" or Marvell's "To His Coy Mistress" are unthinkable without the extraordinarily rich literary tradition that stands behind them—whether the licentious Ovidian elegy, as redefined by Donne, or the Horatian-

10. Louis Martz, *The Wit of Love* (Notre Dame, Ind.: Univ. of Notre Dame Press, 1969), p. 94.

Catullan *carpe diem* poem, domesticated by Daniel, Jonson, Herrick, and a score of others. But both poets bring to the traditions they inherit a new sophistication, a new polish, and a new panache. They are at once more obviously skilled than their predecessors and less committed.

Born at either extremity of the cavalier generation—falling indeed somewhat outside its stricter limits—Carew and Marvell offer perhaps the most exquisitely finished examples of English mannerist verse. But most of those many writers whose births fall somewhere midway between share their addiction to style, to *la maniera*. As one might suppose, the forms in which this common addiction expresses itself vary considerably, ranging from the extreme negligence of Suckling to the extreme virtuosity of Crashaw. But most seek, within the sometimes straited limits of their ability, a union of these qualities. For this is the generation in which the *sprezzatura* and *virtù* of that manual of mannerist behavior, *Il Cortegiano,* find at last their purest English manifestation.

Though not all the cavalier poets were courtiers, the court was the natural home of such poetry. The men who wrote it were nearly of an age with their King and were just the age of his Queen. And the halcyon years of the King's personal rule— the years when style was most prized—coincided exactly with their appearance on the literary scene. In 1629, Carew was already thirty-four and Marvell only eight, but Milton was just twenty-one, Suckling twenty, Davenant, Waller, and William Killigrew twenty-three, and Randolph twenty-four. In the course of the next eleven years, the eleven years between Parliaments, Cartwright, Thomas Killigrew, Crashaw, Cleveland, Denham, and even those two younger companions of the cavaliers, Lovelace and Cowley, reached their maturity. Already in 1629, Cowley, though only a boy of eleven, had written more than a third of his first volume of poetry, which was published a scant four years later, and, to at least one reader, Lovelace's poems when they appeared in 1649 seemed, for all their references to imprisonment and war, to harken back to that more peaceful age. "Our times," Marvell wrote,

> are much degenerate from those
> Which your sweet Muse, which your fair fortune chose. . . .
> That candid age no other way could tell
> To be ingenious, but by speaking well. . . .
> Our civil wars have lost the civic crown.[11]

From Randolph to Lovelace, these men emerged into a world that honored "speaking well." Their King was the greatest connoisseur and patron of art ever to sit on the English throne, and their Queen was a French *précieuse*. Theirs was the age of Anthony Van Dyck and Inigo Jones, of Henry Lawes and William Laud, of Caroline masque and High Church liturgy. And the young men helped make the age what it was. They posed for Van Dyck's portraits. They wrote the plays and masques that Jones staged and the songs that Lawes set to music. Some even supported the Thorough methods of Archbishop Laud, and most shared Laud's antipathy toward Puritans. And in all they did, they cultivated style.

Unlike Jonson, these professed Sons of Ben expressed no disdain for "painting and carpentry." In their work, the arts of spectacle invaded the drama and dominated the masque. No longer did poetry stand high and aloof. Instead it was absorbed into the ornamented life of college and court. Style was everywhere, which meant that it was nowhere in particular. The barriers that had marked off a semi-independent realm of art were down. Most Elizabethan and Jacobean poets had written some occasional verse and some to be set to music, but never before had so large a part of the poetic output of even the most prolific and proficient writers been produced in response to

11. *The Poems and Letters of Andrew Marvell,* ed. H. M. Margoliouth, 3d ed. rev., 2 vols. (Oxford: Clarendon Press, 1971), I, 2–3.

such external promptings. Individual poems in *Astrophel and Stella* suppose specific historical occasions, but the collection as a whole has an autonomy quite lacking in *Lucasta, Castara,* or the various pieces Waller dedicated to Sacharissa. *Poems Upon Several Occasions,* Waller's title, would have equally suited most collections of the period. Even the theater for which these men wrote was occasional. Walter Montagu suited his *Shepherd's Paradise* to the tastes of the Queen and the requirements of a Twelfth Night performance at Somerset House. The court also saw the first performance of Suckling's *Aglaura* and Habington's *Queen of Aragon,* both of which, like Montagu's play, were provided with sets and costumes by Inigo Jones. Other plays, Cartwright's *Royal Slave* or Cowley's *Guardian,* were prompted by royal visits to Oxford or Cambridge. And under Charles, the masque, which had always been occasional, became still more firmly tied to the times. No longer concerned merely to celebrate the ideal virtue of the monarch, Caroline masques increasingly took as their subject the very substance of royal policy. The Queen's "Platonic" philosophy found expression in Davenant's *Temple of Love,* and Carew's *Coelum Britannicum* justified her husband's position on such unpoetic matters as prerogative rule, price control, monopoly, sexual morality, and even tavern closing hours—and all without marring the high polish of its own elegant surface.

Davenant called himself and his fellow poets "Orpheus' sons."[12] And well he might. For not only did the cavaliers keenly feel their filial belatedness, they also found in their stylishness an image of the art that had distinguished Orpheus, Amphion, and Arion. By the sheer beauty of song, more than by the substance of what they sang, those legendary Greeks moved rocks and uprooted trees, built cities, and tamed wild

12. Sir William Davenant, *The Shorter Poems, and Songs from the Plays and Masques,* ed. A. M. Gibbs (Oxford: Clarendon Press, 1972), p. 23.

beasts. They were the poets for a connoisseur king—a king intent on governing by the force of an indomitably superior style, a king who shared the Orphic power. As Waller wrote in "Upon His Majesty's Repairing of Paul's," Charles

> like Amphion makes those quarries leap
> Into fair figures from a confused heap:
> For in his art of regiments is found
> A power like that of harmony in sound.
> Those antique minstrels sure were Charles-like kings,
> Cities their lutes and subjects' hearts their strings.[13]

The very structure of the Stuart masque, with its easy symbolic victory of masque over antimasque, revealed the same expectation—an expectation that was often enforced by the text. "All that are harsh, all that are rude," the chorus of *Salmacida Spolia* sang to the King and Queen,

> Are by your harmony subdued;
> Yet so into obedience wrought,
> As if not forced to it, but taught.[14]

And this in 1640, on the eve of the Short Parliament and the Long! But even after the royalist collapse, the idea persisted that nations could be ruled and battles stilled by song. In 1649, the year of the King's execution, Alexander Brome based his "hopes for Restoration" on the Orphic power of Lovelace's newly issued poems. Since the Puritans' "prose unhinged the state," Brome wonders

> why mayn't your verse
> Polish those souls that were filed rough by theirs?[15]

13. Waller, p. 4.

14. Reprinted in *Inigo Jones: The Theatre of the Stuart Court,* ed. Stephen Orgel and Roy Strong, 2 vols. (London: Sotheby, 1973), II, 734.

15. Reprinted in *The Poems of Richard Lovelace,* ed. C. H. Wilkinson (1930; rpt. Oxford: Clarendon Press, 1953), pp. lxxxvi–lxxxvii.

Behind these conceits stretches a long literary and philosophical tradition, but that tradition was given a new relevance by the mannerist predilection of the cavaliers.[16]

What strikes one about passages like those quoted in the previous paragraph is their curious literalness. Their authors seem almost to believe that a stylishly graceful manner will do the work of masons and soldiers. Perhaps they did believe it. Suckling spent a fortune fitting out a "troop of one hundred very handsome young proper men . . . in white doublets and scarlet breeches, and scarlet coats, hats, and . . . feathers" for a battle that was abandoned almost before it had begun.[17] The resulting Treaty of Berwick was only the first in a long series of royalist humiliations that came from putting style before substance. The cavalier belief in style was not, however, left wholly without vindication. After the King's death, his royal image, as set forth in *Eikon Basilike,* did enjoy a significant success, even in the world of political action. In the words of John Gauden, its actual author, the King's Book "was an army and did vanquish more than the sword did."[18] Milton Eikonoklastes might protest that "quaint emblems and devices, begged from the old pagentry of some Twelfthnight's entertainment at Whitehall, will do but ill to make a saint or martyr."[19] He protested in vain. With the indispensable assistance of an actual execution, the quaint emblems and devices did make the King appear a sainted martyr. In his absence, his "fair and plausible words"

16. For a thorough discussion of the Orphic tradition, see John Hollander, *The Untuning of the Sky: Ideas of Music in English Poetry, 1500–1700* (Princeton: Princeton Univ. Press, 1961), particularly pp. 162–176.

17. Suckling, I, xlvii.

18. Quoted by H. R. Trevor-Roper, *Historical Essays* (New York: Harper Torchbook, 1957), p. 220.

19. *John Milton: Complete Poems and Major Prose,* ed. Merritt Y. Hughes (Indianapolis: Odyssey Press, 1957), p. 784. Subsequent references to this edition will be indicated by page number in the text. Unless otherwise specified, translations from Milton's Latin will be from this edition.

finally succeeded in winning something of "that interest . . . which the force of arms denied him" (784).

In all of this, there is an unusually deep engagement of art in the business of life—an engagement that goes well beyond anything known in previous reigns, including the Elizabethan. Like Charles, Elizabeth carefully tended her image, but she still more carefully tended the substance of power that it expressed. When at the height of the Essex Rebellion her verse-writing godson, Sir John Harington, imprudently came to court, she dismissed him with a sharp "Get home. It is no season now to fool it here."[20] Did Charles ever rebuke a poet so? Had he, he would perhaps have better served both his office and his poets, for as art lost its autonomy so did the artist.

The guises worn by the poets of the previous generations had marked off a space for literature. As shepherd, as prodigal, or as lover, the Elizabethan poet declared himself outside society, at odds with it, or distracted from it. For the amateur, these roles also provided limits within his own life, a period of pastoral otium, of youthful rebellion, or of amorous folly. The confinement of poetry to youth does not figure so obviously in the role of satyr-satirist played by the poets of Jonson's generation, but theirs too was a role that set them off from the world, as it set them off from their immediate predecessors. The cavaliers had no such distinguishing role. They did not need one. They gratefully accepted the literary tradition bequeathed them and were relatively successful and secure members of the ruling establishment. Sons of Orpheus, they suggested by their Orphic identity rather a grace of manner shared with the stylish court than any differentiating characteristic particular to them as poets. Waller is one of the few to remember Orpheus' fate at the hands of the Thracian women, and he remembers it only to deny the tragedy. The ladies did not dismember Orpheus. They

20. *Nugae Antiquae,* ed. Henry Harington, 2 vols. (London, 1804), I, 317.

merely tore up his poems, as Waller, in good amateur fashion, invites his lady and her friends to do to his.[21] And even had the cavaliers recalled Orpheus' fate in all its horror and applied it, as they might well have done, to their own impending doom, it still would not have separated them as poets. While they suffered, their King died. Pope's line better suggests the collective literary identity of these sons of Orpheus. He called them "the mob of gentlemen who wrote with ease."[22]

Here in a phrase we find the leading characteristics of the Caroline poets: their amiable gregariousness ("the mob"), their comfortable social position ("of gentlemen"), and their mannerist *sprezzatura* ("who wrote with ease"). Not even in their verse did they stand apart from society. Rather they were an integral part of it. Theirs was, as Earl Miner has called it, a "social mode."[23] They presented themselves as men in society, men whose pursuit of business or pleasure and whose activity as courtiers, soldiers, or scholars was continuous with their literary engagement.

With the decline in literary autonomy came a blurring of the lines that had separated amateur, laureate, and professional. In declaring that Waller had "surprised the town" by showing himself a poet at an age when most men had given over writing—that is, in his early thirties—Clarendon was remembering the earlier formulae, with their strict identification of poetry and youth.[24] But in Clarendon's own generation, which was also Waller's, such conventions were ceasing to have much effect on the way men actually behaved, though they

21. Waller, sig. A3.
22. Alexander Pope, *First Epistle of the Second Book of Horace Imitated*, line 108. (Twickenham Edition, IV, 203).
23. Earl Miner, *The Cavalier Mode from Jonson to Cotton* (Princeton: Princeton Univ. Press, 1971), pp. 3–42.
24. *The Life of Edward, Earl of Clarendon*, printed with *The History of the Rebellion* (Oxford: at the Univ. Press, 1843), p. 928. "Drooping poetry" is Clarendon's term for the state of English verse in the late 1630s.

might still affect the way they spoke. Waller himself roundly asserted in the preface to his *Poems* of 1645 that this was "not only all I have done, but all I ever mean to do in this kind," and he went on to defend himself with a familiar amateur argument: "Not so much to have made verses, as not to give over in time, leaves a man without excuse."[25] He nevertheless made more verses in the next four decades than in all his youth, publishing a last collection in 1686, a year before dying at the age of eighty-one. Denham did not live so long (he died at fifty-four), but he too published a last volume in his penultimate year. And he was as much an amateur as Waller. According to his Prologue to *The Sophy,* he wrote

> . . . not for money, nor for praise,
> Nor to be called a wit, nor to wear bays,
>   . . . so now you'll say,
> Then why the Devil did he write a play?
> He says 'twas then with him, as now with you,
> He did it when he had nothing else to do.[26]

Other men—Randolph, Cartwright, Suckling, or Lovelace—did stop writing early, but only because they died early. And for the longest lived of these—Lovelace, who died at thirty-eight or thirty-nine—poems survive that can be firmly assigned to his last year.

Sometimes a posthumous attempt was made to wedge a sprawling amateur career back into a tighter mold. Cartwright's publisher, Humphrey Moseley, obviously embarrassed by his author's academic and clerical profession, claimed that "but one sheet was written after he entered Holy Orders, some before he was twenty years old, scarce any after five and twenty, never his business, only to sweeten and relieve

---

25. Waller, sig. A2 and A2^v.
26. *The Poetical Works of Sir John Denham,* ed. Theodore Howard Banks (1928; 2d ed. New York: Archon Books, 1969), p. 234.

deeper thoughts."[27] But the poems themselves tell a different story. According to their modern editor, "at least ten . . . can be shown to have been composed after" Cartwright's ordination.[28] And, as for the "Confession," which Moseley placed last in the collection, it confesses nothing of a literary nature. As a significant marker in the usual amateur career, the palinode had lost its place. Carew, who had much both in his life and his art to repent, appears to have been genuinely affected by his reading of Sandys' translation of the Psalms. "I no more shall court the verdant bay," he resolves,

> But the dry leaveless trunk on Golgatha,
> And rather strive to gain from thence one thorn,
> Then all the flourishing wreaths by laureates worn.[29]

But in subsequent poems, he still courts the verdant bay. And when a Crashaw or a Vaughan does turn from secular to divine topics, he ceases neither to be a poet nor to be an amateur.

The system of differences in terms of which both the amateurs and the laureates of previous generations had presented themselves thus retained little structural integrity. The poet merged with the gentleman, poetry with the gentlemanly activities of court, college, country, and church. In earlier generations, the sharply delineated place allowed literature and the equally sharp distinctiveness of the usual amateur career had provided the aspiring laureate with an obstacle, but also with an opportunity. Though the amateur idea of the poet could not suit him, it could and did furnish a well-established point of reference against which his own claim to distinction might be readily tested. He could meaningfully differentiate himself from the amateur poets of his generation without appearing

27. *The Plays and Poems of William Cartwright,* ed. G. Blakemore Evans (Madison: Univ. of Wisconsin Press, 1951), p. 832.

28. Cartwright, p. 833.   29. Carew, p. 94.

merely eccentric. But what then of the laureate poets born in the first decades of the seventeenth century? There were, as I have already suggested, two men, in addition to Milton, who sought some such distinction, Sir William Davenant and Abraham Cowley. A brief consideration of their attempts at laureate self-presentation should give us a better sense of those cultural determinants which may also, though in other ways, have affected Milton.

Two Cavalier Laureates

Unlike Milton, Davenant and Cowley both belonged to the mob of gentlemen. Davenant spent most of his long career at court or in its near precincts, and Cowley moved from college to court and then to the scientific circles of Restoration London. Between them, their acquaintance included nearly all the writers of their generation and many of the leading courtiers and intellectuals. Both sought the approbation of their coevals and adapted their self-presentation to current tastes. This sensitivity and collegiality make them particularly useful guides to the demands of their moment.

Davenant has a still more particular claim to consideration. Not only did he seek to distinguish himself as a laureate poet. He was, in at least a quasi-official sense, the Poet Laureate. Though the royal pension granted him in 1638 for "service heretofore done and hereafter to be done" was linked to no specific title or office, Davenant's contemporaries agreed in according him the name of "Laureate," and when in 1668 a warrant was issued "for a grant to John Dryden of the Office of Poet Laureate, void by the death of Sir William Davenant," that informal recognition won retroactive sanction.[30] Spenser and

30. Edmund Kemper Broadus, *The Laureateship* (Oxford: Clarendon Press, 1921), pp. 225 and 61.

Jonson had also enjoyed royal pensions (when they could get them paid), and Jonson had called himself the "King's Poet," but neither had attained official recognition so early—Davenant was only thirty-two when his pension was granted—and neither was so commonly allowed the laureate title. How then did Davenant advance so quickly and so surely? The precedence of Spenser and, particularly, of Jonson clearly had something to do with his success. Without the example of their careers, neither vague classical memories nor scattered continental practices would have sufficed to create an expectation that the court would routinely select for special patronage some particular poet—an expectation that did clearly exist in the 1630s. Only at Jonson's request had Selden added a discussion of the laureateship to the second edition (1631) of his *Titles of Honor,* and even then he found no example nearer in time and place than Johannes Crusius, who was given the laurel crown in 1616 by Thomas Obrechtus, "a professor of law and Count Palatine."[31] Obviously Johannes Crusius, who *was* an official laureate, had less effect on the development of the office in England than did Ben Jonson, who *wasn't*. Had Spenser and Jonson not broadened the way to such preferment, Davenant would not so soon have stumbled into it.

The same careless ease that marks his contemporaries' attainment of style characterizes Davenant's laureate advancement, and the ease has the same cause: the pioneering efforts of his predecessors. Unlike Spenser or Jonson, Davenant seems to have felt no pressing need to distinguish himself as a particular sort of man or as a particular sort of poet. From 1627, when at the age of twenty-one he wrote his first play, to 1638, when he was awarded his pension, he wrote ten plays, three masques, and a volume of poetry. Yet in all this considerable mass of work, we find no *Shepheardes Calender,* no Comical Satire, no

31. Broadus, p. 48.

work in which the literary manner of the poet's generation is tested against the demands of his own laureate calling. The echo of that calling is, on the contrary, rarely heard. In the plays and masques, explicit self-presentation is reserved for an occasional prologue or epilogue. The poet "long[s] for wreaths," he says in the Prologue to *The Wits,* but he seems to have no notion that those who would wear them need do more than supply acceptable entertainment. The poems do indulge in a more liberal display of the poet's self, but the basis they furnish his laureate claim is only slightly broader, though it was evidently broad enough. It consists of little more than an impressive list of courtly patrons and a style that can occasionally climb to the heights of his social ambition.

In Tudor and Stuart England, patronage was the chief road to advancement. Whether as courtiers or as poets, most Elizabethan writers traveled that road. But few can have stuck to it as undeviatingly as Davenant. The son of an Oxford vintner and tavernkeeper, Davenant entered the court circle first as a page in the household of Frances, Duchess of Richmond. He then served Fulke Greville, Lord Brooke, before shifting his residence to the Middle Temple, where he shared the lodgings of the future Earl of Clarendon. While living with Hyde, he began his literary career, addressing himself, as one twentieth-century biographer has remarked, "to a phenomenally large proportion of the great, the near-great, the once-great, and the to-be-great, never desisting in his tireless siege of their interest and good will."[32] His earliest plays bear fulsome dedications to such potential benefactors as the Earl of Somerset, Sir Richard Weston (soon to be Earl of Portland), and the Earl of Dorset. His masques show an unusual attention to the tastes of particular court figures, most obviously the Queen. And his poems are, almost without exception, aimed at some individual grandee or

32. Arthur H. Nethercot, *Sir William D'avenant: Poet Laureate and Play-wright-Manager* (Chicago: Univ. of Chicago Press, 1938), p. 71.

another. All this effort had its success—even before the award of his royal pension. By the early 1630s, Davenant had won the friendship and protection of two important courtiers, Henry Jermyn, the Queen's favorite, and Endymion Porter, whom Davenant came to call the "lord of my muse and heart," and he was able to style himself "Her Majesty's Servant." Together Jermyn, Porter, and the Queen account, whether as addressee or subject, for nearly half the poems in Davenant's first volume—poems that ring with a note of personal dependence quite foreign to Jonson's panegyric epigrams. In relation to his patrons, Davenant is at once more intimate and less free. Unlike Jonson, he claims no poetic integrity that does not derive from them. They provide not only protection and material support but also his very inspiration and ambition. There is, of course, an element of conventional hyperbole in all this, but the hyperbole is so consistently maintained that it ends by appearing an essential part of Davenant's authorial stance.

Nor is the lack of an independent justification of himself as poet confined to his early work. It recurs a quarter of a century later in the poems he addressed to Charles II on the King's restoration. "Though poets, mighty King, such priests have been . . . ," begins the most interesting of them, his "Poem to the King's Most Sacred Majesty." The subordinating "though" and the present perfect "have been" tell the story. Though poets have been priests, they are priests no longer. The one-time likeness has narrowed to a single point: both are poor. And even here a significant difference remains. The priest's poverty is voluntary; the poet's is not. Following from this beginning, the poem frets about Davenant's financial position and his relation to the King. Will there be a Poet Laureate in this new regime? Will it be he? Is he too old? Aren't others too young? Will he find some other refuge in the King? Is his lack of merit a possible argument in his favor? None of this is very directly stated. The poem wanders, guided by the poet's own uncertainty, only to catch itself up: "Auspicious Monarch! here I lose my way." It is a sad performance, made sadder no doubt by Davenant's sense of being an old man in a young man's world.

> That heat is spent which did maintain my bays,
> Spent early in your God-like father's praise.[33]

But though made more acute by age, Davenant's uncertainty springs from a deeper source—the loss of literary autonomy that he shared with his generation. Deprived of its priestly function and having no other to put in its place, Davenant's laureate identity can only await the King's unpredictable pleasure.

Davenant followed no Spenserian *curriculum poetae* from pastoral to epic, nor did he display Jonson-like rectitude. His verse did, however, have (or at least was advertised as having) one intrinsic quality that served to distinguish him and to support his laureate pretension. It had an elevated style. Davenant's "soaring language" and "lofty strain," his Orphic power to "amaze the fiery souls of men," are what the commendatory poems affixed to his first published work, *The Tragedy of Albovine,* single out for particular praise.[34] And in the dedicatory epistle Davenant himself suggests that elevation will continue to be his specialty: "I have imaginations of greater height than these." Now, *Albovine* is little more than poor Shakespearean pastiche, a jumble of sensational scenes from *Hamlet, Measure for Measure,* and *Othello.* But its very absurdity of plot and inconsistency of characterization serve to thrust, in good man-

---

33. Davenant, *Shorter Poems,* p. 91.
34. *The Works of Sir William Davenant,* 2 vols. (1673; facsimile rpt. New York: Benjamin Blom, 1968), II, 415–416. Habington compared Davenant explicitly to Orpheus:

> with sad plaints of love
> Famed Orpheus charmed rude heaps, did cedars move,
> Forced mountains from their station, but thy pen
> Hath now amazed the fiery souls of men.

nerist fashion, style to the fore. High style thus becomes Davenant's laureate sign, as stylishness generally was the sign of his generation. Again, nine years later in the commendation of *Madagascar,* style attracts the greatest notice. Endymion Porter asks,

> What lofty fancy was't possessed your brain,
> And caused you soar into so high a strain?

and Habington waxes lyrical on Davenant's "nobler flight / Of poesy"—nobler, that is, than the mere triumphs of kings.[35] Their stylistic flight moved the admirers of *Albovine* and *Madagascar* to place these works above "what we had from Rome or Greece" and to recognize in Davenant the superior of Homer and Virgil.[36] The same quality of elevation in his early verse must have generally contributed to making him the semiofficial laureate of the Caroline court.

Davenant's lofty strain was not, however, easily maintained—as a passage from *Madagascar* suggests. Working himself up for the introduction of his twin heroes, Porter and Jermyn, he cries out,

> Now give me wine! And let my fury rise,
> That what my travailed soul's immortal eyes
> With joy and wonder saw, I may rehearse
> To curious ears, in high, immortal verse![37]

The call for wine and the rehearsal of a tale for curious ears play oddly against the insistence on poetic fury and ecstatic rapture. Is this heroic or mock-heroic? I am reminded of Cowley in the chair made from Drake's ship—and not only by the drink. The good-hearted sociability of these lines, and of the poem generally, undercuts its ostensible heroic ambition. The

35. Davenant, *Works,* I, 201 and 204.
36. Davenant, *Works,* II, 415, and I, 203.
37. Davenant, *Shorter Poems,* p. 13.

couplets alone give him away. The lines immediately preceding these had rimed "call" and "Surveyor-Generall." Davenant is just too much of a good fellow to be taken very seriously —or to take himself very seriously—in the part of the soaring visionary.

His contemporaries' praise of him often succumbs to a similar comic deflation. "His art was high," writes the author of the *Great Assizes Holden on Parnassus,* "although his nose was low."[38] Davenant's famous nose, unhappily altered by converse with a "black, handsome wench that lay in Axe-yard, Westminster,"[39] served as a physical sign of the disabling gregariousness of his verse. The height of his art had constantly to contend with the lowness of his nose. In "A Sessions of the Poets," Suckling, Davenant's close friend and fellow debauché, disallowed Davenant's claim to the laurel for that "foolish mischance" alone.

> Surely the company would have been content,
> If they could have found any precedent;
> But in all their records, either in verse or prose,
> There was not one laureate without a nose.[40]

Davenant, who made clear his literary dependence on Shakespeare, was as much a professional in his theatrical ventures as any man of his generation, and in his personal behavior he was as much a licentious amateur. Like Suckling and Carew, he belonged to that world which his patron in the Middle Temple, Edward Hyde, later described so vividly, a world of discharged soldiers (Davenant was one) and libertine wits. There was, Hyde writes, "never an age in which, in so short a time, so many

38. Quoted by Alfred Harbage, *Sir William Davenant: Poet Venturer, 1606–1668* (Philadelphia: Univ. of Pennsylvania Press, 1935), p. 46.

39. John Aubrey, quoted by Harbage, p. 45.

40. Suckling, I, 73. Suckling attributes Davenant's misfortune not to the Axe-yard wench but rather to an encounter in France.

young gentlemen, who had not experience in the world or some good tutelar angel to protect them, were insensibly and suddenly overwhelmed in that sea of wine, and women, and quarrels, and gaming, which almost overspread the whole kingdom, and the nobility and gentry thereof."[41] The convivial manner of that age, the manner of his generation, irresistibly invaded Davenant's verse, turning even its loftiest pretensions to genial self-mockery. As the lines separating amateur, laureate, and professional faded, so too did the possibility of sustained seriousness.

The exception to much of what I have said so far, the major anomaly in Davenant's career, is his unfinished epic, *Gondibert,* and especially its lengthy preface. Davenant himself insists on the difference. From the vantage point of *Gondibert,* he "take[s] occasion to accuse and condemn, as papers unworthy of light, all those hasty digestions of thought which were published in my youth."[42] And since the Restoration was to restore those "hasty digestions" to his favor, *Gondibert* seems particularly isolated. Written in exile and in prison at a time when the royalist defeat had closed the theaters and disrupted the system of court patronage, it and its preface undertake with far greater deliberation than Davenant elsewhere found necessary the task of laureate self-presentation. Here high style and a friendly patron are not enough. Instead, Davenant now feels he must clearly define and justify in detail his ambition of standing in the line of Homer, Virgil, Lucan, Statius, Tasso, and Spenser.

This string of names, with a paragraph of commentary on the epic poetry belonging to each, occurs in the first pages of Davenant's Preface—and not much of the commentary is favorable. Davenant wants to be one of them, but realizes that he cannot attain comparable fame by doing again what they have

41. Quoted by Nethercot, *D'avenant,* p. 67.
42. Davenant, *Gondibert,* ed. David F. Gladish (Oxford: Clarendon Press, 1971), p. 20.

already done. "Whilst we imitate others," he says, "we can no more excel them then he that sails by others' maps can make a new discovery."[43] Though he recognizes the salutary moderating effect of imitation, the way it keeps a writer from going too far wrong, his ambition allows him no such safe course. He needs some distinguishing novelty. In the choice between "coasters" and "discoverers," between those "whose satisfied wit will not venture beyond the track of others" and those "who affect a new and remote way of thinking, who esteem it a deficiency and meanness of mind to stay and depend upon the authority of example," he must be a discoverer. One may object that Davenant made most of his discoveries in books he does not name, in the heroic romances so popular in France at the very time he was writing (his address was then "the Louvre in Paris"). But clearly he felt he must claim novelty, whether he achieved it or not. And if that meant talking about Homer while writing like Scudéry, so be it.

The pretension of Davenant's strategy, and the support it got from Waller, Cowley, and Hobbes, provoked considerable mirth. "Room for the best of poets heroic," wrote one "friend,"

> If you'll believe two wits and a stoic;
> Down go the *Iliads*, down go the *Aeneidos*,
> All must give place to the *Gondiberteidos*.[44]

But Davenant's quarrel with the ancients had other motives. Conventions that had made sense in Homer's time and that, despite great changes in belief, had been imitated ever since must now, he argues, be abandoned. As a modern poet, Davenant hoped to distinguish himself by the invention of a modern poetic, one responsive to the latest advances in science and philosophy. Particularly objectionable in the older poetry is the whole superstitious paraphernalia of gods and goddesses. In place of this exploded mythology, Davenant lards his poem

43. Davenant, *Gondibert*, p. 7.   44. Davenant, *Gondibert*, p. 273.

with recently uncovered fact. Instead of being sent to heaven or hell, Gondibert is made to visit a Baconian research institute. This aspect of the poem and of Davenant's program most appealed to the two wits and the stoic. As Cowley wrote,

> Methinks heroic poesy till now,
> Like some fantastic fairyland did show;
> Gods, devils, nymphs, witches, and giants race,
> And all but man, in man's best work had place.
> Thou like some worthy knight, with sacred arms,
> Dost drive the monsters thence, and end the charms.
> Instead of those, dost men and manners plant,
> The things which that rich soil did chiefly want.[45]

And with this demythologizing of poetry went a demythologizing of the poet. No more would he, as Homer had done, interrogate "his muse, not as a rational spirit, but as a familiar, separated from his body."[46] The claim to inspiration, already under attack in Jonson's generation and now made still more suspect by its association with Puritan fanatics, is definitively rejected. Rather, Davenant follows Jonson in making hard work the sign of his laureate seriousness.

By his insistence on hard work, on "painfulness" and "slow pace," Davenant not only draws a line between himself and the ancient "ethnic" poets who had relied on inspiration. He also distinguishes himself from the amateur poets of his own generation and distinguishes *Gondibert* from his own earlier work. For it is in this context that he condemns his youthful "papers." Experience has taught him, he says with apparent reference to passages like the one I quoted from *Madagascar,* that "those must need prophesy with ill success who make use of their visions in wine. . . . Such posting upon Pegasus, I have long since forborne."[47] Furthermore, his description and rejection

---

45. Davenant, *Gondibert,* p. 270.   46. Davenant, *Gondibert,* p. 3.
47. Davenant, *Gondibert,* pp. 19–22. Other quotations in this paragraph come from the same pages.

of that form of wit particularly incident to youth describes and rejects the typical cavalier manner: "Young men . . . imagine [wit] consists in the music of words, and believe they are made wise by refining their speech above the vulgar dialect. . . . From the esteem of speaking they proceed to the admiration of what are commonly called conceits . . . and from thence . . . grow up to some force of fancy." The refinement of speech, the admiration of conceits, and the free flight of fancy, though not necessarily in the progressive order in which Davenant here places them, figure among the most obvious characteristics of cavalier poetry in general and of Davenant's own early verse in particular. In place of these qualities, he now promotes "the laborious and the lucky resultances of thought"—with much emphasis on the labor and the thought. For, he asserts, "'tis a high presumption to entertain a nation . . . with hasty provisions." To entertain and, still more, to instruct a nation was the task Davenant set himself in *Gondibert*. And "next to the usefulness of . . . ripe age," he writes, "I believed pains most requisite to this undertaking."

As further evidence of "the difficulties and greatness of such a work," Davenant cites his many "assistants," and particularly those three friends with whom he met regularly in Paris to discuss the progress of his poem, Hobbes, Waller, and Cowley. The presence of Cowley's name on this list is of special interest, both because he too was a poet of laureate ambition and because he arrived at the meeting in Paris by a significantly different career path, one that reveals another section of their shared generational terrain. In the decade of their close acquaintance, the decade that saw the composition of *Gondibert* and the revision of Cowley's *Davideis,* Davenant and Cowley had in common a considerable set of artistic and self-presentational problems, and to these we shall wish to attend. But before doing so, let us consider the particular configuration of Cowley's career. Unlike Davenant's, his laureate claim was not endorsed by a royal pension. When Jonson died and there was talk of who might succeed him as chief poet to the Stuart court, Cowley's name was not even mentioned. Though his first volume of verse had already entered its third edition, its youthful author was only just entering Cambridge. By the time he emerged with the degree of Master of Arts five years later, the bright decade of the King's personal rule was over and the Civil Wars had begun. He thus had no chance to achieve laureate standing by the ready path of patronage and promotion that had served Davenant. Like Milton, who was similarly cut off from the court in its days of easy affluence (though by religious and political conviction, rather than by age), Cowley was obliged to be more deliberate in his laureate self-presentation than Davenant had been.

Cowley's career began with the fact of precocity. But what does precocity mean? Does the mere fact of writing competent verse at an extraordinarily early age mark one off as a laureate poet? In trying to understand and communicate the sense of his life and of his literary profession, Cowley was eager to answer questions like these. The precocity itself was, of course, culturally determined. No child writes poems of any sort, much less romantic epyllia in six-line iambic stanzas, without some prompting. In an autobiographical essay written late in his life, Cowley credited the influence of Spenser. "For," he wrote,

I remember when I began to read, and to take some pleasure in it, there was wont to be in my mother's parlor ... Spenser's works; this I happened to fall upon, and was infinitely delighted with the stories of the knights, and giants, and monsters, and brave houses, which I found everywhere there (though my understanding had little to do with all this) and by degrees with the tinkling of the rime and the dance of the numbers, so that I think I had read him all over before I was twelve years old, and was thus made a poet.[48]

48. Abraham Cowley, *Essays, Plays and Sundry Verse,* ed. A.R. Waller (Cambridge: Cambridge Univ. Press, 1906), pp. 457–458.

We may, however, suppose that not even the reading of Spenser would have made Cowley a poet quite so early had the writing of verse not been a regular grammar school exercise. Westminster—the school not only of Cowley, but also of Jonson, Corbett, Herbert, Randolph, and Cartwright—put particular emphasis on such activity, and other humanist foundations were not far behind. It is thus not surprising that a sixteenth- or seventeenth-century child should produce passable verse.

What is surprising is that so much should have been made of Cowley's early efforts. Though verse making had been a part of the humanist curriculum for over a century by the time Cowley reached grammar school, poets in earlier generations had neither published their school-age poems nor drawn any particular attention to their existence. The partial exception of Spenser tends to prove the rule. A set of translations was published when he was only seventeen, but they appeared anonymously, and when, some twenty-five years later, the same poems did at last come out under his name, he made no allusion to their early composition. In marked contrast to this Elizabethan reticence, the title, frontispiece portrait, and commendatory poems in Cowley's first volume all proclaim its author's extreme youth, and, as his career proceeds, Cowley himself talks again and again of his precocious start.

In his own generation, Cowley was not, however, alone in claiming at least some measure of precocity. Just a year after the appearance of the *Poetical Blossoms,* his future friend Richard Crashaw, who was later to devote a poem to the praise of Cowley's "April-Autumn," wrote of his own "infant muse" bearing "the flowers of a tender age."[49] And, as we have noticed, Humphrey Moseley advertised the early composition of some of Cartwright's poems. But in precocity, it is Milton who most resembles Cowley. Many of the poems in Milton's 1645

49. *The Complete Poetry of Richard Crashaw,* ed. George Walton Williams (Garden City, N.Y.: Anchor Books, 1970), pp. 494–495, 628, and 630.

volume are assigned to a period before his twentieth year, some coming as early as age fifteen. In the famous autobiographical passage from *The Reason of Church Government,* he tells how in his "first years ... it was found that whether aught was imposed me by them that had the overlooking, or betaken to of mine own choice in English or other tongue, prosing and versing, but chiefly in this latter, the style, by certain vital signs it had, was likely to live" (667). To be known as having lisped in numbers, and lisped well, had for these men an evident appeal not much shared by their predecessors. Cowley's reference to the music of verse and Milton's mention of style suggest the generational basis of this appeal. Having written early was a sign of that mannerist virtuosity which characterized their generation. In this, precocity shares a place with the production and dissemination of large quantities of Latin verse. Both Milton and Cowley showed their prowess in the ancient tongue, as did Cartwright, Fane, Randolph, Crashaw, and Marvell. This too was a skill fostered by the century-old methods of humanist education, but here again earlier English poets had not made so much of it. For Sidney or Spenser, for Marlowe, Jonson, or Donne, writing gracefully and/or wittily in English had been challenge enough. And they met that challenge brilliantly. Their very accomplishment forced their successors to excel in other languages and in other ways, by extreme smoothness, extreme negligence, or extreme precocity.

Starting early does not, however, necessarily get one very far, particularly not when the goal is a laureate career. Cowley took another step with the publication of *The Mistress* in 1647. As he was later to write, this was his way of satisfying a traditional expectation. "For so it is," he explained, "that poets are scarce thought freemen of their company without paying some duties and obliging themselves to be true to love. Sooner or later they must all pass through that trial, like some Mahumetan monks, that are bound by their order once at least in their life to make a pilgrimage to Mecca."[50] This Renaissance tradition had its more narrowly generational basis as well. *The Mistress* put Cowley in the company of Waller, Suckling, and Shirley, each of whom had paid his duty to love in the preceding year or two. In promising to fix his mistress's "title next in fame / To Sacharissa's well-sung name," Cowley specifically evoked Waller, and in modeling many of his poems on Donne's, he joined the mannerist game of stylish imitation played by all three.[51] He out-Donned Donne, winning by the extravagance of his conceits that reputation as a latter-day metaphysical that has stuck with him since the late seventeenth century—the only reputation he has with most modern readers of English poetry. But in his generation this was a natural turn for him to take—natural, that is, if one accepts the definition of youthful wit that Davenant was to provide three years later in the Preface to *Gondibert*. After essaying the "music of words" in his *Poetical Blossoms,* Cowley advanced in *The Mistress* to the "admiration of conceits." And in the subsequent Pindaric odes, Davenant might have been satisfied to see him "grow up to some force of fancy"—though Cowley himself had something greater in mind.

If *The Mistress* established Cowley's credentials as a poet of the cavalier generation, it also began to distinguish him from his amateur contemporaries. Compared to the love poems of Suckling, Waller, Shirley, Habington, or Lovelace, Cowley's is a more nearly free-standing collection. The only nonfictional occasion it supposes is literary—a moment in its author's career and in the development of English poetry. Cut off from historical event ("It is not the picture of the poet, but of things and persons imagined by him," Cowley wrote),[52] it is also cut off

50. Cowley, *Poems,* p. 10.
51. Cowley, *Poems,* p. 70. James G. Taaffe discusses Cowley's imitations of Donne in *Abraham Cowley* (New York: Twayne, 1972), pp. 49–59.
52. Cowley, *Poems,* p. 10.

from his other work by a traditional gesture of closure. The final poem is entitled "Love Given Over" and begins:

> It is enough; enough of time and pain
>   Hast thou consumed in vain;
>   Leave wretched Cowley, leave
>   Thyself with shadows to deceive;
> Think that already lost which thou must never gain.[53]

And then he adds, as pendant to *The Mistress,* another poem, "The Motto," in which, having paid his duty to love, he abruptly announces his distinguishing ambition:

> What shall I do to be forever known,
>   And make the age to come my own?
> . . . What sound is't strikes mine ear?
>   Sure I Fame's trumpet hear.
> It sounds like the last trumpet, for it can
>   Raise up the buried man.
> Unpast Alps stop me, but I'll cut through all,
>   And march, the Muses' Hannibal.
> Hence, all the flattering vanities that lay
>   Nets of roses in the way.
> Hence, the desire of honors or estate,
>   And all that is not above fate.
> Hence love himself, that tyrant of my days,
>   Which intercepts my coming praise.[54]

Unlike the cavalier amateurs, Cowley intends to be more than the author of a few witty occasional poems. As the opening echo of the *Georgics* intimates and as the later invocation of "the Mantuan swan" makes explicit, his ambition is Virgilian.[55]

53. Cowley, *Poems,* p. 151.
54. Cowley, *Poems,* p. 15–16.
55. The motto of "The Motto" and the inspiration of its opening lines is a passage from the *Georgics* (3.8) whose opening words Cowley quotes. In full the relevant lines read: *Temptanda via est, qua me quoque possim / tollere humo victorque virum volitare per ora.* ("I must essay a path whereby I, too,

When in 1656 Cowley published his collected *Poems,* he moved "The Motto" to the head of the volume. Here it pointed not to what he would do, but to what he had done. *The Mistress* was still there, as the second part of a four-part book, but now it was preceded by a selection of miscellaneous poems and followed by the *Pindaric Odes* and *Davideis.* On these two works Cowley's laureate claim primarily depended.

Like *Gondibert,* Cowley's odes and epic were programmatic undertakings. As Davenant strove to rid heroic poetry of the trappings of pagan myth, so Cowley sought to reform one heroic genre and to supply another. He was the first in English to attempt a Virgilian epic on a Biblical theme and the first to write odes in "the style and manner" of Pindar.[56] And as *Gondibert's* lengthy preface eclipsed its poem (originally the preface appeared alone—"a porch to no house," one wag remarked),[57] so too Cowley's heroic compositions are shadowed by a preface and notes that together bulk larger and are more fully realized than the poems they surround. Furthermore, the poems themselves advertise the program. The odes celebrate the glory of the ode, and the epic vaunts its own reforming mission.

> Too long the Muses' Land have heathen been;
> Their gods too long were devils, and virtues sin.
> But Thou, Eternal Word, hast called forth me,
> Th' apostle, to convert that world to thee,
> T'unbind the charms that in slight fables lie,
> And teach that truth is truest poesy.[58]

---

may rise from earth and fly victorious on the lips of men"—trans. H. R. Fairclough in the Loeb edition.) Not only Virgil's expression of ambition would have attracted Cowley; the Roman poet's situation also resembled that of the belated Englishman. Virgil writes of agriculture because, he says, "other themes, which else had charmed with song some idle fancy, are now all trite."

56. Cowley, *Poems,* p. 153.   57. Davenant, *Gondibert,* p. 273.
58. Cowley, *Poems,* p. 243.

Obviously Cowley felt, as Davenant had, the difficulty of making a place for himself as a laureate poet in a belated generation. Simply to demonstrate his self-justifying novelty cost him an extraordinary effort.[59] For Spenser and Jonson, writing the poem had still been the first job. Compared to the programmatic statements of Davenant and Cowley, Spenser's letter to Raleigh and Jonson's preface to *Volpone* seem casual afterthoughts. The energy in them falls far short, as one supposes it should, of that in the works they introduce. With Davenant and Cowley, it is the other way around. Their programmatic intentions were expressed with more imaginative vigor than their poems and have, as a result, figured more prominently in the history of English literature. Cowley himself came eventually to see that this was the most he could expect. Of the abandoned *Davideis* he wrote, "I shall be ambitious of no other fruit from this weak and imperfect attempt of mine, but the opening of a way to the courage of industry of some other persons, who may be better able to perform it thoroughly and successfully."[60] We, of course, think of Milton.

Cowley's disappointed reassessment of his hopes for the *Davideis* concludes the Preface to his 1656 *Poems*. Something of the same note of defeat dominates his presentation of the whole volume and of himself. The ambitions so boldly set forth

59. Cowley makes the need for novelty part of his defense of the Biblical epic. Of themes from classical literature and mythology, he writes: "Were there never so wholesome nourishment to be had (but, alas, it breeds nothing but diseases) out of these boasted feasts of love and fables, yet, methinks, the unalterable continuance of the diet should make us nauseate it. For it is almost impossible to serve up any new dish of that kind. They are all but the cold meats of the ancients new-heated and new set forth. I do not at all wonder that the old poets made some rich crops out of these grounds. The heart of the soil was not then wrought out with continual tillage. But what can we expect now, who come a gleaning, not after the first reapers, but after the very beggars" (*Poems,* p. 13).

60. Cowley, *Poems,* p. 14.

in "The Motto," the ambitions with which his various poetic ventures began, have not been realized. His precocity gave rise to unfulfillable expectations. He now sees his schoolboy poems "as promises and instruments under my own hand, whereby I stood engaged for more than I have been able to perform."[61] So much are they a reproach to him that he omits them from this collection. Also omitted is *The Civil War,* which had gotten "as far as the first battle of Newbury, where the succeeding misfortunes of the party stopped the work."[62] Cowley's defeat thus derives in part from the King's. But even the *Davideis,* which he does include and into which he worked the *dejecta membra* of *The Civil War,* remains uncompleted.[63] He has, Cowley admits, no "appetite at present to finish the work or so much as to revise that part which is done." And of the *Pindaric Odes,* he confesses himself "in great doubt whether they will be understood by most readers."[64] The collection as a whole he publishes as his "posthumous" works. Though the man is not yet dead, the poet is. "For to make myself absolutely dead in a poetical capacity, my resolution at present is never to exercise anymore that faculty."[65] Instead he plans to retire "to some of our American plantations," where, he feels assured, poetry will be as out of place as "Doctor Donne's sun dial in a grave."[66]

Cowley did not go to America, nor did he stop writing poetry. But the *Poems* of 1656 do mark the death of his Virgilian ambition. In retrospect, *Davideis* seems as much an anomaly in his career as the also unfinished *Gondibert* does in Davenant's. The laureate ideal, as Cowley and Davenant understood it, demanded such works of them, but neither the literary nor the political situation of their generation seemed to permit their achievement. Even before the Restoration, Davenant

61. Cowley, *Poems,* p. 9.   62. Cowley, *Poems,* p. 9.
63. Allan Pritchard discusses the relation of the two poems in his introduction to *The Civil War* (Toronto: Univ. of Toronto Press, 1973), pp. 52–54.
64. Cowley, *Poems,* p. 10.   65. Cowley, *Poems,* p. 6.
66. Cowley, *Poems,* p. 8.

abandoned his epic plans and returned to the more comfortable role of professional dramatist, stage manager, and court poet. And Cowley too made a return. He returned to the early signs of his literary vocation and discovered in them a new meaning. He was destined to write not of love and war, as he had mistakenly supposed ("Not sedulous by Nature to indite/ Wars," Milton was to say of himself at about the same point in his career), but rather of that very alienation from "wealth, honor, pleasures, all the world" that came of his literary precocity. His calling set him apart, made him a eunuch for poetry. Now that isolation becomes his subject.

In the last and perhaps the most attractive of his works, his *Essays in Verse and Prose,* Cowley looks back over his career and finds in it repeated pointers toward the solitary, retired life, toward the "small house and large garden" that even in *The Mistress* he had longed for.[67] As evidence "that I was then of the same mind as I am now (which, I confess, I wonder at myself)," he quotes verses he made when he was only thirteen, verses very different in tone from the conquering ambition of the Muses' erstwhile Hannibal:

> This only grant me, that my means may lie
> Too low for envy, for contempt too high.[68]

And in the light of this newly recovered sense of himself, even his special mastery of the ode takes on new meaning. It now seems a sign less of his poetic elevation than of his freedom.

> If life should a well-ordered poem be
>   (In which he only hits the white
> Who joins true profit with the best delight)
> The more heroic strain let others take,
>   Mine the Pindaric way I'll make.
> The matter shall be grave, the numbers loose and free.[69]

67. Cowley, *Poems,* p. 88, and *Essays,* p. 420.
68. Cowley, *Essays,* p. 456.   69. Cowley, *Essays,* p. 391.

Liberty, solitude, obscurity, and the country life are his themes now. In talking of them he presents the essential meaning of his poetic career. If he remains a laureate—and his reference to life as a well-ordered poem suggests that he does—it must be in terms of these largely Horatian values.

Had Cowley considered not only his own early poems but also the verse of his cavalier contemporaries, he would have found generational as well as personal support for his retirement. As a recent student of Waller has remarked, "the poems of the Cavaliers express an intellectual quietism, a recurrent emphasis on retreat, on rejection, on limitation and exclusion."[70] Carew's refusal to write of heroic subjects provided one early symptom of this tendency, and the sustained cavalier devotion to the "good life," as found in the society of a few friends or in the domesticated nature of a garden retreat, confirmed it.[71] Even the heroic *Gondibert* sets retiredness, figured in its protagonist's love for the simple country girl, Birtha, against, and perhaps above, military and political power, represented by Princess Rhodalind's love for him. And Davenant himself, though one of the least retiring of the cavaliers, could write of the attraction "all the silent privacies of rest" held for him.[72] Still more evident in poets like Fane, Randolph, Habington, and Waller, this love of what Fane called "Blest privacy! Happy retreat!" becomes central in the work of Cowley's immediate contemporaries, the poets who came of age only as the Civil War began.[73] Cowley, Lovelace, Vaughan,

70. Warren L. Chernaik, *The Poetry of Limitation: A Study of Edmund Waller* (New Haven: Yale Univ. Press, 1968), p. 61. Chernaik goes on to say of the cavaliers that "they are constantly drawing magic circles that will shut the world out, seeking to find an autonomous realm of love and art, a court immune to change." This autonomy is not, however, specifically literary.

71. See Earl Miner's discussion of the "good life" in *The Cavalier Mode*, pp. 43–99.

72. Davenant, *Shorter Poems*, p. 35.

73. Mildmay Fane, *Otia Sacra* (1648), sig. B1ᵛ.

and Marvell are alike in this, if in nothing else: much of their best verse celebrates a private withdrawal from the tumult of their age.

According to Thomas Sprat, the founders of the Royal Society were first brought together by a similar desire for quiet, by "the security and ease of a retirement amongst gown-men."[74] The enthusiasm for natural philosophy that made those meetings so fruitful was shared by many of the poets. In Randolph its bases are still Aristotelian, but, nevertheless, his "Eclogue to Master Jonson" presents the study of nature, enjoyed in pastoral retirement, as the answer to Jonson's question, "What is't can move/Thy mind once fixed on the Muses' love?"[75] Fane, more in tune with the Baconian spirit of the Royal Society, leaves Aristotle unopened and concentrates instead "on nature's book." In "To Retiredness," he imagines himself, removed from "fears or noise of war," observing

> by reason
> Why every plant obeys its season;
> How the sap rises, and the fall
> Wherein they shake off leaves and all;
> Then how again they bud and spring,
> Are laden for an offering.[76]

Other poets' interest found expression in a still more formal adhesion to the new science and a more deliberate advocacy of its advancement. Cowley and Denham were among the early members of the Royal Society, and Waller sat on a Society committee "for improving the English tongue." After humanism, government service, overseas exploration, poetry, and politico-religious controversy, natural philosophy was in its turn becoming the most dynamic area of cultural expansion.

74. Thomas Sprat, *History of the Royal Society*, ed. Jackson I. Cope and Harold Whitmore Jones (Saint Louis, Missouri: Washington Univ. Studies, 1958), p. 53.
75. Randolph, II, 609.   76. Fane, sig. Y3^v.

Cowley's involvement was particularly intense. In 1661 he issued a detailed proposal for the foundation of a college devoted to "the advancement of experimental philosphy," and already in the *Davideis* he had presented a fictional image of such a college—an image that finds its likeness not only in Bacon's *New Atlantis* but also in *Gondibert*. Like the Prophets' College, where David takes refuge from the anger of Saul, Davenant's House of Astragon is both a place of retreat and a center for scientific research. But on Davenant experimental philosophy exercised a merely transitory hold. Its place in Cowley's work and in his literary self-presentation never ceased to increase, until toward the end of his life he became the Poet of Natural Philosophy in much the way that earlier laureates had been the King's Poet. Where Spenser and Jonson had found the divine order mirrored in the monarch, Cowley finds it rather in the order of nature, as that order was being revealed by scientific investigation. In his work, odes to Hobbes, Harvey, and the Royal Society take the place of panegyrics on Elizabeth or James. He could thus reconcile his retirement and his laureate calling. "He withdrew himself out of the crowd," Sprat wrote,

with desires of enlightening and instructing the minds of those who remained in it. It was his resolution in that station to search into the secrets of divine and humane knowledge, and to communicate what he should observe. He always professed that he went out of the world as it was man's, into the same world as it was nature's and as it was God's. The whole compass of the creation and all the wonderful effects of the divine wisdom were the constant prospect of his senses and his thoughts. And, indeed, he entered with great advantage on the studies of nature, even as the first great men of antiquity did, who were generally both poets and philosophers. He betook himself to its contemplation as well furnished with sound judgment and diligent observation and good method to discover its mysteries as with abilities to set it forth in all its ornaments.[77]

77. Quoted by Taaffe, p. 114.

As the program of the *Davideis* had been, in the words of the hostile but accurate Meric Casaubon, to "exclude ancient mythology" and "erect a new kind of poetry, grounded upon the scriptures," so Cowley's program in his later work is to ground the new poetry on "knowledge of nature and experiments."[78]

But when one puts this program into effect, what becomes of the poet? What can he do that the scientist can't? What independent authority has he? Here in still another guise is the central problem of Cowley's generation, the problem of literary autonomy. If the poet accepts, as Cowley does, the superiority of this new scientific truth based on observation and experiment, his art retains no autonomous epistemological function. If he no longer pretends to create worlds transcending this but rather reports on the material facts of this world, on "things, the mind's right object,"[79] he has no way of distinguishing himself from the experimentalist. These difficulties seem not to have worried Sprat. For him it was enough that the ancient philosophers were also poets. The rhetorical skill of the one complements the judgment, observation, and method of the other. Yet Sprat's own theory of language leaves little place even for the art of ornamentation to which he reduces poetry. A language fit for science should, he argues, be strictly denotative, delivering "so many things almost in an equal number of words, . . . bringing all things so near the mathematical plainness as they can."[80] Could this be a language of poetry?

Cowley sensed the conflict. Philosophy, he wrote in his ode "To the Royal Society," a poem that prefaced and puffed Sprat's *History,* had for centuries been kept from full possession of the knowledge rightfully his by jealous guardians.

78. Robert B. Hinman, *Abraham Cowley's World of Order* (Cambridge: Harvard Univ. Press, 1960), p. 142. Hinman's is the most thorough discussion of Cowley's use of the New Science in his poetry.

79. Cowley, *Poems,* p. 450.

80. Sprat, p. 113.

That his own business he might quite forget,
They amused him with the sport of wanton wit;
With the desserts of poetry they fed him,
Instead of solid meats t'increase his force;
Instead of vigorous exercise, they led him
Into the pleasant labyrinths of ever fresh discourse;
    Instead of carrying him to see
The riches which do hoarded for him lie
    In nature's endless treasury,
    They chose his eye to entertain
    (His curious but not covetous eye)
With painted scenes, and pageants of the brain.[81]

"Sports of wanton wit," "painted scenes," "pageants of the brain"—it all sounds suspiciously like the poetry of Cowley's own generation, the poetry of the Caroline court. But could this poetry or any other be now turned to the service of that very science it had so long abused? Cowley, lacking other subjects worthy his laureate ambition, felt compelled to answer "yes." The testimony of his poems nevertheless gives reason for doubt. As natural philosopher, the poet of the 1660s had no greater autonomy than the poet of the 1630s had enjoyed as stylish ornamentor of court and society. On the contrary, his predicament remained largely unchanged. The substance of his discourse, and thus of his self-presentation, belonged to another realm.

Toward the end of his *Proposition for the Advancement of Experimental Philosophy,* Cowley describes a textbook he would like to see put together for his philosophical college. "Because the truth is we want good poets (I mean we have but few) who have purposely treated solid and learned, that is, natural matters (the most part indulging the weakness of the world, and feeding it either with the follies of love or with the fables of gods and heroes), we conceive that one book ought to

81. Cowley, *Poems,* p. 448.

be compiled of all the scattered little parcels among the ancient poets that might serve for the advancement of natural science, and which would make no small or unuseful or unpleasant volume."[82] Such a volume does now exist. The excerpted authors are English and the focus is less exclusively scientific than Cowley wished, but it does contain many poems on natural phenomena—poems on liquidity and azotic gas, on the habits of elephants, moles, lizards, and lampreys, on gastric indigestion and the economy of vegetation. It is called *The Stuffed Owl,* and, as its title suggests, its editors' purpose was not to advance science.

Assembled in 1930 by D. B. Wyndham Lewis and Charles Lee, *The Stuffed Owl* is an anthology of comically bad verse. But for us it has an interest that goes beyond its humorous intent. For the first author to appear in this chronologically ordered volume—"the first," the editors concluded after some fairly extensive hunting, "to be bad comically"—is none other than Cowley himself.[83] How did he get there? In the opinion of Hugh Kenner, the novel preeminence of fact in the later seventeenth century explains his presence—the preeminence of fact coupled with the desire to write poetically.[84] Cowley heads *The Stuffed Owl* precisely because he sought to be the laureate poet of science, because he sought to be serious in the wrong way about the wrong thing. His presence is laughter's revenge. What makes the passage Lewis and Lee quote from Cowley's "Ode upon Dr. Harvey" ridiculous, Kenner explains, "is the rhetoric of the Grand Style. For verse is supposed to present prose sense with a heightened decorum. . . . It requires that the poet climb onto a pedestal, so that we can tell he is writing

82. Cowley, *Essays,* p. 256.
83. *The Stuffed Owl,* ed. D. B. Wyndham Lewis and Charles Lee (London: J. M. Dent, 1930), p. xix.
84. Hugh Kenner, *The Counterfeiters: An Historical Comedy* (Bloomington: Indiana Univ. Press, 1968), p. 60.

poetry. That is what comes of the Restoration emphasis on clarity; it leaves nothing whatever for the poet to do but strike a bardic posture and elevate his language."[85] English poets prior to Cowley were relatively immune to this failing. They could be dull or turgid, but they were not often bathetic. Beginning with Cowley's generation, bathos became a constant danger. In *Gondibert,* Davenant topples repeatedly, and even Milton ("No fear lest dinner cool"—*Paradise Lost,* V, 396) can slip.

Striking a bardic posture and elevating his language are just the faults many earlier twentieth-century critics found in Milton. And though their accusations have been effectively answered, one can nevertheless see that Milton (or Cowley, or Davenant) makes a more likely target than would Spenser, Sidney, Jonson, or Donne. What the earlier poets wanted to say required poetry. It took no effort for them to be poetical. They were thus unlikely to discover inadvertently what Pope later called "the Art of Sinking in Poetry." So long as poetry retained its autonomy, they were safe. But when prose sense replaced mythopoetic vision as the mark of seriousness, then the poet, "soaring in the high region of his fancies with his garland and singing robes about him" (667), risked a funny fall.

For Davenant and Cowley, the risk was too great. Unlike Milton, they are at their best when they soar least, when they descend to chatty, informal poems or to the still lower element of prose. But without soaring, they could hardly achieve the laureate distinction they sought. Davenant's ambition was the more easily satisfied. A pension, a job, and a quasi-official title took the pressure from his self-presentation. Cowley aimed higher and worked harder. His efforts were, however, only marginally more successful. Perhaps even in an earlier generation, neither would have been a great poet. But they would have been bad in quite other ways. For the difficulties they encoun-

85. Kenner, p. 53.

tered, difficulties that profoundly shape their work, were as much a function of their time as of their talent.

Opening the Way to Paradise Lost

How to be a laureate poet in a belated literary generation, in a generation distracted first by an artificial peace and then by civil war, in a generation whose most concerted efforts were devoted to politics, religion, and natural philosophy? This was the problem that confronted not only Davenant and Cowley, but also Milton. In discussions of Milton we do not, however, hear much of it. So complete was his success in transcending the difficulties inherent in his temporal location that any possible likeness he may have to the other writers of his generation is regularly ignored. Born five years after the death of Elizabeth, nearly ten years after the death of Spenser, and twenty-two after that of Sidney, Milton still figures in our histories and in our imaginations as "the last Elizabethan."

The magnitude of Milton's accomplishment has made him appear an anachronism among his literary coevals. If he must be assigned to any time, it should, we instinctively feel, be to an age greater than his own. Even students of the cavaliers back off from an attempt to locate Milton by likeness. Instead they apologetically contrast their time-bound subjects with their timeless coeval. Cowley, writes one, "as a man of his own age rather than of all time, may be taken to reflect contemporary sentiments more closely than Milton," and Davenant, in the view of another, "was not, like Milton, a plant strong enough to thrive in any soil, and that he wrote during a period of spiritual and artistic exhaustion is apparent in his works."[86] On the

---

86. Basil Willey, *The Seventeenth Century Background* (1934; rpt. London: Chatto & Windus, 1950), p. 229, and Harbage, p. 287.

other side, the Miltonists neglect even to notice the difference. For them Milton belongs either alone or with his peers—with Homer and Virgil, with the authors of the Pentateuch and the Book of Job, with Plato and Saint Augustine, with Dante and Tasso, with Spenser, Blake, Shelley, and Yeats. We often hear that Milton thought Spenser a better teacher than Scotus or Aquinas, but how often are we reminded that Cowley was one of his three favorite English poets? In a large book on *Milton's Literary Milieu*, G. W. Whiting found place for only one passing reference to Cowley and another, scarcely more substantial, to Davenant. For the rest of Milton's literary coevals, he found no place at all.[87] At about the same time, E. M. W. Tillyard was arguing against the notion of Milton's isolation from "what his English colleagues thought and did," but even Tillyard gave far more attention to such distant "colleagues" as Spenser, Daniel, Drayton, Heywood, Phineas Fletcher, and William Browne than to any cavalier.[88]

In the forty years since Tillyard wrote, literary historians have refused even his modest lead—as two recent compendia suggest. Don M. Wolfe's handsome picture book, *Milton and His England,* shows many soldiers, statesmen, scholars, and divines, but not one poet closer in age to Milton than Andrew Marvell and none at all other than Marvell.[89] One wonders: Were Dr. John Bastwick, Algernon Sidney, and Prince Rupert really so much more important to the author of *Paradise Lost* than Cowley or Davenant? The massive *Milton Encyclopedia,* a work which prides itself on being "a study of English civilization in Milton's time," surely does nothing to strengthen the

87. George Wesley Whiting, *Milton's Literary Milieu* (Chapel Hill: Univ. of North Carolina Press, 1939).

88. E. M. W. Tillyard, *The Miltonic Setting: Past & Present* (Cambridge: Cambridge Univ. Press, 1938), p. 168.

89. Don M. Wolfe, *Milton and His England* (Princeton: Princeton Univ. Press, 1971).

claim of the poets.[90] Its eight volumes include entries for no cavalier other than Cowley and Davenant and allow them together no more space than a relatively minor Elizabethan like Sir Walter Raleigh has all to himself. The Fletchers get twice as much and Sidney even more. Again one wonders: Wouldn't there have been room between Clement of Alexandria and Georgius Codius for John Cleveland, who was Milton's contemporary at Christ's College and whose first published poem appeared in the same volume as *Lycidas*? Obviously the editors thought not, and their choice faithfully reflects the practice of the profession. Whether scholars discuss Milton's literary relations and move away from the mid-seventeenth century or his relation to his own time and move away from literature, the result is the same. They ignore the cavaliers.

In one respect this neglect is certainly justified. Milton himself had little to do with the other poets of his generation and said even less of them. The remark about Spenser's qualities as teacher occurs in *Areopagitica* as an explicit profession of Milton's respect for his "sage and serious" predecessor (728). But we learn of his taste for Cowley only indirectly, through the report of his widow, Elizabeth Minshull.[91] And if Milton rarely referred to any of the cavaliers (never by name), they were equally silent about him. On the basis of commendatory poems alone, we can draw lines connecting, directly or indirectly, virtually all the cavalier poets, and, if we add other poems and nonliterary documents, we end with as tightly woven a net of personal relations as one could produce for any Renaissance generation. Milton stands outside that network. He was, in his immediate relations with his literary coevals, the most isolated English poet of any significance in the sixteenth or seventeenth

90. *A Milton Encyclopedia,* ed. William B. Hunter, Jr., 8 vols. (Lewisburg, Pa.: Bucknell Univ. Press, 1978–1980), I, 5.

91. Mentioned by William Riley Parker, *Milton: A Biography,* 2 vols. (Oxford: Clarendon Press, 1968), I, 584.

centuries—one of the most isolated in English literary history. And that isolation, already marked in the 1620s and 1630s, was later made still more absolute by differences in politics and religion. If, as Christopher Hill has recently proposed (to the general scepticism of reviewers), Milton was more "clubbable than is often thought," the cavalier poets were clearly not members of his club.[92]

But perhaps he regarded with attention the proceedings of theirs. At least one striking coincidence would seem to suggest as much. Less than two years after Cowley published his unfinished *Davideis* with the hope that it might open "a way to the courage of other persons . . . better able" to give England a Virgilian epic on a Biblical theme, Milton took up *Paradise Lost,* transforming his originally projected tragedy into a classical epic, an epic that resembles the *Davideis* more closely than it does any previous English poem. Not only do Milton's revised intentions correspond closely to the program Cowley defined, but his poem follows Cowley's in moving from invocation, to Hell, to Heaven, and thence to earth. Furthermore, *Paradise Lost* contains at least a sprinkling of more specific borrowings from the *Davideis.* A modern biographer of Cowley lists as examples "the digression on the fatal qualities of gold, the sonorous use of proper names, the description of the division of labor in building Pandemonium, and the picture of Satan and his staff, 'Which Nature meant some tall ship's mast to be' (in Cowley's phrase)."[93] At certain moments, Milton seems even to suppose that his readers will catch the echo—as, for example, when he invokes

92. Hill, *Milton and the English Revolution,* p. 9. Though his main interest is in political and religious controversy, Hill refers more often to the other poets of Milton's generation than does almost any literary critic that I am aware of.

93. Arthur H. Nethercot, *Abraham Cowley: The Muse's Hannibal* (1931; rpt. New York: Russell, 1967), p. 52. At least one of the items on Nethercot's list, "the sonorous use of proper names," could easily have come from many other sources, including the Bible itself.

> Thou O Spirit, that dost prefer
> Before all Temples th' upright heart and pure. (212)

At precisely the same point in the *Davideis,* Cowley had assured the deity whose inspiration he invoked

> Lo, this great work, a temple to thy praise,
> On polished pillars of strong verse I raise.
> A temple, where if thou vouchsafe to dwell,
> It Solomon's and Herod's shall excell.[94]

Read after Cowley's, Milton's lines seem both an imitation and a correction. As Cowley's temple excels those of Solomon and Herod, so Milton's excels both theirs and Cowley's too.

The inward turn—the turn toward "th' upright heart and pure"—that Milton gives his self-presentation and the presentation of his poem depends in part on his literary isolation. That grandly imposing solitariness figured among the most persistent and most powerful signs of Milton's laureate transcendence. His isolation allowed him to sing "high and aloof," as neither Jonson nor his cavalier "sons" ever quite managed to do. The very sensitivity to social interaction that so distinguishes Jonsonian and cavalier verse forbids the laureate his lonely eminence. We noticed the limitation in the witty couplets of Davenant's *Madagascar,* and one feels it again in the couplets of the *Davideis.* As Waller anticipated and as Pope so consummately realized, the heroic couplet itself puts the poet in the company of other men. Perhaps that is why Milton vigorously rejected "the troublesome and modern bondage of riming" (210).[95] But though Milton avoided the other poets of his

94. Cowley, *Poems,* p. 243.
95. On the couplet and Milton's rejection of it, see Lorna Sage, "Milton in Literary History," in *John Milton: Introductions,* ed. J. B. Broadbent (Cambridge: Cambridge Univ. Press, 1973), pp. 299–302. Sage is one of the very few critics to have considered Milton in conjunction with his literary coevals. Though I disagree with her conclusion that *Paradise Lost* had no "working relationship to current poetic idiom," I have found her essay helpful and suggestive.

generation and rejected the verse form they convivially cultivated, he did not, as we are beginning to see, necessarily remain
unaffected by what they were doing.

If, however, Cowley opened Milton's way back to *Paradise
Lost,* he did not do so alone. The project of a Biblical epic had
deep roots in England and abroad, roots that have been traced
by numerous scholars.[96] What the scholars have less often noticed is that there was in Milton's own generation, and particularly in the years immediately prior to his renewal of work on
Paradise Lost, a widespread programmatic interest in the long
poem. Davenant's Preface to *Gondibert* appeared in 1650 and
a year later the first books of the poem itself came out, followed
in 1652 by Benlowes' *Theophila,* in 1655 by Fanshawe's translation of *The Lusiads,* and in 1656 by the *Davideis*—each of
which, like *Gondibert,* came accompanied by an extensive
prefatory statement of literary purpose.[97] Those statements
may in fact outweigh the significance of the poems they introduce, the more so because they find their collective fulfillment
not in the relatively feeble poetic performances of Davenant,
Benlowes, Fanshawe, and Cowley, but rather in *Paradise Lost*
itself. Milton's poem achieves the formal union of drama and

96. See, in particular, Tillyard, *Setting,* pp. 141–204; Grant McColley,
"Paradise Lost": An Account of Its Growth and Major Origins (1940; rpt.
New York: Russell, 1963), chs. 1–8; J. B. Broadbent, *Some Graver Subject: An
Essay on "Paradise Lost"* (London: Chatto, 1960), pp. 15–24; and Barbara
Kiefer Lewalski, *Milton's Brief Epic: The Genre, Meaning, and Art of "Para-
dise Regained"* (Providence, R.I.: Brown Univ. Press, 1966), pp. 3–129.

97. A further sign of the cavalier enthusiasm for the epic was the publication
in 1656 of Denham's translation of the second book of the *Aeneid* and in 1658
of Waller and Sidney Godolphin's version of Book IV. Though both were
written earlier (as, for that matter, was much of the *Davideis* and of
Theophila), their appearance in the 1650s swelled the tide of the cavalier epic.
Furthermore, these poets (with the exception of Godolphin who died in 1643)
maintained their interest in the epic into the 1650s. Waller was among the most
prominent defenders of *Gondibert*; Denham, among its most conspicuous
detractors.

epic sought by Davenant, the visionary exaltation desired by Benlowes, the "ebullition of . . . prophetic truths" in the context of a poem responsive to history as defined by Fanshawe, and the Biblical subject of Cowley.[98] "Man is thy theme," Waller said to Davenant (with Cowley echoing the commendation), and Milton announced his theme to be "Man's first disobedience."[99] "A hallowed poet's muse is the holy dove," Benlowes proclaimed, and Milton invoked a muse that "from the first . . . dovelike satst brooding on the vast abyss."[100] Davenant and Cowley alike stressed the importance for poetry of the New Science, and Milton consecrated a large part of one book to an exposition of the two world systems—a book that ends by raising questions from the old science about the physical nature of angels very like those that fascinated Benlowes. *The Lusiads* proved its commitment to history with a concluding vision of Portuguese conquest, and Milton (drawing on the

---

98. On Milton's use of Davenant and his idea of a five-act epic, see Arthur E. Barker, "Structural Pattern in *Paradise Lost*," *PQ*, 28 (1949), 17–30. Louis Martz has argued that the ten-book structure of *Paradise Lost* reflects rather the influence of Camoens. See Martz's *Poet of Exile: A Study of Milton's Poetry* (New Haven: Yale Univ. Press, 1980), pp. 158–160. I see no need to decide between the two. Both were part of the text milieu in which *Paradise Lost* was written and both may have contributed to Milton's initial choice of a ten-book division. For Edward Benlowes, see *Minor Poets of the Caroline Period*, ed. George Saintsbury, 3 vols. (Oxford: Clarendon Press, 1905), I, 315 *et passim*. For Sir Richard Fanshawe, see *The Lusiads*, ed. Geoffrey Bullough (Carbondale: Southern Illinois Univ. Press, 1963), p. 37.

99. Davenant, *Gondibert*, pp. 269 and 270. Milton stresses the word *man* not only at the beginning of *Paradise Lost* but also in the opening lines of *Paradise Regained*:

> I who erewhile the happy garden sung,
> By one man's disobedience lost, now sing
> Recovered paradise to all mankind,
> By one man's firm obedience fully tried.

Paradise Lost echoes the *Odyssey* and the *Aeneid*; *Paradise Regained*, Romans 5.19. But both respond as well to the literary program defined by Davenant, Waller, Cowley, and Hobbes.

100. Benlowes, I, 334. In Benlowes' Latin, "hallowed poet" becomes *vates*.

language of Camoens) concluded *Paradise Lost* with a strikingly similar vision of Biblical history.[101] There may be some truth (though less than is usually supposed) in the familiar claim that *Paradise Lost* was a glorious anachronism, that at the time of its appearance there existed in England no audience prepared to receive it. But if so, that is only because by 1667 Milton's own generation had largely passed from the scene. Coming after *Gondibert, Theophila, The Lusiads,* and the *Davideis, Paradise Lost* was clearly not *written* in a vacuum.

Not since the generation of Spenser, Sidney, Warner, Chapman, Daniel, and Drayton had any group of English poets manifested so decided an ambition to write heroic poetry as the cavaliers. But where the Elizabethans had been prompted by political settlement and military success, the later poets seem to have been moved rather by defeat. Louis Martz has recently called Milton a "poet of exile."[102] The phrase might equally be applied to Davenant, Cowley, Benlowes, and Fanshawe. The fall of Charles I made political exiles of them all, as the fall of the Cromwellian regime was later to make an exile of Milton. And it was during their period of exile that they produced their heroic poems. The Preface to *Gondibert* and most of the poem were written in Paris, where the *Davideis* was revised and extended. *Theophila* came from a royalist captain of horse living in a county held by parliamentary forces, and the English *Lusiads* from a royalist diplomat confined to his patron's estate by order of the interregnum council. Furthermore, each of the authors alludes, whether in a preface or in his poem itself, to the defeat of the cause he had supported and to his own alienation. Defeat and alienation were, one comes to feel, necessary conditions for the cavalier outpouring of heroic verse.

101. Martz discusses the relation of the two passages in *Poet of Exile,* pp. 155–168.
102. Martz, *Poet of Exile,* pp. 79–94.

More than seventy years earlier, in the work that in England initiated the laureate enterprise, Spenser had lamented poetry's failure to find a secure place at court. According to *The Shepheardes Calender,* the age lacked the Augustus and the Maecenus needed to countenance and sustain a modern Virgil. Moved by this disappointing realization, Piers exclaims,

> O pierlesse Poesye, where is then thy place?
> If not in Princes pallace thou doe sitt:
> (And yet is Princes pallace the most fitt)
> Ne brest of baser birth doth thee embrace.
> Then make thee winges of thine aspyring wit,
> And, whence thou camst, flye backe to heaven apace.[103]

Clearly, Spenser intends the suggestion that poetry fly back to heaven as a counsel of despair. Laureate poetry, in his view, belongs at court where it can contribute to the fashioning of an ideal community, and the laureate poet belongs at the side of the monarch. That is precisely where both Spenser and Jonson strove to place themselves. But though both enjoyed a considerable measure of success, neither found the position very satisfying. Spenser, as we have seen, ended his career by taking that flight back to heaven, by withdrawing into the world of his own inspired imagination, and Jonson ended his in self-righteous anger at the world of power that neglected him and in pitiful self-depreciation. If Davenant, Jonson's successor as King's Poet, suffered less disappointment, it was because he expected so much less. Already in the cavalier generation the laureate ideal had slid far down the ramp toward those birthday odes that in the eighteenth century were to disgrace it forever. Both Jonson and Davenant wrote such poems, and both knew, Jonson most acutely, that in doing so they degraded the high office

103. "October," lines 79–84, in *The Works of Edmund Spenser: A Variorum Edition,* ed. Edwin Greenlaw, C. G. Osgood, et al., 11 vols. (Baltimore: Johns Hopkins Univ. Press, 1932–1957), VII, 98.

to which they had been called. The very idea of a laureate poet harbored a contradiction that the passage of time made increasingly conspicuous. Yes, the laureate belonged by the monarch. But when placed there, he and his work seemed inevitably to decline toward mendacious flattery and triviality. Perhaps the true laureate could only be a poet of alienation and exile.

This momentous revelation, the reversal of a seventeen-hundred-year-old idea, was slow in coming and has never been fully accepted. We still dream of an ideal union of imagination and power. We are still moved by the image of poet and ruler together, by Tennyson reading to Victoria or Frost to Kennedy. But with the careers of Milton, Pope, Blake, and the early Wordsworth behind us, we can more easily conceive of the great writer as a figure of opposition, as "another government" in Solzhenitsyn's phrase, than could men for whom Virgil remained *the* Poet.[104] The shock of civil war and the King's execution gave the cavaliers a first glimpse of another possibility. Defeat made them exiles, and in their exile they found their poetry assuming a new seriousness and dignity. So, in a commendatory poem he wrote from the Tower for Benlowes' *Theophila,* Davenant sets poetic elevation—the very quality that he, as aspiring laureate, had most eagerly sought—against association with the court.

> Till now I guessed but blindly to what height
> The Muses' eagles could maintain their flight!
> Though poets are, like eaglets, bred to soar,
> Gazing through stars at heaven's mysterious power,
> Yet I observe they quickly stoop to ease
> Their wings, and perch on palace-pinnacles.

104. The literary tradition inherited by the English Renaissance did include at least two great poets of exile: Ovid and Dante. Neither seems, however, to have contributed much to the English idea of a laureate career. Ovid was seen rather as a prototypical amateur and Dante was largely ignored.

From thence more usefully they courts discern,
The schools where greatness does disguises learn.[105]

Where Spenser had thought princes' palaces most fit for soaring poetry, Davenant begins to see that those very palaces tempt poetry down from its most exalted flight. The clarity of this insight is, however, lost as Davenant's poem proceeds, just as the insight itself was lost to Davenant himself and to the other surviving cavalier poets with the restoration of Charles II. As we have already noticed in our examination of the careers of Davenant and Cowley, the moment of heroic poetry quickly passed. But not for their great Puritan coeval, whose political exile was sealed by the same Restoration that drew the cavaliers back into the courtly orbit.

Like his predecessors and his contemporaries, Milton initially conceived of the laureate not as an exile but as a poet of established power. Though the breach that first opened between king and parliament just as he was coming of age may have kept Milton from ever imagining himself as the King's Poet, he did think of himself as the destined laureate of the English nation. His great poem, whether devoted to Arthur or to some other "king or knight before the conquest" (668), was to have expressed and extended the glory of England as the *Aeneid* had done for Rome. And by its subject it would, whatever Milton felt about Charles, almost inevitably have had a royalist bent.[106] From the first Milton considered himself a divine poet, yet he saw no necessary opposition between God's ordinance and the order of the state. On the contrary, he, like Spenser and Jonson before him, saw the great poet as at once God's spokesman and the spokesman of national power. Nor

105. Davenant, *Shorter Poems,* p. 177.
106. See Malcolm Ross's discussion of Milton's early epic plans in *Milton's Royalism* (Ithaca: Cornell Univ. Press, 1943), pp. 50–57.

did his increasing alienation from the established church and the royal government radically change that understanding. It simply meant that before he could assume his destined role there would have to be a new church and a new government. Whatever kinship Milton may have felt with the Hebrew prophets—those voices crying out in the wilderness against the sins of the chosen people—he continued until the final collapse of the Puritan Commonwealth to work for a state in which God's poet would be a figure neither of exile nor of opposition. His ideal thus remained the Virgilian one he shared with poets of laureate ambition from Petrarch to Davenant. It was this ideal, and the manifest impossibility of its accomplishment in the England of Charles I, that for so long kept Milton from proceeding in the literary career to which he felt himself called. And it was this ideal that made him mistake his *Defense of the English People* for the great work that as laureate he was destined to write. Church-outed by prelates, Milton was laureate-outed by a political, religious, and literary situation that first gave him nothing to do and then gave him too much.

An extraordinary delay marks Milton's progress as poet. Though he promised to undertake a major literary career as early as 1628, he did not finally set to work on the poem that was to fulfill his promise until 1658, thirty years later. In the meantime, he spoke often of his poetic ambition, but he wrote less and less verse, finally stopping altogether, except for a few sonnets and some translations from Psalms, in 1640. Striking enough in itself, this pattern of "long choosing and beginning late," as Milton himself was to call it in Book IX of *Paradise Lost,* appears still more conspicuous when Milton's career is set by those of Spenser and Jonson. Though these previous laureates each fell some six to eight years behind Milton in announcing his literary ambition, both completed work that justified such pretension twenty years earlier than he. Spenser began *The Faerie Queene* in his late twenties and brought out its first three books before he was forty. By the time he was forty, Jonson had written all the plays and most of the poems and masques that were to appear four years later in his collected *Works*. Milton did not begin the epic version of *Paradise Lost* until he was fifty and did not publish it until he was almost fifty-nine.

To some extent this delay must be attributed to the effect of other preoccupations—to study and travel, to pamphleteering and blindness. But these are not, I think, sufficient to explain away those missing decades. The lives of Spenser and Jonson were also filled with distracting preoccupations, yet they kept writing—and neither was more energetic, ambitious, or talented than Milton. In Milton's case, moreover, the distractions themselves, with the exception of the blindness that came late and did little to slow the production of prose treatises, figured in his long choosing and beginning late. Study and travel were part of his search for a fit subject; controversial writing was a plausible substitute for it. And even with all this activity, there remain years that appear merely blank. The void in the late 1640s tempted William Riley Parker to move *Samson Agonistes* there, taking it from the later period to which it had always seemed to belong.[107] Like most students of Milton, I think Parker was wrong. But one can see how he, as Milton's biographer, would have been bothered by so large a gap in his story.

The gap bothered Milton himself, as his allusion to "long choosing and beginning late" suggests. Already in 1632, in the sonnet on the passing of his three-and-twentieth year, Milton was worried that his "late spring no bud or blossom showeth" (76). Yet when he wrote this sonnet, he had completed nearly three-fourths of the poems he was finally to gather and publish

107. Parker, *Milton*, II, 900–917. For a recent defense of the traditional dating, see Mary Ann Radzinowicz, *Toward "Samson Agonistes": The Growth of Milton's Mind* (Princeton: Princeton Univ. Press, 1978), pp. 387–407.

thirteen years later, including the *Nativity Ode, L'Allegro* and *Il Penseroso,* the brief epic *In Quintum Novembris,* the Latin elegies and Italian sonnets, and the various obituary poems in Latin and English. If at twenty-four this seemed too little, what must the still smaller product of the next decade have seemed at thirty-four? Or the almost invisible product of the next at forty-four? In the final lines of Sonnet 7, Milton had schooled himself in patience:

> Yet be it less or more, or soon or slow,
>   It shall be still in strictest measure even
>   To that same lot, however mean or high,
> Toward which Time leads me, and the will of Heaven;
>   All is, if I have grace to use it so,
>   As ever in my great task-master's eye.   (76–77)

But for a man of Milton's ambition, patience was not a lesson easily learned.

Of the five most substantial poems Milton wrote between "How Soon Hath Time" and the publication of his collected juvenilia in 1645, four are deeply marked by the sense of great expectations still unrealized. *Comus,* where genre and occasion forbad direct self-presentation, is the only exception, and even it, as its thematic likeness to the autobiographical passage from the *Apology for Smectymnuus* suggests, had a place in Milton's preparation for a laureate career. The others, whatever their ostensible occasion, all strive to project Milton into a future that refuses to assume any dependably coherent shape. *Ad Patrem* and *Lycidas* defend and question the value of a life devoted to literature, picture Milton sitting "with the ivy and laurel of a victor" (85), and fear that death may come before such glory can be achieved. *Mansus* and the *Epitaphium Damonis* describe a particular epic project, a project that Milton had already abandoned long before the poems were printed. All four look forward to the writing of some much greater poem. They thus anticipate the "debt" Milton was formally to assume in the autobiographical digression of *The Reason of Church Government,* where he talks at length of his literary plans. Yet even as they contract and renew this vocational debt, a debt Milton had owed implicitly by reason of his talent and his understanding of its meaning since the late 1620s, the poems and the prose treatise alike show how far he was from feeling himself able to pay. And so he "covenant[s] with [the] knowing reader, that for some few years yet I may go on trust with him toward the payment of what I am now indebted" (671). Before he finally paid in the promised poetic currency, those few years had stretched into a quarter of a century.

Much later, something of Milton's long choosing found retrospective expression in his depiction of another great young man, the Son in *Paradise Regained.* Like Milton, Jesus feels himself called to a high office. And, again like Milton, he finds no satisfactory way of fulfilling its requirements. Victorious deeds flame in his heart, as the thought of celebrating such deeds flamed in Milton's, but he quickly discovers their inadequacy. Neither military conquest nor secular rule will do, yet no other model of heroic accomplishment seems immediately relevant either to his situation or to the situation of his people. Thus we find Jesus early in the poem

> Musing and much revolving in his breast,
> How best the mighty work he might begin
> Of savior to mankind, and which way first
> Publish his Godlike office now mature. (487)

The office itself is not in doubt. He knows its name and something of its elevated nature. He is the Son of God, Messiah, the Anointed, the King of Israel, Savior to Mankind. But, as Satan later says to him, such titles bear "no single sense" (527). Their precise meaning thus remains uncertain, and so too does the set of actions appropriate to their fulfillment.

Jesus responds to this uncertainty by reviewing the signs of his calling, by considering in succession his early thoughts and actions,

> What from within I feel myself, and hear
> What from without comes often to my ears.   (487)

To find out what he must do, Jesus "reads" his own life. In much the same way and for much the same reason, Milton also read his. "What besides God has resolved concerning me I know not," he told his friend Charles Diodati, "but this at least: He has instilled into me, if into any one, a vehement love of the beautiful."[108] His love of the beautiful was to him a sign of God's purpose, as were many other attitudes and experiences that in passages scattered throughout his work he read for their vocational significance. The fullest of these passages and the one most like Jesus' meditation in *Paradise Regained* is that autobiographical introduction to the second book of *The Reason of Church Government* from which I have already quoted. Here, telling how he has been "led by the genial power of nature to another task" than the composition of polemical treatises in prose, Milton summarizes the evidence of his poetic calling, and in doing so he reveals an intense self-consciousness very like that which he would later attribute to Jesus.

After I had from my first years by the ceaseless diligence and care of my father (whom God recompense) been exercised to the tongues and some sciences, as my age would suffer, by sundry masters and teachers both at home and at the schools, it was found that whether aught was imposed me by them that had the overlooking, or betaken to of mine own choice in English or other tongue, prosing or versing, but chiefly this latter, the style, by certain signs it had, was likely to live. But much latelier in the private academies of Italy, whither I was favored to resort—perceiving that some trifles which I had in memory, composed at under twenty or thereabout (for the manner is that everyone must give some proof of his wit and reading there) met with acceptance above what was looked for, and other things which I had shifted in

---

108. *The Works of John Milton*, ed. Frank Allen Patterson, 18 vols. (New York: Columbia Univ. Press, 1931–1938), XII, 27.

scarcity of books and conveniences to patch up amongst them, were received with written encomiums, which the Italian is not forward to bestow on men of this side the Alps—I began thus far to assent both to them and divers of my friends here at home, and not less to an inward prompting which now grew daily upon me, that by labor and intent study (which I take to be my portion in this life) joined with the strong propensity of nature, I might leave something so written to aftertimes, as they should not willingly let it die. (667–668)

The whole course of his passage—its attention both to feelings from within and to encouragement from without, its careful chronological ordering of evidence, its movement from home and school to a wider and more expert world—closely resembles Jesus' meditation on himself, and so too does its air of objective detachment. Each looks at his life and finds in it traces of divine purpose. And each proceeds from this self-examination to a systematic consideration of "how and in what manner he shall dispose and employ those sums of knowledge and illumination which God hath sent him into the world to trade with" (665).

But here, as I have been suggesting, both Milton and Jesus encounter difficulty. Neither finds it possible to decide on any particular course of action. Jesus hesitates between heroic conquest, humane teaching, and redemptive suffering; Milton, between the various subjects and generic forms available to a laureate poet. By the end of *Paradise Regained,* Jesus' choice has narrowed considerably, though he determines nothing other than continued obedience to God's as yet unspecified will. Milton's choice in *The Reason of Church Government* remains wide open—as open as it had been fourteen years earlier when he first announced his intention of seeking out "some graver subject." For at least that long Milton had felt the call to a major poetic career, but he had come very little closer to its realization.[109]

109. I agree with John Spencer Hill that Milton's decision to become a poet did not depend on the rejection of his ministerial vocation. See Hill, *John*

Private jottings that Milton made about the same time he was writing *The Reason of Church Government*—jottings now bound in the Trinity Manuscript—make that distance still more apparent. In seven closely written pages, Milton noted down titles, sources, and in some cases character lists and even plot outlines for ninety-seven possible tragedies, two pastoral poems, and one epic. Clearly he was still far from knowing what in particular he should do. He did make four starts on a tragedy about Adam's fall, and these inevitably appear to us charged with promise. But none of the four satisfied him and none much resembles the poem he eventually wrote. Given what we know of his future development, the remaining ninety-nine possibilities seem still less likely. The temptation of Jesus does not even appear, and "Dagonalia, Jud. 16," our first glimpse of *Samson Agonistes,* is only one of fifty-three Old Testament topics and not one of those Milton stops to elaborate.[110] The very thoroughness of his search, moving book by book through the Bible and century by century through British history, reveals the lack of any specific aim—a lack equally apparent in the extraordinary reading program that had occupied much of his time during the preceding decade.

Midway through that decade Milton reported to Diodati: "I have by continuous reading brought down the affairs of the Greeks as far as to the time when they ceased to be Greeks. I have been long engaged in the obscure business of the state of the Italians under the Longobards, the Franks, and the Germans, down to the time when liberty was granted them by Rudolf, King of Germany: from that period it will be better to read separately what each city did by its own wars."[111] This is the same letter in which he talks of his vehement love of the beautiful and reveals that he is thinking of immortality, "grow-

---

Milton, pp. 51–76. For an opposing view, see John T. Shawcross, "Milton's Decision to Become a Poet," *MLQ,* 24 (1963), 21–30.

110. Milton, *Works,* XVIII, 236.   111. Milton, *Works,* XII, 29.

ing . . . wings and meditating flight." Dare one find an incon-
gruity (that Milton would have no doubt denied) between the
poetic aspiration and the painstaking course of study? A man
who knows where he is going can usually find a more direct
way of getting there. At the very least, one might expect an
intending poet would take some time from his reading to write
poetry—unless, of course, he did not know what to write. That
was, I think, Milton's situation from the first recognition of his
literary vocation to the beginning in earnest of *Paradise Lost*
nearly thirty years later. Pressing occasion did draw some fine
small poems from him "before the mellowing year." But neither occasion nor his reading provided a larger subject worthy
of his laureate ambition. Less immediately purposeful than is
sometimes supposed, the strenuous course of study that filled
so many of his middle years served primarily to keep him uncommitted and prepared while he stood and waited. But standing and waiting could be a worrisome pastime. Thus the intensity of Milton's introspection.

Puritans commonly meditated introspectively on the signs
of their calling. But in Milton's case, the literary situation of his
generation must also be held responsible. Anglican Cowley was
similarly introspective. And even Davenant, who wasn't, gave
more attention to defining his literary project than to writing
his poem. Born at about the same time, Milton crossed the
same literary terrain as these men and encountered some of the
same obstacles. For all three the development of a subject and
the related task of fashioning an authorial self appropriate to
its exploitation proved particularly difficult. It is precisely here
that Spenser and Jonson were favored by their placement near
the center of dynamic lead generations—generations possess-
ing a sure sense of the autonomous place and function of poetry. Spenser, as lover, shepherd, and prodigal, and Jonson, as
satirist and dramatist, had something to do. Their generational
location provided a language, an attitude, and a set of forms—

provided, in short, an enabling idea of what it meant to be a poet. In neither generation was that idea designed to accommodate a laureate. There thus arose those self-presentational tensions we have observed in the careers of both Spenser and Jonson. But if these poets had to transform the idiom of their generation, at least an independent literary idiom existed. They spoke it and their friends spoke it. It identified them as poets and gave them the outline of a subject. *The Shepheardes Calender* and *The Faerie Queene, Everyman Out of His Humor* and the *Epigrams* are each the product not only of an individual creative act but also of a communally established structure of differences in terms of which the individual act had purpose and meaning. The Orphic idiom of the cavaliers provided no such distinguishing role. Rather it left the poet with a merely ornamental function, one incapable of sustaining more than an occasional effusion.

Only final and irremediable defeat gave Milton the subject he had so long sought—or rather it gave new relevance to a subject he had considered years before but had not known how to develop. Defeat taught him to sing "with other notes than to th' Orphean lyre" (258). It freed him from the ancient idea that the laureate's task was to "embellish . . . the heroic actions of [his] countrymen."[112] Neither the King's laureate nor the laureate of the English people, Milton was freed by defeat to assume the prophet's posture of divinely inspired alienation, a role adumbrated but never fully realized in his earlier work. He could now present himself as God's Poet, "fallen on evil days,"

> In darkness, and with dangers compast round,
> And solitude. (346)

Passing "through weakness to the greatest strength," as he had talked of doing in his *Second Defense,* he could, moreover, at

112. Milton, *Works,* XIII, 253.

last profit from the example of his cavalier coevals, who in their own moment of defeat had also turned to heroic verse.[113]

The full breakthrough to a new idea of the laureate poet was Milton's own. Davenant and the others glimpsed it. But no cavalier practitioner of the long poem made exile and alienation his subject and his stance. Only Milton expressed the new idea in a finished poem and in an accompanying set of self-presentational gestures. But if *Paradise Lost* finally stands alone, it stands alone as the unique solution to a shared problem. Though in its transcendent accomplishment it seems to put its own time aside, its "answerable style" responds precisely to the demands of its generational moment. Davenant and Cowley had talked in their prefaces of the need to remain within the epic tradition yet to supersede it. *Paradise Lost,* a poem at once Virgilian and anti-Virgilian, Homeric and anti-Homeric, met this requirement as neither *Gondibert* nor *Davideis* could. The cavaliers set stylistic elevation as the chief mark of the great poet, but Milton alone soared "with no middle flight." Furthermore, Milton satisfied, as none of the cavaliers had done, the other chief articles of their literary program. He displaced pagan mythology, respected Biblical, historical, and scientific truth, and centered "man in man's best work." But perhaps more important than any of these accomplishments and more crucially relevant to the literary problem of his generation, he found in blindness and defeat a new autonomy for poetry and the poet. The establishment of a place for his work—a place at once apart and engaged—is perhaps the supreme challenge facing the poet at any time, but in a belated literary generation that challenge is particularly difficult to meet. And where poetry has no sovereign territory, there can be no laureate. Davenant and Cowley faltered at just this point. And it was at this point that Milton so wonderfully succeeded.

113. Milton, *Works,* XIII, 73.

The nature and precise measure of his success is not, however, best discovered from *Paradise Lost* alone, nor is it there that Milton's relation to his generation is most open to view. The shape of his career, the long delay we have been examining and its reflection in *Paradise Regained,* better suggests the distance he traveled. So do his early poems. If, as I have been arguing, Milton was a son of Orpheus in something of the cavalier sense, if he shared the problems inherent in that identity, we are most likely to find the evidence in his early work. For it is there, if anywhere, that he explored the literary idiom of his age, hoping to find in it an opening that would lead toward the laurel crown and the accomplishment of his vocation.

Poems in an Age Too Late

Poems of Mr. John Milton, Both English and Latin, the volume gathered and published in 1645, occupies in Milton's career a position comparable to that of *The Shepheardes Calender* in Spenser's or the three Comical Satires in Jonson's. Though it came in his mid-thirties rather than his mid-twenties, it too was its author's first public display of his literary prowess and pretension. Three years earlier in *The Reason of Church Government,* Milton had discussed his poetic ambition, but he had then provided no poems to substantiate his claim, nor would a curious reader easily have found any. *Comus* had been printed, as had *Lycidas* and a few slighter poems, but none had been accompanied by its author's name. And whatever manuscript circulation Milton's work enjoyed, it had not sufficed to win him any general reputation as a poet. The 1645 volume thus marks his poetic debut. Its publication was a self-presentational gesture of greater import than any he had previously made. Yet it was a gesture whose meaning was largely ignored.

Where the laureate pretensions of Spenser and Jonson were immediately noticed, Milton's were not. So far as one can now tell, his book met with the silence of misunderstanding or indifference. Either its first readers did not see what he was getting at or they did not care.[114]

Looking forward from the *Vacation Exercise* and *The Reason of Church Government* and back from *Paradise Lost, Paradise Regained,* and *Samson Agonistes,* we have no trouble grasping his meaning and no inclination to minimize its importance. From the title-page motto, a passage from Virgil's *Eclogues* that identifies Milton as the *vates futurus,* to the concluding *Epitaphium Damonis,* with its echo of Virgil's farewell to pastoral poetry and its account of Milton's epic plans, the volume comes to us heavy with intimations of laureate grandeur. In his preface, the publisher, Humphrey Moseley, assures us that this collection of verse "bring[s] into the light as true a birth as the Muses have brought forth since our famous Spenser wrote," and Milton obviously agrees.[115] His "trembling ears" have, he tells us, been touched by the hand of Phoebus and his lips "with hallowed fire" from the "secret altar" of God (122 and 43). In his *Canzone* he has his friends speak of the "immortal guerdon of undying leaves" now "putting forth its shoots to crown his locks," and in *Ad Patrem* he pictures himself "sitting with the ivy and laurel of a victor" (55 and 85). He reprints commendatory poems from his Italian acquaintances ranking him above Homer, Virgil, and Tasso, and then in his own poems to these acquaintances he draws attention to their praise. And more significant perhaps than any of these explicit

114. On the reception of the *Poems* of 1645, see William Riley Parker, *Milton's Contemporary Reputation* (Columbus: Ohio State Univ. Press, 1940).

115. *John Milton's Complete Poetical Works Reproduced in Photographic Facsimile,* ed. Harris Francis Fletcher, 4 vols. (Urbana: Univ. of Illinois Press, 1943–1948), I, 156. (Cited hereafter as *Facsimile.*)

pointers, he arranges the volume to make apparent the strong pastoral undercurrent that links him to Virgil as surely as the fountain Arethuse is linked to the river Alpheus.

Moved by the unerring prescience of these signs of future greatness, we may, however, forget that Moseley also compared Cartwright to "Tully and Virgil" and called Shirley "summus vates," that William Browne and Phineas Fletcher were hailed as the Spensers of their age, that Davenant and Crashaw were seen looking down "upon poor Homer, Virgil, Horace, Claudian, &c.," that Wither advertised his own *furor poeticus-propheticus,* and that pastoral imitation was as much the province of amateurs as of laureates.[116] In forgetting the commonplace and debased uses to which these signs had been turned, we block out the static that for seventeenth-century readers would surely have interfered with the clear reception of Milton's laureate meaning. So obvious does that meaning now seem, so obvious and so prophetically true, that we may even grant laureate significance to aspects of the book that could not then have had it—to its very publication, for example, or to its physical appearance. "This was a collected edition," J. W. Saunders has written, "an act of *braggadochio* which no poet before Jonson would have dreamed of committing. And, utterly revolutionary, following the custom established in *posthumous* editions of Shakespeare and Donne, the book was prefaced by a portrait of the author; it was a bad one and Milton amused himself by writing rude lines about it but he clearly sanctioned the innovation in principle. In short, this edition was presented with an *éclat* and brazen determination

---

116. Cartwright, p. 831; James Shirley, *Poems* (1646), frontispiece; William Browne, *The Whole Works,* ed. W. Carew Hazlitt, 2 vols. (1868–1869; rpt. New York: Johnson, 1970), I, 9 and 12; Fletcher, *Poetical Works of Giles and Phineas Fletcher,* ed. Frederick S. Boas, 2 vols. (1909; rpt. Cambridge: Cambridge Univ. Press, 1970), II, 8; Davenant, *Works,* I, 203; Crashaw, p. 651; and George Wither, *Furor-Poeticus (i.e.) Propheticus, A Poetick Phrensie* (1660).

impossible in earlier times."[117] But how much *éclat* would these gestures have had in 1645? The answer is "very little"— however brazenly determined Milton may have been.

Saunders has things backwards. Only in "earlier times" could *éclat* be attained by such means. Jonson was not the first to publish a collected edition of his literary works (Daniel and Drayton had both done so before him), but it remains true that in doing so he accomplished a distinctively laureate act. In the first decades of the seventeenth century, the use of a frontispiece portrait was similarly reserved. There is one on Daniel's *Works* in 1601, another on the 1619 edition of Drayton's *Poems,* and still another on Chapman's *Whole Works of Homer* in 1616, but none on the work of any living amateur or professional.[118] The distinction was thus maintained. Even as late as 1626 George Wither could clearly signal laureate aspirations by gathering his scattered *Juvenilia* and publishing them in an edition headed by his portrait. Though by no means revolutionary (much less "utterly revolutionary"), such gestures might in the mid-1620s still be understood.

Not so in the 1640s. After 1633, after the posthumous editions of Donne and Herbert and the nonposthumous ones of Marston, Cowley, and Phineas Fletcher, a collected edition no longer meant "laureate." Moseley tells us that he brought out Milton's *Poems* encouraged by the success of Waller's. To his mind they belonged in the same category, and a collected edition was equally appropriate for either. As for the frontispiece portrait—in decades that saw portraits heading the

117. J. W. Saunders, "Milton, Diomede and Amaryllis," *ELH,* 22 (1955), 268–269.

118. The much earlier portrait of Gascoigne on the back of the title page of *The Steel Glass* (1576) did not set a precedent that later poets followed. The only exception to the no-amateur rule that I know of between 1576 and 1633 is Harington's portrait on his translation of *Orlando Furioso* (1590). But if Harington was not a laureate poet, *Orlando Furioso* was a laureate poem.

poems of Donne, Herbert, Sylvester, Cowley, Randolph, Ur-
quhart, Shirley, Suckling, and Herrick, it was equally useless in
distinguishing the dead from the living and the laureate from
the amateur or professional. And what the mere fact of a portrait could not do, the details of portrait iconography did only
slightly better. The distant pastoral scene and the muses encir-
cling Milton's head on the 1645 frontispiece might, one supposes, have served to identify his laureate ambition. But what
then does one make of the wreaths of laurel surrounding the
amateur Suckling and the professional Shirley? William Marshall engraved all three for books published by Humphrey
Moseley, and clearly Marshall's artistic incompetence and
Moseley's editorial pretensions did more to determine their
appearance than did any self-presentational intention of the
authors. The one really distinctive portrait on which Marshall
and Moseley collaborated heads Cartwright's *Poems* of 1651.
Of it, Moseley wrote in his preface: "Some perhaps may quarrel with the frontispiece (a man in a gown before a book of
poems). Such may know 'twas done on purpose. We could have
dressed him with chaplets and laurel, cloaked and embroi-
dered, as well as others. But, since he first went to the King's
School at Westminster till he went out of the world, he was ever
in a gown. Give them a cloak whose works need one. He writ
nothing contrary to the laws of art or virtue, nothing but what
the gown may own."[119] Since Milton, Suckling, and Shirley are
each given a cloak, one must assume that they fall indiscriminately into the class of authors "whose works need one." I
don't suppose Moseley seriously thought this of Milton's
poems. If he did, he had not read them. But neither did he think
they required a presentation that would call attention to their
laureate character. They thus appeared *sans éclat*.

Gestures that earlier might have been depended on to make
one's laureate identity known no longer had that power. This

119. Cartwright, p. 830.

seepage affected Milton as much as any member of his generation, as did other changes that rendered difficult the unequivocal adoption of a laureate stance. Not only were the lines between the various categories of poet blurred. A similar loss of
distinctiveness smudged the boundary that had separated the
writing of poetry from other activities. As amateur, professional, and laureate melted into one another, poetry itself
melted into the common business of court and college. We need
go no further than Milton's 1645 title page to find a first sign of
that change. "The songs," we are there told, "were set in music
by Mr. Henry Lawes, gentleman, of the King's Chapel and one
of His Majesty's Private Music." An almost identical notice
appears on Carew's *Poems,* on Suckling's, on Waller's, and on
Cartwright's, and a similar, if briefer, message adorns many of
the individual poems of Lovelace. In no earlier generation had
the marriage of poetry and music been so conspicuously advertised, and in none was the courtly function of both so much a
matter of course.

Whatever Milton's political views may have been by the
mid-1640s, his *Poems* show themselves to have been deeply
engaged in the world frequented by his cavalier contemporaries. The volume's largest work, the masque we now call
Comus, is prefaced by an epistle from Henry Lawes dedicating
the masque to John Egerton, Viscount Brackly, from whose
"noble family," says Lawes, it "received its first occasion of
birth." A few months before their appearance in *Comus,* Egerton and his younger brother Thomas had performed as
masquers in Carew's *Coelum Britannicum,* in which Lawes
had also acted and for which he had composed the music. Still
earlier, Egerton's sister, Lady Alice, who played the Lady in
Comus, had taken part in Townshend's *Tempe Restored*
(1632). It is probable that Lawes too figured in *Tempe Restored* and that, in the same stretch of years, he participated in
the preparation and production of the other chief masques of
the Caroline court: Jonson's *Love's Triumph through Callipo-*

lis (1631) and *Chlorida* (1631), Townshend's *Albion's Triumph* (1632), Shirley's *Triumph of Peace* (1634), and Davenant's *Temple of Love* (1635). Milton's own contact with the Egerton family and with the masque-makers and other masquers of these years may have been slight, but through Lawes he and his work were drawn toward the orbit in which they turned. By its genre and structure, by its themes and style, by its social, political, and professional affiliations, *Comus* declares itself a work of its time.[120] If it strains against the limitations of conventional form, attaining a thematic coherence and a dramatic development rare in a masque, even that may be less a function of Milton's laureate self-presentation than of the particular demands of production in a private castle where the more elaborate splendors of carpentry and paint were lacking. The poetry does more because it had more to do. But certainly the published version contains no echo of the Jonsonian claim that poetry is the soul of masque—a claim that, as Jonson himself angrily admitted, could no longer be sustained in the 1630s.[121]

The requirements of an occasion foreign to any self-presentational purpose of its author mark *Comus* as no early work by either Spenser or Jonson was marked. External circumstance binds *Arcades,* the entertainment Milton helped fashion to honor the Countess Dowager of Derby, still more inextricably.[122] And what is true of these poems is also true in varying measure of most of the others in Milton's volume. Remove the

120. The relation of *Comus* to the court masques of the early 1630s has been studied by John S. Demaray in *Milton and the Masque Tradition* (Cambridge: Harvard Univ. Press, 1968). For a discussion of Lawes' role in these masques and in the making of *Comus*, see Willa McClung Evans, *Henry Lawes: Musician and Friend of Poets* (1951; rpt. New York: Kraus, 1966), pp. 57–112.

121. *Ben Jonson*, VIII, 404.

122. For a careful discussion of the occasion of *Arcades,* see Cedric Brown, "Milton's *Arcades*: Content, Form, and Function," *Renaissance Drama,* 8 (1977), 245–274.

occasional poems and only *L'Allegro* and *Il Penseroso*, the fifth and seventh elegies, and the first six sonnets remain. In the class of occasional poems with *Comus* and *Arcades* obviously belong the funeral elegies in memory of the Vice Chancellor at Cambridge, the University Beadle, the University Carrier, the Bishops of Winchester and Ely, the Marchioness of Winchester, Edward King, and Charles Diodati—all of whom, with the single exception of Milton's close friend Diodati, were also lamented by numerous other poets. Equally occasional are the university exercises, *In Quintum Novembris, Naturam Non Pati Sensum,* and *De Idea Platonica*; the commendatory sonnet on Shakespeare; the epistolary poems addressed to Milton's father, to Diodati, and to Thomas Young; and the poems of thanks to the Italians, Salsilli and Manso, who had favored him with their notice. Even the *Nativity Ode* and *The Passion* seem to have needed the help of a specific occasion, Christmas or Good Friday, to get going—though even with that help *The Passion* didn't get far. So pervasive is the occasional nature of this volume that when in 1673 a second edition finally appeared it was renamed *Poems, &c. Upon Several Occasions*. Few collections of verse written by members of either Spenser's generation or Jonson's would have deserved such a title. Few written by members of Milton's wouldn't. To be a poet in the 1630s and 1640s was, to a far greater degree than had previously been the case, to be at the service of occasion. To that service Milton, though neither a courtier nor a cavalier, devoted the best energies of his fledgling muse. There was nothing else for a poet to do.

Milton's poems do, of course, repeatedly rise above their ostensible occasions, turning external occasion into an occasion for poetic meditation as profound, and as profoundly moving, as any our language can show. But that artistic transcendence does not change the historical fact that Milton, as much as any of the cavaliers, depended on occasion to furnish his subjects. He complains in the opening lines of *Lycidas* that "bitter constraint and sad occasion dear" compel him to write "before the mellowing year." Yet without such compulsion *Lycidas* would not exist, nor would any other original poem of Milton's, with the exception of a few translations, between "At a Solemn Music" in 1633 and the beginning of *Paradise Lost* a quarter of a century later. From his twenty-fifth to his fiftieth year, Milton produced no original work in verse that does not owe its existence to some quite definite occasion. *Elegia Quinta,* written when he was only twenty, suggests what might happen when the inward motion of inspiration touched Milton in the absence of an occasion more specific than a change of seasons.

The poem begins with the return of spring and then moves quickly to the accompanying return of poetic power.

> Fallor? an et nobis redeunt in carmina vires,
> Ingeniumque mihi munere veris adest?
> Munere veris adest, iterumque vigescit ab illo
> (Quis puter?) atque aliquod iam sibi poscit opus.

> Am I deluded? Or are my powers of song returning? And is my inspiration with me again by grace of the spring? By the spring's grace it is with me and—who would guess such a thing?—it is already clamoring for some employment.   (37-38)

The next lines express the eagerness of his inspiration, the sense of exaltation and power, but they fail to find the work for which his *ingenium* clamors. Rather the lines lead to a question:

> Quid tam grande sonat distento spiritus ore?
> Quid parit haec rabies, quid sacer iste furor?

> What mighty song is my soul pouring from its full throat? What is to be the offspring of this madness and this sacred ecstacy?   (38)

In answer the poem doubles back on itself and chooses for its subject the source of its own inspiration. *Ver mihi, quod dedit ingenium, cantabitur illo.* "The spring shall be the song of the inspiration it has given me." The poet creates a self-reflexive occasion that can then become the subject of his song. To some extent this is what poets often do. The lover sings the beloved who moves him to sing; the satirist attacks the society that has taught him to snarl. But more than most, Milton's is a poem of inspiration in search of a subject. The lover and the satirist each have a conventional role capable of generating not only a nonce poem *in adventum veris,* but a body of work and with it a career. The counterpart to Milton's elegy—or, better, to the experience that stands behind it—is to be found neither in the love poetry of Spenser's generation nor in the satire of Jonson's, but rather in a poem of his own generation, in Cowley's "Motto," where, after announcing his towering ambition and after likening himself to Cicero, Aristotle, and Virgil, Cowley remains baffled by the distance he must travel to attain the peaks inhabited by those figures of accomplished glory. Like Milton, Cowley has heard the trumpet of fame, but, again like Milton, he does not know quite how to respond.

One response—perhaps the most frequent in the cavalier generation—was to redo more perfectly what had already been done, to make oneself a poet by the virtuosity of one's stylistic imitation. This is the mannerist response, the response of Cowley, Suckling, Crashaw, Waller, Davenant, and many others, including Milton. Moseley's one substantive remark in his introduction to the 1645 *Poems* directs attention to just this aspect of Milton's verse. "Let the event guide itself which way it will," he writes, "I shall deserve of the age by bringing into the light as true a birth as the muses have brought forth since our famous Spenser wrote, whose poems in these English ones are as rarely imitated as sweetly excelled."[123] The rare imitation

123. *Facsimile,* p. 156.

and sweet excelling of Spenser begins on the very next page with the ode *On the Morning of Christ's Nativity.* Spenserian diction, description, prosody, and mythopoesis mark the poem and declare its lineage. Even the image of its poet, running to "prevent" the Magi with his "humble ode" and "lay it lowly" at the feet of Christ, draws on the mixture of eager ambition and self-depreciation characteristic of Spenser's own self-portrayal. Yet, for all its Spenserian qualities, the *Nativity Ode* attains a polish, a high finish of virtuosity, quite foreign to Spenser's rustic manner. In this respect, it has more in common with "Music's Duel" or the Sacharissa poems than with *The Shepheardes Calender, Colin Clouts Come Home Againe,* or even the *Fowre Hymnes.* And the same high finish, the same easy stylistic mastery, that one finds in the *Nativity Ode* also distinguishes Milton's Jonsonian, Petrarchan, Ovidian, and Virgilian imitations.

The Milton of the *Poems* of 1645 was as much a mannerist as any of his cavalier coevals. He shared with them the plight of the latecomer. In his verse, as in theirs, *la maniera* becomes, if not quite an end in itself, nevertheless an unusually conspicuous means—one whose effect is heightened by frequent reminders of precocity and polyglot facility. At fifteen, the book lets us know, Milton translated psalms into English; at seventeen he produced good Latin verse; before he was twenty-three, he wrote sonnets in Italian; and somewhere along the way he made verse in Greek. Virtuosity thus figures importantly in Milton's self-presentation. And even *sprezzatura,* its mannerist and cavalier complement, finds a small place. As the poems on Leonora and Hobson show, Milton could respond to a slighter occasion with becoming grace and wit. And something of that light touch is meant to be seen in the volume as a whole. *Munditieque nitens non operosa*—"shining with unlabored elegance"—is what Milton himself said of it in his presentational ode to John Rouse (146).

It will be objected (and rightly) that Milton's mannerism differs not only in quality from that of the cavaliers but also in kind. Where the cavaliers trivialize their heritage—sitting and drinking in the relics of Elizabethan literature—Milton enriches his. Even so minor a poem as his "Epitaph on the Marchioness of Winchester" loads its frail Jonsonian bark with a heavier freight of sensuous description, narrative complexity, and transcendent meaning than it was designed to bear.[124] And what is true in a small way of this poem is still truer of many others. *L'Allegro* and *Il Penseroso* greatly extend the range of the Jonsonian plain style; *Comus* gives new thematic depth to the masque; *Lycidas* adds to the personal and prophetic resonance of the Virgilian materials from which it derives.[125] Milton never made "verbal curiosities the end" of his poetry. That, he thought, "were a toilsome vanity" (668). But he did nevertheless read verbal style as the sign of his poetic election. It was, we remember, the style of his childhood exercises that convinced him he should become a poet. In the self-presentational idiom of his belated generation—including the idiom in which the self presents itself to itself—mannerist style had a particularly large part. And though Milton attempted to say more in that idiom than did his coevals, it remained the one in which he had to speak if he wished to be heard at all.

In his virtuosity and stylishness, Milton bears a fraternal relationship to the cavalier poets of his generation. It is here particularly that we find in him another son of Orpheus. Nor

124. See A.H. Tricomi, "Milton and the Jonsonian Plain Style," *Milton Studies*, 13 (1979), 134–138.
125. On the mannerism of *Lycidas* and *Comus*, see Roy Daniells, *Milton, Mannerism and Baroque* (Toronto: Univ. of Toronto Press, 1963), pp. 19–50. Daniells uses a more complex definition of *mannerism* than the one I borrowed from Martz, and thus considers as relevant to his discussion elements of *Lycidas* and *Comus* that are not essential to mine. The same reservation applies to Wylie Sypher's discussion of *Lycidas* in *Four Stages of Renaissance Style* (Garden City, N.Y.: Anchor Books, 1955), pp. 174–175.

does he fail to aid us in making the connection. As Don Cameron Allen remarked, "Milton accents the legend of Orpheus in a way that suggests self-identification."[126] Allusions to Orpheus abound in his work, and, initially at least, he puts the emphasis just where the cavaliers do—on the magical power of Orphic song, on the moving force of its enchanting style. Thus already in the sixth prolusion he compares his oratorical manner to the music of Orpheus and Amphion, and in the seventh he recalls that even the trees and rocks responded to "the elegant music of Orpheus" (614 and 628). In similar fashion he later likens his program of educational reform to such "melodious sounds on every side that the harp of Orpheus was not more charming" (632). The "soft Lydian airs" of *L'Allegro* awaken Orpheus; the more solemn notes of *Il Penseroso* bid him sing; and *Ad Patrem* rallies him to Milton's side in the defense of poetry (72, 74, and 84). Elsewhere in the *Poems* of 1645, though with no specific reference to Orpheus, the moving power of music and verse is celebrated in ways strongly reminiscent of the usual Orphic themes. "At a Solemn Music" makes the "mixed power" of "voice and verse" its subject; the second epigram to Leonora Baroni alludes to the healing power of song; *Ad Salsillum* imagines the Tiber calmed by Salzilli's verse; and the great central panel of the *Nativity Ode* talks of "holy song" causing Time to "run back and fetch the age of gold."

The terms Milton chooses to present this vision of restored harmony suggest the literary and cultural milieu to which in his generation the Orphic most obviously belonged.

---

126. Don Cameron Allen, *The Harmonious Vision,* enlarged edition (Baltimore: Johns Hopkins Univ. Press, 1970), p. 127. See also Caroline W. Mayerson, "The Orphic Image in *Lycidas,*" *PMLA,* 64 (1949), 189–207; Clifford Davidson, "The Young Milton, Orpheus, and Poetry," *English Studies, 59* (1978), 27–34; and Mason Tung, "Orpheus and Milton," in the *Milton Encyclopedia.*

Yea, Truth and Justice then
Will down return to men,
   Th' enameled arras of the rainbow wearing,
And Mercy set between,
Throned in celestial sheen,
   With radiant feet the tissued clouds down steering,
And heaven, as at some festival,
Will open wide the gates of her high palace hall.   (47)

Written in 1629, this stanza describes a scene that would have fit easily into the great court masques of the next five years. Its conceit, action, allegorical figures, and architectural setting would all be at home in a masque, where, as here, the stylistic polish of music and verse would find a visual equivalent in such props as the enameled arras, the celestial sheen, the radiant feet, and the tissued clouds. One art merges into another, and all merge into the ceremony of the high palace hall. In the masque, the mannerism of the Caroline court achieved its fullest expression, and it was there too that the Orphic theme was most pronounced.

Like the *Nativity Ode,* Milton's more direct contributions to the genres of entertainment and masque move in this Orphic field of reference. The sheer beauty of their verse reveals an identity that is both generic and generational. In a letter to Milton reprinted in the *Poems* of 1645, Sir Henry Wotton calls particular attention to the *ipsa mollities,* "softness itself," of *Comus.* "I should much commend the tragical part," Wotton writes, "if the lyrical did not ravish me with a certain Doric delicacy in your songs and odes."[127] Much the same delicacy, though perhaps in a lighter mode than the Doric, characterizes *Arcades.* Furthermore, both works give thematic emphasis to the Orphic power of verse. They thus reflect on the meaning of their own style even as they draw attention to it. "Such sweet compulsion doth in music lie," says the Genius of *Arcades,*

127. *Facsimile,* p. 191.

> To lull the daughters of Necessity
> And keep unsteady Nature to her law,   (79)

and he illustrates the precept by governing his assigned bit of forest "with puissant words and murmurs made to bless" (78). In *Comus,* the Lady herself is an Orphic singer, whose song breathes "divine enchanting ravishment" (96). Prompted by such passages, Donald Bouchard has read *Comus* as an expression of the "mythic antagonism" between Dionysus, "the god of crowds, of the 'rout of Monsters,'" and Orpheus, "the harmonizer of misrule and undisciplined crowds."[128] Even without unmasking the unnamed Orphic presence in *Comus* quite so completely, we can readily see that for Milton, as for the poets of the Caroline court, the idea of Orpheus as master of style and enforcer of civility had an extraordinary appeal. It entered deeply both into his poetry and into his presentation of himself as poet, for it gave sense to the stylistic virtuosity that figured among the most conspicuous signs of his late-coming generation.

None of the passages mentioned in the last several paragraphs is likely, however, to spring first to mind when one thinks of Milton and Orpheus, nor is the power of Orphic song likely to be the dominant theme. Rather than power, one thinks of vulnerability; of *Lycidas* and *Paradise Lost* rather than *L'Allegro, Il Penseroso,* and *Ad Patrem.* In *Lycidas* and again in the invocation to Book VII of *Paradise Lost,* Milton recalls, as the cavaliers almost never do, the tragic fate of Orpheus. "What," he asks in *Lycidas*

> could the Muse herself that Orpheus bore,
> The Muse herself, for her enchanting son
> Whom universal nature did lament,
> When by the rout that made the hideous roar,

128. Donald Bouchard, *Milton: A Structural Reading* (Montreal: McGill-Queen's Univ. Press, 1974), p. 24.

His gory visage down the stream was sent,
Down the swift Hebrus to the Lesbian shore?   (121–122)

And this image of vulnerability prompts him to question all arduous devotion to poetry, including his own.

Alas! What boots it with uncessant care
To tend the homely slighted shepherd's trade,
And strictly meditate the thankless Muse?   (122)

A quarter of a century later and midway through *Paradise Lost,* this questioning is past. Milton has fully embraced his vocation as poet. But still the threat remains. In "evil days . . . in darkness . . . and solitude," the threat has in fact assumed a new immediacy. And so Milton calls upon his muse to

drive far off the barbarous dissonance
Of Bacchus and his revellers, the race
Of that wild rout that tore the Thracian bard
In Rhodope, where woods and rocks had ears
To rapture, till the savage clamor drowned
Both harp and voice; nor could the Muse defend
Her son. So fail not thou, who thee implores;
For thou art heavenly, she an empty dream.   (346–347)

In "Bacchus and his revellers" some readers have caught a glimpse of the Restoration court of Charles II, while in those "others," mentioned in *Lycidas,* who, instead of meditating the thankless muse, "sport with Amaryllis in the shade," other readers have seen the cavalier poets.[129] Such identifications, as lightly as we may stress them, suggest a systematic opposition between Milton and the sometimes tipsy and always sportfully convivial poets of his generation. The opposition is adumbrated in *Elegy VI,* where the aged Orpheus stands for sobriety and solitude against Bacchic merriment, and it underlies the

129. See Hughes' note on *Paradise Lost,* VII, 32–33, and Saunders, 255–256.

confrontation at the center of *Comus*. As laureate, Milton not only claims a larger share of the Orphic inheritance. He attempts to exclude his cavalier siblings from it altogether—to deny their Orphic descent and label them rather sons of Belial and of Bacchus. Yet, though he may labor to obscure it, we continue to remark a family resemblance.

Wherever one looks in the *Poems* of 1645, one finds Milton speaking the literary language of his generation, but speaking it with an accent that reveals his laureate ambition. Waller's has been called "the poetry of limitation."[130] The term might equally well be applied to much cavalier verse. Milton repeatedly strains against such limitation. He makes more of his occasions, more of the styles he imitates, more of the figure of Orpheus. He built this laureate expansiveness into the very sequential structure of the 1645 volume. In it, one can observe, as Louis Martz has demonstrated, a series of emergences.[131] The volume presents its author as "the rising poet"—a Virgilian phrase that gives Martz's article its title—and we can watch the author rise as his book proceeds, until in its last poem, the *Epitaphium Damonis,* he bids farewell to pastoral poetry, to Latin, and to his own youth and announces his plans for a great Arthurian epic. Prior to this ultimate emergence, there are a number of others. The seven numbered elegies end, for example, in a palinode that retrospectively defines them as "monuments to my wantonness" and claims that their author has put such things behind him. The "Jonsonian" poems lead from the narrow conventionality of the "Epitaph on the Marchioness of Winchester" to *Il Penseroso's* concluding intimation of a quite Miltonic "prophetic strain." The group of sonnets closes with

130. Chernaik, *The Poetry of Limitation.*
131. "The Rising Poet, 1645," in *The Lyric and Dramatic Milton,* ed. Joseph H. Summers (New York: Columbia Univ. Press, 1965), pp. 3–33. This article reappears in a slightly expanded version in Martz's *Poet of Exile,* pp. 31–59.

several that, as Martz says, form "a tacit contrast" with the Petrarchan mode with which the series began.[132] And the English poems as a whole rise first to the "lofty rime" of *Lycidas* and then to the book's single largest poem, the only one presented with its own title page and prefatory matter, the Ludlow *Maske.*

Martz's observations seem to me both accurate and significant. Milton does present himself as the rising poet, and the order of his book contributes to that self-presentation. Yet to leave it at that is to miss the strong countermovement, a movement that must be perceived if we are to understand the larger configuration of Milton's career—not only the laureate triumph of *Paradise Lost* but also the many years of poetic inactivity that preceded it.[133] Paradoxically, each emergence represents a deeper involvement with that from which the poet would emerge. The two monodies, *Lycidas* and the *Epitaphium Damonis,* may bid farewell to pastoral poetry, but they are also Milton's most explicitly pastoral poems, the only poems in the 1645 volume that closely imitate the form of the Virgilian eclogue. Milton would seem to have chosen the genre precisely because it was one that could be left behind. The traditional association of pastoral poetry and youth, an association that he emphasizes in each of the poems, allows him to make a statement of poetic maturity. But Milton finds that such statements have to be made over and over. Writing in a generation that had lost its sense of clearly marked boundaries, he has to keep drawing a line. For until the line is drawn, he cannot cross it. Thus the seventh elegy, the one that immediately precedes his palinode and the one to which the palinode most obviously refers, comes last (out of chronological order) pre-

132. Martz, *Poet of Exile,* p. 45.
133. Something of this countermovement in the *Poems* of 1645 has been described by George W. Nitchie in "Milton and His Muses," *ELH,* 44 (1977), 75–84.

cisely because its emphasis on the youthful theme of sensuous love makes it the elegy most deserving renunciation. In like manner, *L'Allegro,* the Jonsonian poem most devoted to the pleasures of youth, provides an impulse for the countermovement of *Il Penseroso.* But despite all this line drawing, Milton's acts of closure never quite close. No emergence sets him definitively on his way. Each time he strips off one inadequate poetic guise, he finds another underneath.

Like the middle class, Milton is always rising and never getting anywhere. Or rather he gets no closer to his laureate object. His book begins at a moment of successful emergence, with the ode *On the Morning of Christ's Nativity.* Here the birth of Christ and the beginning of the Christian era are made to coincide with the new poet's introduction of himself. But just as "wisest Fate says no" to the immediate return of the Golden Age, so Milton's own laureate apotheosis is rebuffed. From the precocious triumph of the *Nativity Ode,* he declines to its failed sequel, *The Passion,* which "the author finding to be above the years he had when he wrote it . . . left it unfinished" (63).

A series of emergences, Milton's volume is also a series of deferrals. The satisfaction of ambition keeps being put off. *Il Penseroso* holds the promise of the "prophetic strain" for "weary age." *Lycidas* turns toward "fresh woods and pastures new," woods and pastures as yet unattained. Sonnet VII at once marks Milton's escape from the Italianate poetry of youth and teaches the lesson of patience. *Ad Patrem, Mansus,* and the *Epitaphium Damonis* all relegate their speaker's longed-for glory to an undefined and distant future. And at the very end of the book, as at the beginning, we are told of an experience of poetic failure.

> Ispe etiam—nam nescio quid mihi grande sonabat
> Fistula—ab undecima iam lux est altera nocte—
> Et tum forte novis admoram labra cicutis,

Dissiluere tamen, rupta compage, nec ultra
Ferre graves potere sonos.

And myself—for I do not know what grand song my
pipe was sounding—it is now eleven nights and a
day—perhaps I was setting my lips to new pipes, but
their fastenings snapped and they fell asunder and
could carry the grave notes no further. (137)

Though the speaker goes on to tell of his epic plans, their
realization clearly remains "above the years he then had." Like
The Passion, this new "grand song" snaps the fastenings of his
still unready pipe. And, as readers of *The Reason of Church
Government* would have known, the Arthurian project, announced here with such hope and determination, had been
abandoned at least three years before the publication of the
Poems of 1645, and even the more general laureate undertaking had been adjourned *sine die.*

In the arrangement of the *Poems* of 1645, neither *Lycidas,*
which concludes the series of shorter English poems, nor the
Epitaphium Damonis, which holds a similar place with respect
to the Latin poems, nor any of the poems that close the various
subsections can, however, be said to occupy the place of choice.
That honor is reserved rather for *Comus.* Coming after *Lycidas,* set apart by its own title page, dedication, and commendatory epistle, Milton's masque is presented as the chief product
of his literary apprenticeship. If the book contains an example
of what the rising poet can do in a larger way, this clearly is it.
Yet, as we have already noticed, *Comus* is as much involved
with those aspects of the cavalier poetic that in Milton's generation impeded the development of a laureate career as any
work in the 1645 volume. *Comus* is an Orphic poem, a mannerist poem, an occasional poem, a poem dependent on the
systems of patronage and artistic collaboration. As such, it
could not serve to distinguish a poet of laureate ambition.

Rather, it caused him and his book to blend into their surroundings—as they do in this extract from Moseley's catalogue:

> 91. Poems with a Masque by Thomas Carew, Esq., Gentleman of the Privy Chamber to his late Majesty, revived and enlarged with additions, 8°.

> 92. Poems of Mr. John Milton, with a Masque presented at Ludlow Castle before the Earl of Bridgewater, then President of Wales, 8°.

> 93. Poems, &c. with a Masque called The Triumph of Beauty, by James Shirley, Gent. 8°.[134]

"Poems with a Masque," "Poems . . . with a Masque," "Poems . . . with a Masque"—the same formula fits the amateur, the laureate, and the professional. A masque was as likely to be the featured item in the collected poems of any one of the three. *Comus* itself, according to the report of Sir Henry Wotton, had already played that role "in the very close of the late R[andolph]'s poems, printed at Oxford, whereunto it was added (as I now suppose) that the accessory might help out the principal . . . and to leave the reader *con la bocca dolce*."[135] But though it might sweeten his mouth, the inclusion of *Comus* would not significantly alter the reader's idea of the vocational category to which the poet belonged—if indeed readers in the 1630s thought of contemporary poets in such terms at all.

134. In Waller, sig. a4ᵛ–a5. Number 90 on this list is Davenant's *Madagascar*; number 94 is Cowley's *Mistress*. The catalogue as a whole gives a rare sense of the text milieu to which Milton's *Poems* of 1645 belonged. It furnishes our nearest approach to a mid-seventeenth-century bookstall.

135. *Facsimile*, p. 191. The enforced loan of *Comus* paid with heavy interest a debt to Randolph contracted years earlier when Milton took a line and perhaps a few ideas for *L'Allegro* from *Aristippus, or the Jovial Philosopher*. (See the entry on Randolph in the *Dictionary of National Biography*.) These reciprocal borrowings are another small element in that system of relations that connected Milton and his *Poems* to their moment.

Like *The Shepheardes Calender* and the Comical Satires, Milton's volume of 1645 represents the crossing of a laureate ambition, whose inspiration was largely diachronic, and a synchronic literary system, a crossing of the then and the now. Milton aspired to be in his age what Homer, Virgil, Ariosto, Tasso, and Spenser had been in theirs. But such a project inevitably has a touch of the Quixotic about it. There remains always a suspicion that in this modern world the laureate may be as much out of place as a knight errant in seventeenth-century Spain. Continuing to speak the self-presentational language of one's own time is a necessary proof of sanity. In his *Poems,* Milton gives that proof. But he does not prove himself the *vates futurus*—except, of course, to us for whom he is already, by virtue of his later work, a *vates praeteritus.* He claims the role and shows he has the skill it requires. But he provides no convincing evidence that he can reclaim for poetry and for the poet the autonomy his generation had been content to let go. And without such autonomy his laureate career could proceed no further.

Laureate Redux

Literary autonomy is precisely what the works Milton produced in the 1640s and 1650s most obviously lack. By the time the 1645 volume was published, he had given up verse—even occasional verse. Only three of its poems, three sonnets, belong to the preceding five years. The other most recent English poem, *Lycidas,* dates all the way back to 1637, and the most recent work in Latin is the *Epitaphium Damonis* of 1640. In the meantime, Milton had turned to prose, finding there a use for the studies that had so far borne little poetic fruit. At first he was inclined to regard these controversial writings as labors of the left hand, works required of him by duty, but ill-suited to achieve the undying fame that was properly the laureate's meed. But early in the 1650s, following the execution of King Charles, the institution of the Commonwealth, and his own appointment as Latin Secretary to the Council of State, he began to think differently. If he was not a King's Poet, he was nevertheless the divinely inspired spokesman of the nation, and, as such, he was acting the laureate part for which he had so long prepared himself. In his *Defense of the English People* he had, he said, "performed ... the service which [he] thought would be of most use to the commonwealth" and in doing so had erected a "monument which will not speedily perish."[136] "It is not possible for me, nor can it ever be my desire, to ascribe to myself anything greater or more glorious."[137] Responding to an opponent who had mocked him for his lack of renown, he wrote:

The truth is, I had learned to be long silent, to be able to forbear writing ... and carried silently in my own breast what, if I had chosen then, as well as now, to bring forth, I could long since have gained a name. But I was not eager for fame, who is slow of pace. . . . . It was not the fame of everything that I was waiting for, but the opportunity.[138]

Milton's development depended, to a degree unequaled by that of any previous laureate, on opportunity, on the chance of a favorable occasion. In the English revolution he found that opportunity—or so he thought.

He was mistaken. His *Defense* did not outlive the government for which it was written. Nor could it fairly have been expected to do so. Where Milton saw an epic account of the English struggle for liberty, later readers have been hard put to find more than a violently partisan diatribe heavily charged with *ad hominem* abuse, a book so dependent for its emphases and structure on the work of its opponent that it can scarcely

136. Milton, *Works,* VIII, 253.   137. Milton, *Works,* VIII, 19.
138. Quoted by Parker, *Reputation,* p. 32.

claim an independent existence. Even a critic intent on tracing common aesthetic principles in the prose and the verse finds himself obliged to complain of "the disparity between Milton's ambitious claims for [the *First Defense*] and our feeling of disappointment at the delay, if not the squanderings, of his genius."[139] That Milton should have erred in just this way is, however, not surprising. His mistake was the product of tendencies strong both in his generation and in the laureate tradition. I have said enough already of the preemption of the cavalier poets and their work by interests inimical to the maintenance of literary autonomy. Davenant's devotion to the royal court and its occasions and Cowley's to the Royal Society and its are but two signs of an erosion of autonomy that affected amateur, professional, and laureate alike. But even without the erasure of boundaries characteristic of his belated generation, Milton, as laureate, might have been susceptible to the blandishments of power—so long, that is, as he could convince himself of its legitimacy. The very process of differentiation by which the laureate defined and presented himself—a process whose result was enforced by the authoritative example of Virgil and by the Renaissance tradition of civic humanism— led him to make the reason of state the reason of his work. Already in earlier generations this inclination had decisively and, often, destructively manifested itself. Spenser's defense of English policy in Ireland went a long way toward ruining Book V of *The Faerie Queene*. Only the pastoral retreat of Book VI and the reintroduction of Colin Clout restored his poetic integrity, but that restoration was accomplished at considerable cost

139. Thomas Kranidas, *The Fierce Equation: A Study of Milton's Decorum* (The Hague: Mouton, 1965), p. 82. For other similar complaints about the *First Defense*, see Samuel L. Wolff, "Milton's 'Advocatum Nescio Quem,'" *MLQ*, 2 (1941), 559; James Holly Hanford, *A Milton Handbook*, 4th ed. (New York: Crofts, 1946), p. 110; and E. M. W. Tillyard, *Milton* (1930; rev. ed. London: Chatto, 1966), p. 159.

to his laureate identity. A similar inclination drew Drayton toward topography and Daniel toward history and prose. And from the same laureate sources came Jonson's abandonment of drama in favor of masque. To serve a monarch, or a policy, or simply a body of established fact, Spenser, Drayton, Daniel, and Jonson each gave up something of his artistic autonomy and with it the role of poet current among the amateurs and professionals of his own generation. But perhaps the most extreme example, and the one closest to Milton both in time and in partisan sympathy, is George Wither. Born in 1588, Wither renounced the pastoral and satiric guises of his youth to emerge in the early 1640s as the indefatigable poet, prophet, and pamphleteer of the English revolution. "Wither had," as one critic has remarked, "the ability to delight, but it deserted him when he decided that his duty was to teach. He is, in a sense, a casualty of Renaissance poetic—. . . of the Horatian, Sidneyan, Bartasian notion of the poet's function."[140] Though a far more sophisticated interpreter of that notion, Milton too fell victim to it. Unlike Wither, he had the good sense to write his pamphlets in prose. But his good sense did not keep him from thinking those pamphlets the great work he was destined to produce—the great work that aftertimes would not willingly let die.

Had Milton stopped here, aftertimes would surely not have allowed him the laureate standing he claimed. As a poetry of promise, a poetry that constantly looks forward to something that it is not itself, the work collected in the *Poems* of 1645

140. Joan Grundy, *The Spenserian Poets* (London: Edward Arnold, 1969), p. 161. Grundy draws on an important article by Allan Pritchard, "George Wither: The Poet as Prophet," *SP*, 59 (1962), 211–230. Both Grundy's chapter and Pritchard's article discuss Wither in terms very suggestive for the student of laureate self-presentation. Christopher Hill has recently examined the similarities in career and ideas between Milton and Wither. See "George Wither and John Milton," in *English Renaissance Studies, Presented to Dame Helen Gardner,* ed. John Carey (Oxford: Clarendon Press, 1980), pp. 212–227.

depends for its richest resonance on a fulfillment that comes only with *Paradise Lost, Paradise Regained,* and *Samson Agonistes.* Lacking that fulfillment, Milton's early verse would have remained unnoticed in his lifetime and might not have enjoyed even the posthumous attention accorded the work of such amateurs as Marvell, Crashaw, or Vaughan. But of course Milton did not stop. With the decline of the Commonwealth and the approaching defeat of the political and religious positions he had defended, his attitude again changed. Moved in part by the example of Cowley, Davenant, Fanshawe, and Benlowes, he returned to poetry and began work on the epic that was to be *Paradise Lost,* a poem that would acknowledge no patron but God. Gone was the expectation that the laureate's position depended on official recognition. "Not sedulous by nature to indite / Wars, hitherto the only argument / Heroic deemed," Milton shifted the action of the epic from the outer world of history to the inner world of the individual mind, to "the better fortitude / Of patience and heroic martyrdom," and made the poet responsible only to his own inspired vision (379). No longer was he prompted—as Spenser had been in *The Faerie Queene,* or Jonson in his masques, or he himself in his pamphlets—by reason of state. In the epilogue to the second edition of the *Defensio Prima,* Milton used the term *public reason* to explain why he had written the book with such haste, *pro eo ac ratio tum reipub. postulabat.*[141] In *Paradise Lost,* the term reappears in the mouth of Satan, who uses it to justify his temptation of Adam and Eve (287). The difference suggests the distance Milton traveled as laureate.

History, as Milton portrays it in the opening and concluding books of *Paradise Lost,* constitutes a series of betrayals, acts of individual and collective disobedience to God, countered in each age by one man chosen of God and obedient to his commands—"the one just man alive,"

141. Milton, *Works,* VII, 554.

the only son of light
In a dark age, against example good,
Against allurement, custom, and a world
Offended; fearless of reproach and scorn,
Or violence.   (451–452)

Noah, Abraham, Moses, Joshua, David, Josiah, Jeremiah, and Ezekiel were such men, and so too were Samson and Jesus, the protagonists of Milton's last poems. It is in this line that Milton inscribes himself. Once again the chosen people have betrayed their sacred trust, and once again the just man of God has risen up "in darkness and with dangers compassed round" to illustrate and justify God's ways. Though an epic poet, he is an epic poet with a difference. He imitates the genealogical-historical catalogues of Virgil, Ariosto, Spenser, and Camoens, but, where they celebrated a family, a race, or a nation and led to the glory of a particular patron, he records the sins of humanity and leads to the coming of Christ. He has no other patron.

The laureate's new isolation from the institutions of power shapes the presentation and substance of *Paradise Regained* and *Samson Agonistes,* as it did those of their predecessor. Like *Paradise Lost* and unlike virtually all other previous laureate verse, these works appear with no sign of a connection between poet and state. Rather, they ignore the political dispensation under which their author lived and express contempt for any change that is not also a change in heart. Jesus disdains an earthly kingdom and Samson, though a hero of action rather than of suffering, knows that his deeds can deliver Israel only if Israel is inwardly prepared to accept deliverance. "The deeds themselves, though mute, [speak] loud the doer" (557). Inspired deeds have a self-presentational value. But "in nations grown corrupt"—and from Milton's point of view such corruption has characterized most of human history, including finally the history of his own time—they are likely to have no other effect.

Milton's laureate self-fashioning deeply informs each of these last poems. *Paradise Regained,* as I have already suggested, draws on the experience of his early years, on the experience of the great young man, sure of his calling but unsure how to fulfill it. In a similar manner, *Samson Agonistes* reflects the experience of the older man whose work in the cause of liberty had failed to achieve its expected end and who seemed denied a second chance.[142] The crisis of his defeat, his blindness, and his captivity forces Samson, as the crisis of 1660 must have forced Milton, to review the signs of his vocation. Can this be what was meant? "Why," Samson asks,

> was my breeding ordered and prescribed
> As of a person separate to God,
> Designed for great exploits . . . ?
>   . . . Promise was that I
> Should Israel from Philistian yoke deliver;
> Ask for this great Deliverer now, and find him
> Eyeless in Gaza at the mill with slaves,
> Himself in bonds under Philistian yoke. (552)

Like *Paradise Regained, Samson Agonistes* discovers a gap between the apparent meaning of the signs of special election and the situation in which the protagonist finds himself, a gap between God's plan and man's understanding.

Milton had known such a gap in the development of his own career. At various times in the years that stretched between the first announcement of his laureate ambition and the writing of *Paradise Lost,* he must have felt that the "one talent which is death to hide," was, as he said in reflecting on his blindness, "lodged with me useless" (168). Though he was always eager to serve therewith his maker and present his true account, the means of service were often lacking. At first the literary tradition failed him. What use was a great poetic talent

142. See Frank Kermode, "Milton in Old Age," *The Southern Review,* n.s. 11 (1975), 513–529.

in an age when poetry had lost its autonomy, when there remained nothing for the poet to do but demonstrate stylistic virtuosity while adorning the ordinary occasions of public and private life, nothing for him to be but another son of Orpheus? And then the cavalier world was swept away by a revolution in church and state, a revolution that made demands on him no less destructive of his laureate purpose. What use a great poetic talent in an age that required prose? Neither the Caroline peace of the 1630s nor the civil war and Puritan Commonwealth of the 1640s and 1650s provided a way of achieving a laureate career, a way of being at once poet, prophet, and spokesman of the governing order.

Never was Milton able to combine all three functions. But sometime in the late 1650s he began to forge a new role for the laureate based exclusively on the functions of poet and prophet. No longer need the laureate model himself on "wise Demodocus" singing "at King Alcinous' feast" (31) or on Virgil reading to Augustus. Henceforth exile and alienation would be the signs of his calling. Elements of this new role begin appearing in Milton's work as early as the *Nativity Ode,* but only much later do they come together to constitute an altered idea of the laureate poet. What we have commonly ignored has been the difficulty of that coming together and, more particularly, the way in which Milton's generational position contributed both to the problem and to its solution. As the coeval of Davenant and Cowley, Milton suffered from the diminished autonomy of poetry, and, as their coeval, he wrote *Paradise Lost.*

Like Spenser and Jonson, though with still greater effect, Milton inscribed in the text of our culture a new self-presentational message. And, like them, he did so by placing himself in a strongly marked historical sequence—or rather, in his case, at the converging point of two such sequences, one of vatic poets, the other of Biblical prophets. The very weakness of his own literary generation, its insufficiency as foundation for a great poetic career, required that such diachronic pointers be all the more emphatic. But for all his explicit emphasis on his likeness to and his rivalry with the prophets and poets of Hebrew and pagan antiquity, Milton, like his Elizabethan and Jacobean forebears, also related himself, however unobtrusively, to his literary contemporaries. As we have already noticed, *Paradise Lost* resembles the heroic poems of the cavaliers at so many points that it comes finally to seem the fulfillment of a generational ambition. Such resemblance was not, however, what his contemporaries were quickest to notice. They were struck rather by the differences that lifted Milton above his age. The most obvious of these was that unsociable avoidance of rime to whose significance I earlier alluded. It alone would have sufficed to put Milton in a class apart not only from the cavaliers but also from their younger, Restoration followers—including, as Marvell pointed out, both the newly appointed "Town-Bayes," John Dryden, and Marvell himself.

> I too transported by the mode offend,
> And while I meant to praise thee must commend.
> Thy verse created like thy theme sublime,
> In number, weight, and measure, needs not rime.   (210)

As Marvell here suggests, the neglect of rime was caught up in a still more powerful—more powerful because more pervasive and less obviously intended—sign of Milton's unique eminence: his sublimity. Other poets of his generation—Davenant and Cowley among them—had striven for such elevation. Milton alone achieved it. So convincing is that achievement that even now we are more likely to read it as symptom than as sign, as a reflection of Milton's nature rather than as a conventional construct whose meaning derives from a socially determined and largely arbitrary play of signifiers and signifieds. But nature does not make one arrangement of words lofty and another low, nor does it decide which will say "laureate." In

1579 Spenser's homely shepherd talk conveyed this meaning. In 1616 Jonson's epigrammatic middle style did it. And in 1667 it took Milton's Latinate sublimity. What unites these radically differing modes is the dialectical relation each had to the poetic idiom of its author's generation.

Self-presentation is inevitably the reflex of a particular moment—even when the moment seems as unpropitious as Milton's. The differences by which the self declares its identity must necessarily be located in a synchronic system, in a communally established sense of social reality, a sense renewed and revised with each successive generation. The aspiring laureate comes on stage, his mind filled with lines that in earlier ages have served Homer or Virgil or Horace, only to find that the script has changed, that the laureate part has been eliminated or must be played in a costume and with gestures that utterly transform it. Yet such transformation is precisely what the laureate in his devotion to a fixed standard of moral worth can least afford to admit. No wonder that Jonson's work is riven by irreconcilable paradox, that Spenser's ends in a sustained meditation on mutability, or that Milton's turns repeatedly to the uncertainties of greatness in history. Whatever the answer, the question could not be avoided. How in this generation can I respond to the laureate summons my talent imposes on me, and how can I make my high office known?

Index

Designer: Wolfgang Lederer
Compositor: Innovative
Printer: Braun-Brumfield
Binder: Braun-Brumfield
Text: 10/13 Sabon
Display: Sabon Italic